M000286705

Awakening To Home:

A Partnership of Sidhe, Star and Stone

AWAKENING TO HOME:
A Partnership of Sidhe, Star and Stone

© Copyright Anne Gambling 2016

All rights reserved, including the right to reproduce this book, or portions thereof, in any form. Anne Gambling has asserted her right to be identified as the author of this work and photographer of her interior images.

Cover Art: Giovanni Giacometti (1868-1933), 'Autumn' 1903, Oil on Linen, 80.5x54.5cm, Reproduced with the kind permission of Kunstmuseum Solothurn, Switzerland.

Interior Photographs by Anne Gambling
Page 18 Art by Jeremy Berg

Book design by Jeremy Berg

ISBN-13: 978-0-936878-87-4

Library of Congress Control Number: 2016937853

Gambling, Anne
Awakening To Home:
A Partnership Of Sidhe, Star And Stone/Anne Gambling

First Edition: April 2016

Printed in the United States of America,
the United Kingdom and Australia

Awakening To Home:

A Partnership of Sidhe, Star and Stone

Anne Gambling

Lorian Press
6592 Peninsula Dr
Traverse City, MI 49686
www.lorian.org

Dedication

"Well, bless me, the legends are true!
Giants – stone giants!"

Bofur of Khazad-dûm

"Three hundred lives of men have I walked this Earth and
now I have no time"

Gandalf the White

In honour of the Ancestors,
In honour of Hope,
In honour of the Alliance
between Humanity and Faerie,
We 'companions of the way' dedicate this text to

~ Gaia ~

Acknowledgments

I have it on good authority that it is challenging to be the son or daughter (or partner) of one with such a Huxleyian mode of being. Nevertheless they (and I) (as well as the four-legged members of our tribe) persevere. For their collective as well as individual support and good humour (including every sigh of 'here we go again') in advance of as well as throughout each adventure to which they are subjected, my eternal thanks and undying love.

To the spirit of Giovanni Giacometti, thank you for crossing my path years past and for your most recent 'popping-up' in the wake of this winter's dark in the paper shop downstairs. Truly are you an inspirational *Amici della Montagna della Luce* and I am deeply grateful for your gift of love.

To David and Jeremy, thank you for your valuable commentary on the text, and for its acceptance into the esteemed Lorian stable.

And finally, to my Cousins of the Commons, thank you for entrusting me with this task. It has indeed been an honour ...

Contents

Prologue

Through your eyes I see myself.

This text documents a journey in the company of Sidhe, and the tasks arising in its wake.

Specifically it documents how the Lorian publications – *Card Deck of the Sidhe* and its companion volume *Conversations with the Sidhe* – were instrumental in crystallising and focusing a swirling hub (or node) of Faerie-energy of which I had been vaguely aware and with which I had had intermittent contact over the years, most latterly manifesting in a merry band linked to a specific region of the Alps I am blessed to call home. Attuning to this troupe in my own trial-and-error way, I had undertaken a task in autumn 2014 to complete (what I considered to be) a three-year 'self-apprenticeship' in working with light and its flow into the world. The Annex houses two essays describing this adventure – *Amici della Montagna* and *Amici della Luce*. Rivers of emergent relevance running through these texts provide contextual background to the chapters that follow.

Expecting that Lorian's Sidhe resources would deepen my connection with this particular group, I ordered the double-pack as Christmas reading, and gradually brought the energy of the *Card Deck* into my meditations in the months following. But instead of refining attunement to this troupe, the *Card Deck* released a network of alternate potential collaborators into my miniscule orbit, with an invitation to participate in shared worldwork in service of Gaia's evolutionary consciousness. The rollercoaster ride this set in motion was gleefully compounded

1

by said Sidhe companions' 'prodding' me (for want of a better word) to write the story of our unfolding liaison over the course of the past year, with especial reference to the process of engagement facilitated by the *Card Deck*.

In taking up the mantle of reportage, my companions and I are excited by the possibility to support the manifestation of more alliances based on Lorian's resource bank, for which our methodology stands as evidence of the *Card Deck*'s value. We also offer this methodology as potential guidance or (at least) thought-prompts for others' own journeys into the realms of Faerie. The issue, of course, lies in awakening (or re-awakening) the energy housed in stone. Standing or otherwise, they are containers of mountain sentience pure, and central to the process. As Mariel describes to David in one of their Conversations (pp.37-38):

> *The crystal matrix of planetary forces is still as available to you as it is to us. As we who became Sidhe retreated, and you who became human expanded upon the world, you carried with you the memory of the telluric technology of node, connection, and flow, shaped by song and dance and ritual. Guided by this memory, you discovered new ways to tap the sites of power. The practice of building stone circles and erecting standing stones began. What once was done by a person became embodied in stone. This worked as long as the stones were alive, but as the descent into matter continued, and much more importantly, as you lost the ability to form connections with the livingness of matter, the stones have become just what you see today, dormant and in some cases truly dead to the ancient powers.*

The quote defines my work of late, together with Sidhe companions, a truly collaborative effort and one to which I am humbled to offer a small (human) contribution. With thanks to the foundational work of David and Jeremy together with Mariel and her team, this text offers a building block to their approach, the results of ethnographic fieldwork if you like, one way amongst the many that humanity may engage with subtle energies toward a shared vision of Gaian holism. And, as the task to produce this text was truly gifted into my care as a result of working with the *Card Deck*, I happily gift it on (and back) to Lorian, closing the circle and (hopefully) enriching the association's coffers in the process.

Perennial blessings,

Anne

Chapter 1: A (Brief) Introduction

When the Spirit is once again at One with the Third ...

Like most stories, this one has a long and rich pre-history. Further, like most stories, it begins *in medias res*, looping back (and forth) on itself like a warp in Einstein's space-time, its various rhizomatic tendrils (or threads in the telling) making a Han Solo-like leap to hyperspace whenever, wherever, whimsical mood takes this writer's equally whimsical whim. Such it is to dwell amongst the ranks of Faerie, to night-walk becoming landscapes, to return and document tales, insights and instructions with all the colour and texture of re-found becoming myths ...

Indeed are the realms of Faerie as organic, fluid and complex an ecology as any on this side of the veil. While I have enjoyed contact with a variety of these different characters over time, this text shall concentrate on my engagement with humanity's 'cousins' – whom Tolkien described as 'Elven' folk, and Lorian, in the spirit of Irish Celtic roots, 'Sidhe'. Meanwhile, a group with which I align introduced themselves to me as 'Pixie'; in Australia my companions call themselves 'Shining Ones'; my original merry band I know as '*Amici*'. The reader shall therefore find such expressions used interchangeably dependent on context, just as we may use human, person, man, woman similarly, or European, American and so on to delineate location.

But at the outset – a caveat. In describing the journeys into subtle realms which populate this story, as well as the presences encountered therein, the reader may find the raft of symbolic imagery and language used a little heavy on the senses (and tenses). The fact is that I am presented with information in complex (and densely compacted) ways, and while trying to tease out the various threads of import as best I can for a third party, at times such translation can be unwieldy – I am only human, after all. What is presented, of course, makes sense to me because our communication is honed to the shared wiring of consciousness that has evolved over time to enable said communication. Understanding thus emerges from a shared dance toward meaning, toward a cumulative 'a-ha' moment in the spirit of TS Eliot's return to the beginning, and knowing it for the first time.

A wiser soul than I (and one whose words I appropriate with Sidhe-like glee) expressed the process this way: '(It) is generally one in which they present me in various ways with a body of information and experience and I work to translate it into a form that other people can access. My attempts to understand and interpret properly what I experience or am shown is part of the process because if I can translate it into a felt sense, I can then translate it into words." Thus spake (like Nietzsche's *Zarathustra*) Lorian's own wizard, David Spangler, directly mirroring my experience, yet in text assuredly more accessible than mine. Please accept my apology up-front, therefore, if the writing which emanates from my 'mode-of-being' (see Glossary) is far less congruent with ease of understanding than dear David's.

A second caveat while I think of it: None of the following will gel for the reader without engaging the *Card Deck of the Sidhe* him or herself, together with its practical companion guide. So too communing with David's volume of *Conversations* with Mariel in advance to gain a flavour for what may follow in the field. A lot of the play and early forms of establishing connectivity with Sidhe-energy contained in these Lorian texts is invaluable to uplifting a more cogent (and, dare I say, concrete?) understanding of the ways of Faerie.

I often find that my becoming-relation with a potential collaborator is akin to the slow dance of courtship – eyes meet across a crowded room, and a bow or curtsey of respect follows before any circling of each other's energy-field is commenced. 'Tis a process I call 'reciprocal recognition' (see Glossary), one which may involve soundings-out of intent as well as background checks by tribal elders (on both sides of the veil), long before any jig is fiddle-played to foot-stamping applause or a (Celtic) willow deemed ripe for the stripping.

I would hazard a guess that the reason my process took off like a freight train once the *Card Deck* arrived in the letterbox had a lot to do with the years of sporadic contact and initiation into practices with a distinct orientation similar to Sidhe-like tasks – even if I was blissfully unaware at the time where such soundings-out and learnings would lead. Herein, therefore, I share several threads of relevant pre-history which (re-) awakened ways 'in' in specific company with the *Card*

Deck. Nonetheless, only when both sides were ready could a partnership, or pact, be conceived, one founded on loving intent, in service to the circulation of peace, love and light in our beautiful shared Gaiasphere.

Finally, one area where I hope the reader shall humour me is in the use of specific vocabulary to describe certain aspects of process. These are housed in a glossary at the rear of the text. One example is that my preferred expression for the subtle realms is *Malakut*, the Arabic word for the intermediate world of the soul in Islamic (Sufi) mysticism, the place 'where the body is spiritualised and the spiritual is embodied' in the words of renowned scholar Henri Corbin in his seminal text *The Voyage and the Messenger* (p.125). The reason? Simply because my first major journeys in (many years past) walked in the footsteps of Ibn Arabi, *Alone with the Alone* (see Glossary).

I wish the reader well in his or her own journeys, alone or otherwise, on the way to engaging Sidhe-energy, and with a prospect of potential collaborations unfolding in the future ...

Chapter 2: An Invitation to Participation

I am the vapour, said the snow atop the peak, and I am as light as air.

I am somewhat of a fringe-dweller of the Lorian community, and recently at that. In the lead-up to my winter-dark (solstice) cycle of two years past – a time of musings, ritual and beyond – I subscribed to David's *Views from the Borderlands* journal on the back of reading a book of his from 1984 that had somehow squirrelled its way into the subterranean three million plus volume shelves of the University of Zurich Library. So-armed, I journeyed between symbolism and material reality, between winter-dark and the crystalline clarity of the eastern Alps in January 2014. There, I was drawn to jot down a question on the basis of what I experienced in its majestic terrain coupled with what I had been reading in the pages of David's most recent journal.

But before I reveal my question (and his response), perhaps a little context is required. I am no child of the Alps, but rather of the southern Pacific Ocean. More than a decade past I consciously committed to put down roots in this land after a slow dance of courtship with its terrain, forged principally on a connection to mountain sentience. I had heard *der Ruf der Berge* (the mountains' call) like so many before, an energy of spirit that was to paradoxically lead me into the heart of the felt world, rather than simply skimming her skin.

Several way-markers along this particular (hiking) trail included greeting the soul of each mountain (our family) climbed, spontaneously coming into contact with the wee-folk of the Alps, the *Wildmännli* of many a legend, and traversing

7

(subtle) catacombs on the way to (what was described to me as) the '*kiln room*' deep within the alpine chain, wherein dwelt the mountains' fire, the wisdom of ages (and sages).

Most significant as a way-marker to longer-than purpose, though, was a vision, some years back, of this small land-locked land as a 'peace-sink' – that like a carbon sink, the collective peace and tranquillity of a stable harmonious nation with beautiful natural places long-protected from further ravishment is actually sequestered in the subtle bones of the land. Here, it seemed, an unconscious form of activism was taking place, whereby humanity fed the vibration of their peaceful co-habitation as a natural matter-of-course into Helvetia's reservoir – *wei wu wei*-like (see Glossary).

The opportunity to heighten or extend this vibration through conscious thanksgiving and connection to and for the peace-sink was also clearly communicated by the vision. In the moment I was drawn to remark in my journal: "I can imagine a time when the energy of this sink is actively directed out into the Gaiasphere, fed into the grid so to speak, to be circulated and sent where it is needed most. Maybe my prayer – *for peace, love and the light of grace to infuse every nook, cranny and heart in this world* – could be sent up into the aetheric to rain down elsewhere?"

Context done and dusted (for now at least), we meet the experience of early 2014 which led to my correspondence with David Spangler:

Off I trekked on a day's snow-hike as a self-action to contribute to the peace-sink, my prayer (as mantra) invoked with each rhythmic step. I asked Sun to witness the action, and offered greetings and blessings to each expression of the Sacred encountered along the way, sharing my joy at this task with the All. It didn't happen often that I'd drift in thought, away. But in case I lost touch with intent, Sun was always there to remind me with a kiss to the cheek.

As energy built during the hike, I experienced a swirling vortex of light spiral up through my body from feet to head, growing all the while – faster, wider – till it gushed like a fountain out the top of my head to shower the world in blessing. At one level this manifested as personal (or local) felt-sense; I also engaged a collective (or non-local) visioning as if witness to myself from deep-space. From this (latter) location, 'I saw' (see Glossary) the selfsame vortex of light issue from a pinprick on Earth's surface, spiral up to the far reaches of atmosphere before the fountain gushed forth to 'coat' the whole outer membrane of the world in light, yet remain translucent enough for me to see Earth within. In the moment, I understood this outer coating would gradually infill the membrane with light. It was as if I watched the pinprick of 'me' and what 'her' tiny action could contribute to the whole.

I stopped briefly to catch my breath and consider what I had seen (and experienced). Suddenly, my felt-sense moved, shifted – down. I became aware of a deep connection to Earth-energies far beneath my feet, as if the 'self-vortex' had morphed into a channel or conduit for actively moving energy stored in the peace-sink up and out into the world. In fact, there was so much energy seeking release that I found it escaping from my fingertips and more, spilling out beyond the 'fountain' streaming skyward from my head. The shock of this discovery immediately shut down the connection – something about which I was not unhappy. What had I unwittingly tapped into? And was this OK?

David very kindly offered the following counsel: 'As far as my understanding goes, what happened is OK. We are, after all, as incarnate beings part of the great circulation of these energies in "vertical" and "horizontal" ways. My sense is that there are two things here. The first is to offer one's own energy and attunement to contribute to peace-sinks (lovely concept!) and so on because you are the responsible person and the energy being shifted does so within your scale of being and operation; you're not trying to "move" more than you can understand or handle. But at the same time, you can certainly invite a larger participation on the part of allies and your own larger self as well. In this sense, you're not trying to do something big but you're making yourself part of something big.

'It's been my experience more than once that subtle beings are opportunists: given a chance, they will respond, and often with greater "vigour" than anticipated. We provide the pinprick and they provide the flood. But the pinprick needs to be there. It sounds as if you set yourself up for what happened, but from my perspective it's as if the inner forces assumed an invitation to participation and responded accordingly. My sense is that the inner worlds are seeking every opportunity that presents to both show themselves but more importantly, to, as you say, add to the love in the world and its circulation.

'We are each called to a wondrous partnership which carries many possibilities but also responsibilities to honour our partners and their intents. But it's important in this process to realize that we're dealing with non-human intelligences and thus not to assume immediate and perfect congruency of understanding. In a way, it's like working with someone from a different culture from one's own. There are unconscious and thus hidden assumptions of which both parties may be unaware. Not all inner beings have a good understanding of what it means to be incarnated – or to be human – and what our strengths and limits are. They can project what is normal for them onto us just as much as we can project what is normal to us onto them. This, I've found, is particularly true of many nature spirits, especially if they don't have a lot of daily contact with human beings – or operate at a level of consciousness and being where humans don't often go anymore.

'So it's up to us to establish boundaries, pacing, and so on, which then gives them solid information to know how best to engage with us. That's why I'm so

9

strong on the "standing in sovereignty" piece, both for our protection but also for theirs as it gives a stable boundary with which they can interact. And of course, once engaged and in partnership, everything can change, just as it does in a dance when two partners, having discovered what each are capable of, can blend into the flowing rhythm of the music and let it carry them where it will' (correspondence 10-12 February 2014).

Something which I did not include in my initial query to David was what followed after I shut down the connection. However, armed with his response, I thought it worthwhile to share:

As I made my way back down to the village, my attention was drawn to the ridge opposite, a line of mountains I have often communed with over the years. There 'I saw' its overlighting presence take on the form of a huge eagle, one which I had not seen her assume before. This form straddled the entire ridge, stretched its full length; it looked as if the full force of all subtle energies in her remit had come together – accumulated – into a single shape. Filled with awe at this 'gathering of presence' vis-à-vis miniscule me, I was too drained, depleted (physically and psychically), to attempt any reading of or attunement thereto. What did it mean?

David's take was as follows: 'I think the eagle you saw was an invitation to further exploration and partnership, perhaps on a larger scale. You may wish to investigate this further, assuming you haven't already done so!'

Coincidentally, a week or so prior to my communication with David, yet a month or so following the encounter in the Alps, I had met a subtle being on a *Malakut* night wander who described how she was linked or attuned to a specific line of mountains in her world. And later, following my reading of *Conversations*, especially David's comments on features in Mariel's 'world' which can align with those in our physical (p.24-5, amongst others), I understood this must have been a Sidhe presence. At the time, however, I simply watched as her *StarGeist* (an expression she used to connote the star-spirit of the mountain) rose up out of the rock to connect with her, so they could take flight together.

At the time I found this a very intriguing notion but was unsure of the information's relevance for me. It would stay on a research pile labelled 'stone and mountain sentience' until more puzzle pieces could come into this (jigsaw's) orbit. What this meant is that neither did I connect it to the eagle vision previously related which, at that stage, I considered to be a random line of flight with no potential rhizomatic interconnection regardless of David's 'prophecy'. Indeed, the reader will find many instances in this text of how long it can take for my surface consciousness to catch up with what 'I' (seemingly) have already signed up for in the *Malakut*. At such times, I am reminded of Emerson's observation – that the soul already contains in itself the event that befalls it, 'for the event is only the actualising of its thoughts' (from 'Fate', in *Collected Works*, p.21).

Meanwhile, with thanks to David for helping put the pieces of the (current) puzzle together, I walked into my (then) future continuing to work with the energies of self-light, yet shy about making overtures to spirits of places, *genii locorum*, with which I felt deep connection. I wanted to learn and understand more before issuing any invitation to participation. For the remainder of the year, therefore, my focus was a specific river-valley in the country's south where I had taken root in this land, undertaking a task which, in a way, completed a three-year self-apprenticeship in working with light and its flow into the world.

By coincidence (or, at the time, what I thought was coincidence) my (conscious) history of encounter with Faerie-energy was likewise bound to this valley. As these adventures interconnect strongly with the Sidhe story to follow, they are housed in the annexed *Amici Files* (and if the reader is interested in even more background to my understanding of stone and mountain sentience and Earth-energies, the essays – *Peace Sinks* and *Der Ruf der Berge* – may be accessed from the library of my website: www.nestedfishes.org).

Because of my excitement at the successful completion of this self-assigned task, I felt energised to maintain contact with these *Amici*. We had not collaborated on task, but they were aware of my presence and acknowledged its intent. I had been welcomed by the *genius loci* of the particular watershed and they had stood by her commitment, as well as spoken directly to me about their own tasks within her remit. Heading into my winter-dark 2014 retreat a buzz of energy backdropped my meditations – I felt I was being called to engage but I didn't know by whom or with what. Assuming it was the *Amici*, though, I ordered the *Card Deck of the Sidhe* and David's *Conversations with the Sidhe* in the hope that it may help refine and/or sharpen contact with those energies I perceived as far away from a Zurich-based daily life orbit.

Hence, another question to David about its likelihood or otherwise. His response?

'This is a good question, and I really don't know the answer. My impression is that it varies from Sidhe to (shining?) Sidhe, excuse the pun. That is, there seem to be Sidhe that are, like Hobbits, rooted to their own shire-places, but there are others, like Bilbo and Frodo, who travel. On the other hand, there seems to be a worldwide web of connection, so that the Sidhe here in our area can communicate with the Sidhe in Europe or elsewhere. Again, I don't know how extensive or easy this is. So my advice would be to contact your regular Sidhe friends as always and see what happens, while at the same time acknowledging and blessing any local Sidhe where you are in Zurich. You have nothing to lose here and much to gain. My guess is that you'll "get through" to your regulars without any problem' (correspondence 5 December 2014).

Meeting Mountains

One thing I have consistently found about making plans is the need to be ever-ready to change them. The proverbial spanner in the works meant I had to delay any opportunity to engage the energy of the *Card Deck* for contact till early 2015. My winter-dark retreat would be spent instead meditating on the *I Ching* hexagram which spontaneously revealed itself when the book fell out of the shelf one day. It had opened onto a specific page which, I found to my surprise, I had never read before, and sat on the floor regarding me with an equanimous gaze till I agreed to engage its energy.

Mountain, it said: *Stopping at the back, one does not have a body; walking in the garden, one does not see a person. No fault.* Stillness pure, within and without – thus was its counsel. Mountain above as mountain below: *Joining mountains; thus do superior people think without leaving their place.* Hmmm.

I was reminded of an instruction received years prior, when, as a pure novice in all matters elemental, Mr 1300BC (a dear longer-than subtle friend) explained that as part of my apprenticeship, I needed to climb a mountain. Yet when the mountain appeared, it constellated as exactly my size – no need to climb at all. I stood before the mountain and immediately felt such love, that the only thing I wanted to do was hug it. My arms encircled its vast girth; I kissed and set my cheek to its solidity and strength. I felt very calm; it seemed perfectly natural to be locked in embrace with stone sentience and in the moment, I knew, *deep-knew*, that we were one-together. The lesson, and what it portended (i.e. actualising the mountain of/in/as oneself), is described in the essay *self-naughting* (on nestedfishes. org).

In his *Mountains and Rivers Sutra*, the 13th century Zen master Dogen writes: 'The appearance of the mountains is completely different when we are in the world gazing at the distant mountains and when we are in the mountains meeting the mountains ... From time immemorial ... wise men and sages have all made the mountains their own chambers, their own body and mind.' In his commentary on Dogen's text, John Daido Loori says: 'To realise the mountains as one's own body and mind is transformative ... *Intimacy* is the dwelling place of the great sages ... To realise all form as one's own body and mind is to dwell in a universe that is unborn and inextinguishable, a universe that has no beginning or end'. Intimacy – my embrace of the mountain. During the days of winter-dark retreat, my lesson was to be as still as stone sentience, as silent as the winds during Halcyon's days to make her kingfisher's nest on shore.

Sidhe research would have to wait; yet in the stillness, my *Malakut* wanders were rich in detail, colour, texture and song. As usual, I kept a comprehensive journal of energies encountered and 'becoming landscapes' (see Glossary) walked. Spontaneously I would encounter bands of Elven-folk I had not met before. In the moment I made no conscious link to the *Card Deck* and its companion volumes still languishing in padded envelopes somewhere in the study, but it seems a portal had perhaps been opened with my statement of intent. Somewhere, on their side of the veil, someone had been listening and was mobilising to action, in song ...

I find Sidhe-energy manifests as song, joy, a lightness-of-being *mergent* with the wonders of our glorious world, a connection to beauty we humans oft-bury beneath layers of scrutiny and sobriety. David comments similarly in the *Card Deck* text: '(T)hey seemed to me to walk in music' (p.177). Each time I'm in the company of Sidhe, I feel like skipping, sprite-like, through a springtime meadow hand-in-hand with happy hippy Green Man, backdropped by tinkling (cow) bells. It's not that Sidhe don't take life seriously, but their sincerity is joy-infused, laughter-inflected, innocence-fed, celebration-abundant – things humanity (latterly) seems to have difficulty integrating into task-orientation. When did we forget? I wonder. It is as if in the human lexicon, activity must be earnestly, gravely, stoically pursued in order to be considered work; otherwise perceived as leisure. Another example of where dichotomies pull us asunder from a single keel.

Such it was that during my winter-dark retreat (nine days around the time of the solstice), I kept finding myself in bright-lit landscapes full of healthy shimmering worker-bee types singing up a storm, juxtaposed against human spaces of wan exhausted faces, energy-depleted souls dragging their feet, blind to my presence; seemingly a case of Dante's *Divina Commedia* updated in 20th-21st century dress.

At one point, the doorbell to home was to ring constantly, persistently – a clear sign, for me, of subtle visitors – to which I responded: *You can always come in*! Later, in meditation, I was to stand before a huge tree; amongst its exposed roots was a bounty of treasure (seeds and nuts) from which I was welcome to gather as needed – insights stored from earlier winters, perhaps? I was reminded of previous encounters with a race of 'Shining Ones', how I flew across the sea to the 'Far Isles' or 'Green-Man's-Land' as well as other locales named in symbolic tongue. A ring was my connective thread to these spaces, a ring of glacial blue which rippled like the waves over which I flew, a ring I wore in the *Malakut* but did not yet possess in the material ...

Each day more of the same in the stillness, the silence, of retreat – this time a *Malakut* trek made in the company of my partner, F, to a 'new Maleny' (see Glossary), a place we had agreed to steward on the edge of a forest but with an extraordinarily high (and solitary) crystal mountain above and beyond the space which kept emerging and disappearing from view. It seemed important to take a picture before the mists rose again – we needed to remember this place. Exhilarating to behold, the crystal peak stood like a sentinel over our work here, at a house which needed outfitting to our specifications. Suddenly, the scene shifted to a promenade along a rock-wall flanking the sea; lots of happy shining people. Where was this place; where had we been?

And following – at a station where people connected to different trains according to their work details. As my friends and I parted ways, they said we would all meet up again on our final night together, for a farewell party (and yes, this did actually happen and it was loads of fun). Suffice it to say this went on and on, each of the nine for the nine (days); myriad encounters and scenarios to be shared in the context of the chapters to follow, if and when appropriate. At the time I knew I was encountering Sidhe-energy but without any thought how this could or would integrate with my (existing) work.

As Dogen writes: Enlightenment *unfolds*. It is the key reason I keep comprehensive journals of my *Malakut* wanders. Never have my records of same not been useful to evolving process. Whether in the stillness of meditation or night-walking, pre-dawn is usually the time preferred by my interlocutors to drop by for a chat, or to 'gather up' my consciousness with their own (David's fitting description for the process) for a shared journey to beyond. Nevertheless, if there was an 'invitation to participation' amongst the many encounters presented during this period it was buried far beneath a plethora of symbolic and cryptic clues.

Post-solstice, retreat at end, I entered the material merriment on this side of the veil for the weeks of Christmas, New Year, Three Kings. In mid-January, I assembled the Lorian resources, together with my existing piles of research into the realms of Faerie and several symbolic interlocutors, to begin first forays into actively pursuing connection through the *Card Deck*. Thus armed I boarded the train for the eastern Alps for a fortnight's communion with the *genius loci* in whose domain I had had the vortex experience twelve months prior. She and I had a lot to talk about …

Chapter 3: Establishing Connectivity

In Winter's cradle, I see You, who are everywhere and everything One.

The valley road ends here at the place to which I have come – this village in the eastern Alps a place of semi-annual migration for our family to commune with nature pure. Here we are cradled within a cirque of peaks and while the *genius loci* may rise out of a particular ridgeline on its (south-west) flank, I feel her presence wherever I trek.

A special place, this, where I climbed my first ever mountain in the material – where, as an (old) lass who'd grown up at sea level, I enjoined the high wild on a day of unending blue. Reaching the summit in glorious exhaustion, of course I felt I had 'done good'. But before managing to wallow too long in any self-important sense of achievement, I found myself marvelling instead at how the ridges and crests of countless other peaks rolled off into the distance, seemingly forever. My paltry wander up a hill was suddenly put into perspective; I was as insignificant an actor in the unfolding aeons-old drama of life as the (minor) geological formation on which I stood. We were both part of something much bigger – much broader, taller and altogether more awe-inspiring. My humility in the moment was keen, only made more so when a golden eagle drifted lazily not three metres above my head. Turning a nonchalant eye my way, this emissary of spiritual energy encased in stone enquired: *And your point is?* Exactly.

Now, long years later, an unexpected joy was to be revealed as I turned the key in the lock of our small rented flat – the living room 'wall' was, in fact, a full length plate glass window looking directly onto the cragged and snow-crumpled face of my first mountain: *Hello the House* (see Glossary). It would be my companion each day, each night, each step of the way (from the top of Sekiso's hundred-foot-pole). Recalling the *I Ching* wisdom of some weeks prior, I intoned: Mountain above as mountain below, one does not have a body. Walking in the garden, one does not see a person.

Yes, *Schiesshorn* agreed. *Es ist wie es ist.* Welcome back …

In this space, in the presence of mountain-sentience pure, overlit by a *genius loci* whose energy hums like a well-tuned carburettor, I finally opened the *Card Deck of the Sidhe*. Before reading the Lorian texts, I was drawn to simply lay out the cards and listen for their voices in the stillness.

The first jolt of connectivity was to the 'round stone' Jeremy had decided to paint as the deck's signature image. I had had an encounter with this stone in the *Malakut* once when a subtle contact shared with me the Sidhe legend of a great battle. By way of background, over time I have been witness to the *Malakut* re-telling of several such legends, with a request to collaborate on transcribing these stories here in the material to help heal the wounds, the rifts between Humanity and Faerie. In other words, in the hope that mythopoiesis begets holopoiesis in the spirit of Tolkien's 'blessed are the legend-makers with their rhyme of things not found within recorded time'. 'Tis an ongoing project …

In the moment of this particular encounter, my contact had called his group 'Pixie' and I was to discover (in research, following my direct and harrowing witness of the battle) that Pixie is the name for Sidhe in south-west England, specifically Devon and Cornwall (and the physical location of the stone I encountered in the *Malakut*, so-named *Men-an-Tol*, which bore an uncanny resemblance to Jeremy's painting). The resonance I immediately felt to the *Card Deck* upon finding this stone as the portal or gateway in to its energy cannot be overstated.

I fanned out the cards, to sift and sort them, look closely at their images; it seemed there were other cards amongst the deck I already knew (and/or that already knew me). As aesthetically engaging as it was to commune with Jeremy's beautiful artwork on its own terms, more often than not the images captured inner landscapes and beings with which I had had significant encounters over the years – encounters which had proved integral to the unfolding of my path.

Thus did I find the cards naming themselves in accordance with the tag-lines or text-snatches which described their connection to (my) past *Malakut* events. I had always needed these text-snatches to re-guide entry to the various locales (and the teachings housed therein) as I am hopeless at sketching (such a frustration!). Yet now it seemed Jeremy's paintings were the mirror-mirror-on-the-wall to these (inner) events, resonant with specific place-holders in my consciousness.

How grateful can a girl be for such a wonderful piece of synchronicity! I began to overlay my encounters (copiously recorded in journals over the years) onto the card images, the pattern to reveal, and let the two commune in my psyche. The rest, as they say, is history but in this case a history-in-perpetual-making …

Only later, when reading David's accompanying text to the *Card Deck*, did I discover that he had had an experience of Sidhe arriving while he attuned to the cards in order to name themselves the various visitors to his Stone Circle (pp.88-94 refer): 'It was as if each Dancer Card carried a signature energy or quality to which a particular Sidhe felt attracted.' Similarly for Jeremy, as he painted the Stone Circle images, each stone's voice would arise with a short epigram or message. In reading of their experiences, I realised that what I had found was not only synchronicity-in-action but that the naming process itself revealed the connective thread to manifest our unique way in. David writes: 'What a particular card means to you or what it invokes is for you to determine at that time.' This implies that the naming is dependent on who works with the cards, the energy which arises when in communion with the images as well as the purpose of said communion.

As an intellectual intrigue (chicken and egg-like, what came first: the image or the name?), I found these alternate experiences very interesting. What it meant in actuality, though, is that my intent for the *Card Deck* to help refine contact with the existing group of Sidhe in the country's south, my *Amici*, completely dropped off the radar when the naming process released a raft of alternate potential collaborators into my miniscule pond. Their invitation to participate in shared worldwork in service of Gaia was to emerge slowly like a (star) seed sprouting in the fertile soil of my being long before waking consciousness was engaged. Yet with a beginning like this to our liaison, how could I have ever said no?

Each naming is a long story in itself; I have no plans to bore the reader unduly. However, I crave indulgence while I list the names vis-à-vis the *Card Deck*'s, and place several of the more pertinent naming events in context as the chapters which follow speak to 'my' names rather than those chosen by David and Jeremy. In so doing, the aim is to maintain congruency with and respect for the collaboration set in train by the energy of the *Card Deck* which led to a collective of compatriots aligning themselves with a specific set of working cards in the course of our becoming-relation.

This means that several of the cards are out of order with the formal deck: Gaian Throne (Anne-named: *Companions of the Way*), Ocean and Land, and The Shaping Man. Each spoke its sequence to me – specifically, the first two expressed a desire to join the Stone Circle on a permanent basis together with the three stone Condition cards, while the latter grumbled good-naturedly that he needed to precede the Feast before he could actually join any feasting. To clarify, therefore, the Stone Circle as a working set eventually evolved to comprise the first nineteen cards in the following table, with the fourteen Dancers thereafter offering perspective and counsel as and when required.

Note that the 'Anne-name' column more often than not reads as a verse-text comprising the original tag-lines or text-snatches housed in my consciousness rather than being sedentary names rooted to a single spot or attached to discrete energy streams. Like an Aboriginal songline sung into being as it is walked across the land, this form of strung-prose seeks to individualise the cards, yet always in the context of how each pearl is threaded to its neighbour, on and on, and returned to the beginning as a collective proposition.

In this way, it bespeaks the collaborative, *flowing* energy at the heart of the Circle's *beingness*, as well as being a function of my Huxleyian mode which tends to think in verse as a natural matter-of-course. Over time my tendency to 'versify' develops into mantra – short songs of praise, invocation, offered as greeting and blessing. As such, the *Card Deck* couldn't help but be another recipient of this methodology of connection. And the reader shall find many more examples as we journey further in the text.

The Howe (from the *Card Deck of the Sidhe)*

18

Formal *Card Deck* Name	Anne-name
Howe (The Hollow Hill)	Mountain above as mountain below, one does not have a body; walking in the garden, one does not see a person ...
Gate of Earth	From the gate of the earth,
Gate of Dawn	And the rising sun,
Gate of Stars	Through the gate of the stars,
Gate of Twilight	To the twilight zone:
Altar (Gate of Consciousness)	Here is my kiln room, my ten-foot-square hut within
Gaian Throne	To which you are all most welcome, my companions of the way ...
Wizard Stone	Hello MagicMan,
Artisan Stone	Hello MakerMan,
Bard Stone	Hello MossMan,
Gatekeeper Stone	Welcome VanDiemen'sMan!
Stone of Identity	For a new hawk is born,
Stone of Boundary	Who is centred within,
Stone of Opening	Split open by love,
Stone of Emergence	For the inner to come out.
Ancestor Stone	In honour of the Ancestors,
Fallen Stone	In honour of Hope,
Stone of Alliance	In honour of the Alliance between Humanity and Faerie,
Ocean and Land	Know that I am homecome to the sea ...
A Bird on the Hand	One day the singing bird;
Bear and Stone	We are brothers bear all;
Blossoms and Wheat	When did I forget the beauty of the world?
Dragon and Books	Yes I am a scholar;
Edge	Gravity always gets in the way when we don't make a big enough leap;
Faerie Gold	This we know, dear TreeMother –
Grail and Roses	A rose by any other name would smell as sweet,
Moonstairs	On our stairway to heaven,
Palace	To Laputa, our castle in the sky,
Stag and Pool	Where we drink at the sacred pool,
Stone Raptor	With a stone raptor,
The Shaping Man	And a shaping man,
The Feast	Sharing a moveable feast,
The Tossing Coin	And singing joy to the world ...

Cleaving

During my fortnight in the mountains looking into the face of beauty, I would regularly read (and re-read) sections of the Lorian texts as well as tomes documenting the medieval legends of mountain spirits and Faerie-folk hereabouts. My desire, as always, is to understand the specifics of present location together with the broader context of universal intent. Establishing connectivity, I find, is an organic unfolding to shared purpose – a slow dance of re-entry ever re-engaged. A specific practice thereto I call 'cleaving' – a process whereby (outer) perceptions (research-raw) are adhered (glue-like) to the solidity of (inner) stone sentience (soul-knowing pure – i.e. the things I don't even know I know).

How the word arose to describe my felt-sense of this experience in the first place is a case in point – it wanted to be spoken before I'd even realised I needed a word to describe it. Like most instances of 'words formed' (see Glossary) it was accompanied (simultaneously) by an image. 'I saw' little sea critters cemented to rock pool walls, washed by waves yet remaining undisturbed, living the Taoist *I Ching* wisdom: Let wind enter, keep mountain still. Yet as soon as uplifted to surface consciousness, the imagery shifted – to lichens on the faces of forest boulders or Japanese *rakuware*, ash from its firing wedded to the bowl's skin-self. Thus did the word emerge to meet my sensate boundary with the felt world.

Cleaving – a form of psychoid unity (see Glossary) or symbiotic relation, perhaps? I watched it in action between rock and sea critter, stone and lichen – was it now the turn of higher self mountain and little climber (hugger) me? To cleave: From the Old English or German (*kleben* – to stick) yet with an adjunct meaning to remain faithful to someone or something. This latter definition a lovely piece of synchronicity – the inner coming out, the outer coming in; the result a seamless and mergent (plus vocabularic!) relation of living the one-life-of-the-one-world (see Glossary).

To facilitate cleaving in this particular Sidhe-relevant instance, I had brought with me several symbolic interlocutors – pictures and figurines of *Wildmännli* (literally wild-folk), one amongst the many subtle inhabitants of the Alps, dear sweet souls, no more than 'two-shoes' tall, whom I describe in the annexed essay, *Amici della Montagna*. And then, of course, I cleaved myself onto the felt world herself, walking the landscape each day with Sun as witness, 'singing up country' (see Glossary) in the spirit of my self-action from the previous year.

This time, though, I more consciously attuned to, and specifically named, the spirits of mountains, waters, ancestors, flora and fauna resident of *genius loci* as the recipients of blessing, my intent to deepen connection to the sink rather than inadvertently tap it out. So too did I outreach to stellar energies each night against a backdrop of patient mountains stitched to painted sky with the same purpose to the mantra, effecting reciprocal recognition with each presence who winked welcome in through the glass and/or communing with Moon's (growing) self well into the crystal'd light of morn before her slow wistful set behind *Erzhorn's* ridge.

Daily was I tugged out by the 'unseen hand' (see Glossary), in the spirit of John Muir's observation that 'going out is really going in', rather than being drawn to sit at desk-research or in meditation in benign view of the mountain. Nevertheless, anything and everything seemed fit to purpose in the moment – 'flow' enacted itself; seamless its thread strung from hours to days to weeks.

I sensed Sidhe presence in company of the Sacred even if no specific

20

communications were begun at this time. And in hindsight, I can say that it was as if the grail space within me was being developed (paradoxically being opened, extended and expanded by these cleaving activities) in order to welcome companions to its altar once all causes and conditions sufficiently ripened – which the following chapter documents in more detail.

In the previous chapter I shared Dogen's wisdom about *meeting* the mountains. The great Reinhold Messner is oft-drawn to quote William Blake similarly: 'Great things are done when men and mountains meet'. It is difficult for me to describe the felt-sense of directly encountering the Sacred when likewise in the mountains. To merge with landscape is communion pure, and the blessing tasks I engaged while in this place *wei wu wei*-like; I simply couldn't *not* perform them. Here, an example from my journal as evidence of the focus of these days for which no other word suffices than cleaved ...

2.30pm: Finally home, after hours circumambulating the full bowl of beauty in which this village nestles. As well as the usual mantras, here was the song set to the beat of my footfalls: *I carry Your joy to be in my heart, I mirror Your joy to the face of the sky, with every step I taste Your breath flowing Love out into the world.* I am so grateful to you, Sun, and the All of universal energy that helped me each part of the way! Indeed I felt your kiss, the kiss of the All of the One and how it spurred my movement on.

At last I came to *Schwellisee's* winter cradle to commune with spirit-of-place. Wind – strong, sharp, stinging, chill in its desire to be, to flow, to share blessings out into the world via its own true nature – suddenly miraculously hushed, stilled completely as I finished my prayer so that we may all stand for a moment in divine silence, surround-sounded by the resonant hum of Gaian presence; then, just as suddenly she returned to herald the voices of a boy-band of off-piste snowboarders on her tongue. Time to turn, to go. But never leave. *Schwupp!* as the *blitzschnell* departure of tiny *Wildmännli* would sound:

Wind. High-risen. Snowdrifts plough
the thermals, skate invisible slopes,
fuse with aether far-flung by Breath;
down skid the flakes from Schiesshorn's
crest, to soar, spiral, become the Eagle –
what? – nothing; there to rest like a
calling cloud's kiss. Indeed I am the
vapour, like the snow atop the peak,
and I am as feather-light as air ...

My intent, purely, simply, is outreach to the physicality of the world, to wed myself to the bones of the earth, the life *within* the mountains. Something as matter-of-course as walking – greeting wonder, praising glory, blessing beauty – sends me slip-sliding, sinking into the peace-sink, joining with every other expression of Divine Being to fill it brimful, ready to shower the world, send Love's light flooding into each heart, each nook and cranny; a watershed of liquid light do I see all around, and we all *Amici* to Your divine purpose.

Suddenly a turn of the path and a portal appears in the mist-shrouded meadow down the slope – the most extraordinary effect, Sun haloed at the (low) apex of a whitish-golden archway in the midst of tree sentinels, mantled in white. Simply an atmospheric effect or an invitation to participation? A bit of both, perhaps? In any case a phenomenon I have never seen before, and one which leaves me glowing with intrigued joy.

Later: Starlight. Starlight. The slope to *Scheidegg* a sea of twinkling starlight; your face, Sun, *swimming* in each snow crystal, therein your presence sunk, participant in, brother to the world, sharing your true nature with us all – *wei wu wei* each step of the way. Oh, what it is to be love, be joy, be peace, be light. This is the sovereignty of my humanity, what I offer on behalf of and to the All. I am a connective thread, only one (a single tiny Laleima-inspired firefly: see Glossary) amongst the infinite points, nodes or threads of connectivity between heaven and earth, between stellar and earth energies. I sculpt nestedfishes into the snow, draw the spots through which heaven and earth may commune. I bring an offering of snow up to my mouth; they are crystal containers of starlight here on earth, as am I a vessel of liquid light. I feel the snow melt into me, separate out into water and vapour.

I am the vapour, says the snow atop *Schiesshorn, and you know I am as light as air ...*

Cleaving: I knew little of the lore of the Sidhe until reading David's volume of *Conversations* with Mariel. Not only did it help deepen my intellectual understanding of their world but triggered many 'a-ha – now I get it!' moments. I scribbled away in the book, flooded David's text with corollary notes and remarks. For example: To discover the Sidhe are called the People of Peace, and my work involves connecting to peace-sink energy? Likewise to discover their work with starlight and my induction (for want of a better word) into weaving threads of light between 'heaven' and 'earth' (in its own small way) shares this purpose?

I drew especial inspiration from David's final thoughts:

'Finding in ourselves the human equivalent of the joy, the wonderment, the attunement to life, the skill in connectedness, and the creation of wholeness that mark the Sidhe is really what this work is about ... Whether we call it "finding the Sidhe within" or "finding our deep and sacred humanity", it's what the world needs ... The road to the Sidhe is through the starlit depths of our own humanity as a child of the Earth and a partner to Gaia' (p.170).

I may use different vernacular ('liquid light' for Mariel's 'star blood', 'nestedfishes' for David's 'synthesis') but delving into *Conversations* energised me with the thought that I was on the same page (so to speak) to offer to contribute to the Sidhe's worldwork. During the fortnight, I had read, absorbed, meditated, walked. Insights into the interconnections between our worlds intrigued and excited me, and I experienced the familiar buzziness of energies circulating that would soon make eye-contact across a crowded room.

On the morning we were to take the train back down to the dense fog of the lowlands, the *genius loci*'s home ridge bid fond farewell with a stunning physicality to rival her imposing (subtle) eagle of the year before – rising magically above the thickly-misted valley like a broad crystal pillar shot straight from the earth, up into the sky. An ice palace seemingly carved by God's hand was before me; a kingdom of *bergkristall* (see Glossary) from the innermost heart of the mountain had erupted through her skin to say: I am. And all I could do was marvel, hold the purity of crystal against the blue of the sky – the blue-blue of the sky – in my mind's eye with a vague stirring of cognisance that I had seen this crystal'd mountain in the *Malakut* somewhere before ...

But in the moment I simply stood, gave thanks, and said: *Tschüss* ...

Chapter 4: First Forays

**Gravity always gets in the way
when you don't make a big enough leap ...**

In *Conversations* with the Sidhe, Mariel describes the temple where she works – 'as much a creation of spirit, energy and possibility as it is of form' (p.122); similarly she writes of the altar space she created, where 'I "make space" for you in my life ... (as) only partly solid; it is a blend of energy and substance. ... This altar reflects the true altar which is in my heart' (p.119). Such energy and substance include her experiences and memory, what she learns and brings back from communications with David to further her work.

Mariel says: 'If you dedicate, as I have done, some part of your environment to be an altar to our contact, then the energies of affinity, resonance, and presence can be grounded and enhanced by something concrete in your life; such a place or thing can be an ally between us ... remember you are the stone circle' (p.146). In the *Card Deck of the Sidhe*, a Stone Circle card is called the Altar, the Gate of Consciousness. This card self-named in 'my' deck as: *Here is my Kiln Room, my Ten-Foot-Square Hut within*. As the naming process continued, a Dancer card, Gaian Throne, asked to join the Circle as a permanent member, communicating that it belonged together with the Altar. Its self-naming was as follows: *Companions of the Way*. Thus the full invocation to which the commencement to this chapter bears witness is:

Here is my Kiln Room, my Ten-Foot-Square Hut within
To which you are all most welcome, my Companions of the Way …

As related in the last chapter, the cards had named themselves in accordance with specific place-holders in my consciousness documenting past *Malakut* events, beings or locations. These I had used to re-guide my entry to such spaces. One was called the *kiln room* and while not constellating exactly as Jeremy had painted the Altar (yet – more on that later in the chapter), I felt-sensed the card's deep resonance with the place within the mountain in which I would commune with the heart of the felt world.

I had been led to the *kiln room* in meditation years earlier by Mr1300BC. A guide of longer-than standing (obviously, given his name: see Glossary) and a dear, dear friend, he had gathered up my consciousness with his own for a raft of journeys into the heart of things. It was all part of my learning about Earth-energies, specifically mountain or stone sentience, which led (amongst others) to the peace-sink insights. It meant that, over time, I could see deeper into a sink's differing levels as if I were on subtle archaeological dig. With him, I would witness the work of wise women in certain ceremonial spaces, consult maps to find the source of sacred waters, and traverse labyrinths in preparation to teach myself (as he bluntly put it) how to negotiate the different stages of firing within (what he called) the 'volcano mountain'.

The *kiln room* was central to this proposition – both literally and metaphorically – a representation of the elemental core of Earth herself as I understood it. I stood within the walls of a tall earthern structure of rough brickwork and the occasional square of colour, domed like an egg, its floor dirt or stone-flagged. So, a chamber *within* the chamber of the mountain; fully rendered and reinforced, it reminded me of a vertical kiln, the brickwork like that of a cement kiln I had once stood inside upon decommissioning – cracked, heated, smoke-stained were its refractory bricks but always up to the task at hand. Within the *kiln room*, I heard a strong 'resonant hum' (see Glossary) underpinning and overlaying all (absence) of sound, and was drawn to meditate. The previous night Mr1300BC had instructed me in 'The Way of the Knight' (a teaching included in the annexed essay: *Amici della Luce*). There was much to contemplate …

I have since journeyed to the *kiln room* on my own; now I find therein a chalice in which a huge pulsing heart *breathes* life into the world. Like Mariel's, this altar, where I connect with mountain sentience pure, is a space within a space – deep within the Howe. To be honest, I could barely contain my excitement when I read that the Sidhe recognise the integral nature of mountains to furthering Gaian consciousness; in her *Conversations* with David, Mariel says: '(A mountain) is a major conduit through which the energies of stars and earth meet … (it) is for us not a geographical feature as much as a presence and an energy field' (p.130). She goes on to say that mountains provide points of contact with powerful beings and forces: 'Some are more accessible than others ... (some) prefer to be left alone as they are doing their work in deep solitude ... Most, though, are happy to engage ... When I go into the mountain, then, I am entering into the energy and life of one of the great servants of Gaia, one who itself can perceive the cosmic energies and draw them into our world ... Mountain spirits are among humanity's greatest allies in the changes that you face, though you don't realise it' (p.131).

In the moment I was reminded of the lesson of the *StarGeist* I had seen rise up out of the mountain to collaborate with a (Sidhe?) partner in shared worldwork (as recounted in Chapter 2); I felt more and more resonance with Sidhe-energies and how the constellation of their work-spaces were likewise home-spaces as I conceived – indeed how can it be otherwise when the outer altar we create mirrors the altar of our heart?

Thus, if Mariel's altar could be likened to my *Kiln Room*, her temple would be akin to my *Ten-Foot-Square Hut* – hence the double-moniker for the Altar card within the mountain as much as within me. This particular naming also has a longer-than history (see Glossary). In brief, though, it comes from a 13th century text by the Japanese poet-monk Kamo no Chomei. His *Hojoki*, or 'Record of the Ten-Foot-Square Hut', documented a life of seclusion in his *hojo*, or one-*jo*-square hut (*jo* being a linear measurement equivalent to ten feet). Reading this text, and others in a similar vein, put me in mind of the tiny cottage I had built at Maleny decades earlier in order to commune with her spirit-of-place. It was to be my first consciously-lived experience of immersion *in* and *mergence with* landscape, that which countless mystics have described as their conduit to the divine – in my case the twin joys of immanence and transcendence wrapped up in one delightful Gaian parcel.

Later Mr1300BC would come as an architect of space to help me navigate the energy streams (and signatures) of the *Malakut*. Together we focussed on developing a toolkit for constellating becoming landscapes in which I could meet my interlocutors on equal terms with shared intent – like Mariel's temple such spaces would meld both energy and substance. Yet only with love as my core purpose and the foundation of such spaces' creation would an 'unpolluted' current of energy flow between the worlds. Indeed, this was something I embraced as a natural matter-of-course as the 'way-of-love' (see Glossary) but was sincerely grateful in the moment for how he deepened my understanding of its application.

Companions of the Way

While Maleny may have begun my experimentation with the notion of the ten-foot-square hut as temple, my principal node of connection these days is a grail space 'built' into my home where I write, read, think, dream, meditate. Filled with symbolic touchstones, much love, joy and light, it is where I meet my companions in the grounded presence of the Sacred. Imagine my surprise, then, to find all but one inhabitant of the Gaian Throne image were already dear friends! I shall delight in telling the story of their entry to my life, but first some words about the Throne itself.

Once, years past, on a *Malakut* 'field-trip' in company of others, we were taken on a guided tour of a temple structure hewn deep into the side of a mountain. We wandered past huge sculpted stone crypts depicting great beings from a range of mythic traditions on either side of a vast inner chamber. It was very dark in the space, yet some crypts illuminated in my mind as if by bright daylight, while others remained impenetrable. This I did not question. It seemed to be a function of relevance to my learning and task orientation. The group gradually faded. I walked further and further in; soon I was alone.

Finally I came to an arched crypt at the end of the huge hall, at a place where it seemed to meet the midpoint of the mountain in both height and breadth. Here stood a single (empty) throne, spot-lit at its centre. An absolute masterpiece of ancient carved wood, it was high-backed, with weathered ochre paint. I entered a great silence as I looked upon the throne, and sensed the depth of universal resonance it held on behalf of the felt world. To look upon Jeremy's painting is to therefore enter the same space, and I am immensely grateful for the connection this image invites.

In the *Card Deck of the Sidhe*, David describes the vivid dream experience which led to Jeremy's painting of the Gaian Throne, how the card represents 'in its image of wholeness and service … the aspiration of the soul behind every incarnation' (pp.168-9). In describing how the card resonates for him as a 'meeting place where stars and earth come together' (ibid.), the same essence as that represented by the Howe at the centre of the Stone Circle between the Gates of Stars and Earth, it is little wonder that my *Companions of the Way* chose this place to sit within the Circle. Within the *Kiln Room*, within the *Mountain* – what could be more natural a placement? And once more I am grateful for the congruency of process the *Card Deck* affords my practice, as well as its amplification thereto.

So now to introduce these Companions who surround (my) *Kiln Room's* empty throne.

We begin with 'Eagle-Owl' (so-named – Mr1300BC in one of his many symbolic shape-shifting guises relevant to my learning) who arrived in the 'Garden of the Great Mother' with a young (female) fledgling owl to gift into my care. The Garden was moist and cool, mist-shrouded and green, like a lush rainforest. The fledgling was very tired – learning to fly was hard work! – and dozed in the crook of my arm while I sat in an easy chair. Every now and then she would snuggle closer, look up with her beautiful brown eyes and smile (if an owl can smile). Meanwhile, the Great Mother did the ironing (how's that for symbolism!). All this time, Mr1300BC perched on the high back of my chair and watched. Later he demonstrated how he could shape-shift at will in order to camouflage himself in the world, to blend in with the crowd. Over time I learnt the message of this demonstration – that he (and/or his voice) would appear with insights or wisdoms as and when required. It was as much my work to nurture what he gifted as it was his to make those gifts available. Further, his purpose was to demonstrate how to recognise an energy-signature no matter how the presence constellated in my imagination.

Next, to the beautiful koi swimming in the *sacred pool* at the base of the throne. This took me straight into the territory of the 'nested fishes' of Taoist philosophy, the yin-yang symbol a dear companion to my meditations on the Unity of Being (see Glossary). Indeed, I appropriated the fish (plural) for my website on peace consciousness with the following explanation:

> Why nestedfishes? The perennial Taoist symbol of the yin and yang fishes, nested together to unite the opposites – of heaven and earth, spirit and matter, male and female, and so on – represents my belief that love is the foundation for peace. By hosting a spot of the other's colour within each fish, their respective energies connect and commune, 'speak' to each other, and transform duality into solitary fusion.
>
> In the same way we interconnect with all of creation, whether we are aware of it or not, via the spark of love which is the creative energy that animates all life. We are each unique manifestations sprung from the Ground of Being as love's energy transformed to matter. When we recognise, respect and consciously work toward understanding this commonality, this oneness at the heart of us all, regardless of how different we may seem in our outer forms, love has the capacity to propel each of us toward real and lasting peace – in relation with ourselves, with each other, with the world. ...
>
> To *be* peace, to *think* peace, to *live* peace, we simply need to be love, think love, live love. When we open our hearts to inherent oneness, we shall find that peace is as easy as breathing.

And the wolf? She is dear *WolfMother*, the *genius loci* of the high wild valley where I consciously took root in Swiss soil, where I originally met my *Amici*, where my self-apprenticeship was completed. One day she greeted me, and acknowledged my intent as I walked her domain carrying nought but love in my heart and blessings on my tongue. It is her words – you are welcome here – which are repeated in the card's self-naming. Indeed all my *Companions of the*

Way are 'most welcome' at this fireside, a fireside Mr1300BC himself first lit with burning embers delivered from his pouch to my 'hearth' with the comment: Love in itself is fire.

But who is Spidey? I wondered as I sat with the cards one evening. I teasingly thought to count her legs in homage to the six-legged guardian of Maleny's ten-foot-square hut (it certainly looked the size of a huntsman and without my glasses on definitely appeared short a couple of pins). Perhaps this was she? Deciding as much, I set the cards aside and headed to bed.

Night-walking the *Malakut* some hours later, I had the most extraordinary encounter. I was in a dark space, like a cave, but outfitted like a temple or meeting chamber. I looked from a circular porthole-type window onto the 'world' as it was there, a dark lush jungle or rainforest where two pre-teens, naked, descended thick liana vines out of the canopy in the company of two gorillas. Somehow, in the space, I knew this referenced humanity's connection to its primal roots. The 'family' was happy together, clowning around, hugging, showing each other the tricks of their particular species. I then looked around the cavern – two women were readying the space for a ceremony, lighting candles and torches at the entrance to the temple, where it met a tunnel beyond.

Only later did I realise that the way the space constellated was like the view of the Altar as painted by Jeremy at its entrance; yet my point of view from beyond, within the temple – where, it seems, I was one of several witnesses asked to observe a ceremony. At that moment, in came a spider. Huge. Black. Hairy. She inched slowly in from the tunnel to stand regally at the centre of the room. There was nothing scary about her. She was very elegant, refined; I understood her to be an elder female spirit and felt-sensed her nature as considered and thoughtful, but also firm in conviction. Most interesting were the tiny banks of 'eyes' which came all the way down her legs. There were eyes everywhere; was it because she represented the views of many in her testimony?

She had come to give an account of humanity's fall since I had seen the naked children playing and engaging as 'family'. She was very measured, solemn in what she told, telling of the negligence in humanity's duty of care to the natural world, and how it demonstrated a fundamental lack of respect for the rights of all. I surfaced from this encounter, stunned by the revelatory nature of my witness and with fresh knowledge to counter even the seeming well-meaning stewardship of Earth – in its own way it smacked of arrogance and condescension, the 'we know best' of supposedly righting former wrongs. Only with true partnership, learning from and integrating the views of all could we hope to effectively contribute to holistic outcomes on Gaia's behalf.

So, welcome 'Madam S' (which suits you far better than 'Spidey', methinks!); I thank you most sincerely for joining the *Companions of the Way*!

Taking to the (Faerie) Road

The manner in which I had sat with the cards that evening and the *Malakut* wanders which had brought me into contact with Madam S (definitely an unexpected consequence) was a ritual begun once returned from the fortnight in the eastern Alps at the end of January. In the ten-foot-square hut of my home, I would invoke the full set of the *Card Deck* via their names before setting out (my) Stone Circle – which included all Stones (17) together with, at that stage, a single Dancer, *Companions of the Way* (only later was *Homecome to the Sea*, Jeremy's Ocean and Land, to join the Council).

To commence, I explained to any new voices hovering in the vicinity (witness or potential participant) that they were entering an existing grail space of intimacy and discretion (Chatham House rules applied) where all symbolic interlocutors to Sacred Presence already housed in the space had spun a web of warmth in which universal resonance veritably purred with unguarded delight. I described it as a 'clean well-lighted place' (in Hemingway vernacular), with love as the anchor energy of this ground within the Ground, of this spirit within matter. And I spoke an audible welcome to any who would share its intent.

In making this little speech, I was cognisant of David's notes on 'Safety with the Sidhe' (pp.84-87) in the *Card Deck* guide. My encounters with the subtle realms over many years have followed similar 'rules of the road' – by effecting reciprocal recognition, based on a way-of-love. Such practices evolved organically, over time, yet were seemingly always underpinned by an unconscious knowing to approach the *ganz andere* (see Glossary) with consideration and respect when meeting, and then in whichever way the interrelation continued thereafter.

At the same time, the following comment from David seemed to sum up the intent upon which any forays into new territory could be based: 'I am told by my Sidhe contacts that … this deck is intended and inspired … to be a safe bridge. … In its own way, it is blessed as an expression of their love for the world and their desire to join with human partners in serving the wellbeing of the planet and bringing to birth a Gaian consciousness that allows us to live in the world more ecologically and holistically' (p.85). For my part, I can say with a high degree of confidence that I have felt the inspiration contained in the *Card Deck* and the resonance of its underlying intent. The rollercoaster ride mentioned in the Prologue refers, and shall be dealt with in detail in the chapters to follow.

In this chapter, however, my aim is to set the scene for what follows by describing early forays into such (foreign) territory. In doing so, I was mindful of Mariel's comment in *Conversations* as follows: 'In you, stars and earth meet. … In partnership with us, our desire is for you to become like the Old Ones, who stood and formed the first circles. … You are less child-like than you were then. In some ways you have become darker, but in other ways you shine more brightly and

31

carry a hard-won wisdom and connection to the world … you are in touch with the life within matter in ways we are not. If you will listen, it speaks to you with voices we do not hear. We know the voices of starlight but you hear the voices of the fire within earth and matter' (p.141).

This text was to backbone my daily meditations. Yes, I knew of what she spoke at one level and had clearly experienced same, but within the context of the Stone Circle it meant listening to the voices of the cards as they arose – housed in their material containers was a wisdom already set in train by the intent with which the *Card Deck* had come into being. Of course it manifested initially as the cards' self-naming, but, for example, it also meant that the Condition Cards were not conditional at all in the context of energies wanting to manifest in (my) Stone Circle. They were as keen to be permanent members of the Council as the *Companions of the Way*. This became apparent when the cards' presences were invoked (via their naming) in my home grail space the first time. It was as if an energy-of-interaction had begun at that point with existing 'member-presences' of the grail space (i.e. the symbolic interlocutors the space already housed).

Jeremy's Ancestor Stone was first to speak, basically saying that if I intended to truly *honour* the ancestors (as self-named), then such energy should be ever-present within the Stone Circle, not simply as a conditional witness and/or occasional participant (he'd obviously been talking to the Aboriginal Dreaming artworks in the room as well as the rings 'holding' the energy of my parents' lineage).

Meanwhile, the Fallen Stone was quite disconcerted with his position, and asked me to focus on his self-naming as 'Hope', reminding that despite the warnings and/or caution the stone had counselled Jeremy, it still voiced its ability to grow whole again. As far as this card saw *its* purpose in *my* Circle, hope rested at its energetic core. My commitment to honour same would be by looking ahead (to future bright), at the same time aware of present challenges (as well as whatever loomed on the radar). It was as if it were saying: Yes, all *may* come to naught, but there is always ever hope! I looked to the photos of my children on the dresser, the generations to come who would inherit stewardship of Gaia, and agreed.

Finally to the Stone of Alliance whose message was clear – to engage the energy of the *Card Deck* was to honour alliance in and of itself. Clear, too, was the stone's self-placement in the Circle – at the head of the *Gate of the Stars*. Meanwhile, the Ancestor decided it belonged at the edge of the *Twilight Zone*, while Hope chose to nestle in the cirque of the *Rising Sun*. All fit to purpose, each card had found its home. The full Circle was outlaid before me; all settled into position with a comfortable smoothing of their (ample) matronly laps, as a collective they looked expectantly toward me with an: *And? What next?*

At this I felt the strength in the Stone Circle. Each little piece of printed matter was suddenly, literally, a rock-solid presence. Each contained the strength of commitment, of shared worldwork. Before me stood an invitation to participation (in David's lexicon) but was I ready to don the mantle as Mariel had described in *Conversations* (p.58)? In one respect I already had, long past, with my self-apprenticeship (both learning and tasks); in another when I looked into the face of the *genius loci* in the eastern Alps and promised never not to add my blessings to her watershed of liquid light, never not to be an *Amici* to divine purpose. But to step into a circle of stone, into a grail within a grail and be a grail – 'a Circle for this world' as Mariel says?

David writes: 'It feels like an initiation to me into being one with the Sidhe, of sharing a mantle they have carried but doing so in a new way ... within us as individuals who are also living Grails, living Circles ... (yet) a person needs to be willing to enter into such a covenant and initiation ... and for it to "take", it has to be entered into in right timing' (p.61 & p.59 respectively). Yes, this I knew and understood.

Years earlier I had been witness to a traumatic event 'out of time' which triggered in my mind Margaret Atwood's observation that 'the dead may guard the treasure, but it is useless treasure unless it can be brought back into the land of the living and allowed to enter time once more'; Atwood's text is aptly named *Negotiating with the Dead* (p.178). For my part, compassion propelled negotiation – all because a subtle 'sister' had appeared to me, and said: *There is not enough love in the world.* Entering a covenant with souls of the dead who wanted their story told, in its own small way my work at that time echoed Virgil's plea in the *Aeneid: You gods who rule the kingdom of souls! You soundless shades! ... Grant me to tell what I have heard! With your assent may I reveal!*

Yes, the 'gods' did grant permission, and on occasion I had more subtle guides to the telling (of their treasure) than I knew what to do with. It meant my ethical commitment to honour their trust in me as 'spokesperson' felt like a psychic weight as heavy as any (standing) stone. The experience taught me how it felt to wear a mantle of stewardship in this world on behalf of beings from beyond the veil – the result a dissertation documenting my process of engagement with Virgil's 'gods' to bring inner knowing out onto an external plane together with a major work of prose fiction, *The Taste of Translation* (see Glossary).

The experience also taught me how a 'personal myth' (see Glossary) could be uplifted into the collective (conscious) pool. Indeed, Carl Jung held that because of humanity's common ancestral life, the (collective unconscious) link between and amongst each of us, one's 'personal' myth could never be entirely 'individual'. Extend this notion to the common ancestry shared between humanity and Sidhe and I could see the overarching nature of the mantle and what it could potentially manifest in the world – very exciting on the one hand, perhaps overwhelmingly daunting on the other?

Suffice it to say I had lived previously the felt-sense (or self-imposed obligation, if you like) to honour 'content emerging from the unconscious into consciousness' with the expectation that it 'involved a spiritual or moral task' (another Jungian principle). The question I asked myself was: Could I take on that responsibility again? I felt I needed to learn more, to summon the unveiling of further lessons via the Circle in order to define the intent of any potential engagement before considering entering a covenant for same. Self-doubt also fuelled my concerns in the face of the Circle's collective energy. Would I ever feel *worthy* to share the mantle?

Inviting Lessons

In matters of the *Malakut*, self-guided learning for me has been a longer-than practice, similar in a way to choosing elective classes at Uni to support individual explorations. Specific teachings, therefore, are not forthcoming unless I exhaust all other avenues of research first – a perfect fit to Mr1300BC's mentoring style, and a process which proved no different in this case. Thus, asking the *Circle* to unveil more lessons meant, more often than not, that I was the one being prodded to answer such requests myself.

So, in concert with the self-named cards, I guided myself further into their histories to see what this could reveal – a case of revisiting the past to point a way to the future. Essentially, this related to two distinct sets of cards: the four Heart Stones which, according to David's commentary, always embody the essential power and qualities of their quadrant, and the four Transition Stones which embody dynamic activity between one quadrant and another, a state of unfoldment and flow to carry its conditions forward organically (p.37).

Two of the Heart Stones were known to me – *MakerMan*, aligned with the *Rising Sun*, and *VanDiemen'sMan* of the *Twilight Zone*. Significantly, neither were linked to the Gates of Earth or Stars, the axis line Mariel had described to make the connection between stellar energies and the 'stars within the earth' (p.101). Yes, these stones had self-named, and yes, I had a ritual of connectivity in my own practice of 'threading light' (which I shall describe in the next chapter) but I felt no link to these two stones' energy specifically. Perhaps the story of my 'known' two would shed some light? I investigated:

MakerMan's self-naming referenced the *Malakut* meeting with the subtle being who had demonstrated her attunement to a *StarGeist* that rose up out of a line of mountains in her world so they could 'take flight' together (which I described in Chapter 2). Prior to the demonstration, our discussion had been about the history of human creativity – that making things with our hands, the earthen-textural creation of artefacts, had a greater longevity of practice in the world than latter-day 'virtual' creativity. Her argument was that intellectual pursuits had to be coupled or balanced with an energy of 'making' (see Glossary) for us to not lose touch with reality. There were layers of meaning within our discussion that I was yet to unpack, but this Stone definitely carried her spirit and impetus and named itself accordingly.

VanDiemen'sMan's story is layered in symbolism. He appeared in my *Malakut* orbit years before as a very tall slim dark stranger; immediately seeing Jeremy's artwork for this Stone, I knew who it was. At one point he was a guide, but later when we met, it was as if he had lost his way, had become seriously sad at the state of the world. We wandered cityscapes arm-in-arm while riots raged. I'll never forget his sigh of disappointment and resignation that this is how we treated ourselves and our world. He was a writer, too sad to write, to 'make'.

His right hand was covered in a beautiful mystical tattoo, a compass, and he demonstrated that to find his way 'home' he needed to head West, shown directionally between thumb and forefinger, saying wistfully: *I am following the path of van Diemen*. It was a potent totem, and to help overcome his malaise, my task was to guide him to a huge leather-bound tome, van Diemen's own *Book of Voyage*, which acted as a kind of placeholder for all seekers to state their intent therein.

In coaxing him to try, I said: Let's both write down the deepest thing in our hearts at the same time. Spontaneously each of us wrote: *I promise to write every day*. In spirit, I knew it to mean that whatever each of us wrote each day (for our own self) would be a *gift* to the other, whereby it (so too we) became the other and his/her writing. Like nested fishes, writing was the spot of colour to enable our communion. And in charting this course, we wouldn't lose direction, our compass firmly fixed. A wonderful reminder for my own practice – whenever sad or parched, it is time to troll the depths to hopefully bring healing energies into the *Malakut* too.

I found it interesting how the histories of these two Stones formed an alignment with each other, and with me. But what of the other two? I would need to wait. They had named themselves under my careful scrutiny but had then stood silent within the Circle – stoic, guarded, dormant. Yes, a direct relation was to emerge in time. If not, there would be no story to tell herein, nor methodology of engagement to share in later chapters!

Meanwhile, the four Transition Stones form a seamless story of my path to date, to which various dancers weave in and out of the narrative. An interesting finding, given these Stones are said to foster unfoldment as part of their intended remit. As such it augured well for a future direction integrating the energy of the *Card Deck*. Let me explain.

A *Malakut* landscape years past. A high cliff – I am with an instructor preparing to jump off. No rope, no harness; the instructor simply says: *Hold my hand*, and we leap into nothing, to arrive safely at the bottom after an exhilarating freefall. There I watch as others with ropes and harnesses practice jumping (forwards, not abseiling) from about three metres in height; they tumbleturn, get bumped and bruised, hooked up on things, stuff falls out everywhere. The instructor turns to me and says: *See? Gravity gets in the way when you don't make a big enough leap* (hence the Dancer Edge's self-naming). I was so excited with the success of our jump, a 'radical' methodology with trust at its core, I asked to immediately repeat it. Of course, he said. *I'm always happy when a new hawk is born.* So did the Stone of Identity self-name.

This lesson was part of a string about operating more consistently at a different vibration in order to strengthen communication to, and connection with the subtle realms. The instructor amply demonstrated that 'gravity' could be an issue, causing more problems or injuries than a simple leap into the unknown. Later I would understand how this was akin to being 'buoyed by aether', something I can thank Sidhe companions (through the energy of the cards) for sharing with me. At the time, though, Mr1300BC backed this up with specific guidance in what it would mean to 'belong' in the 'beyond' – of critical importance was the need to be 'centred within'. So did the Stone of Boundary self-name. In the moment of its arising voice, I was reminded of David's practice, standing-in-sovereignty, which is essentially an act of 'centring'.

But it was the following card, the Stone of Opening, which really clinched the deal, so to speak. Its self-naming was soul-knowing pure – a case of Emerson's observation revealed to the blinding light of day. *Yes*, it proclaimed, to any who would listen. *You were 'split open by love'. Do not deny it. For see what has emerged in its wake?* its voice continued, passing the baton to the Stone of *Emergence* in a lovely segue reminiscent of the dynamism at the heart of the Transition Stones. Indeed, 'the inner' had come 'out' – no longer was my soul prepared to hide its strengthening light under the bushel of little me.

Hence the invocational string of verse for these cards proceeds thus:

For a new hawk is born
Who is centred within
Split open by love
For the inner to come out

Into the space of this self-knowledge, I continued my process of ritual attunement to the full *Card Deck*, laying out the Stone Circle as part of my morning meditations, as well as evening, with an invitation, during the latter, for any within the Circle to feel free to take me 'night-walking' if they happened to be in the neighbourhood …

A significant encounter during this early sounding-out period proceeded thus:

The connection faint but a female Sidhe presence visited to introduce herself and her work, and how it could intersect with mine. The proviso, however, was that I needed to ensure I organised my time appropriately so that nothing fell off the table as it were. She seemed to know that I had three areas of focus in my work, one of which connected with hers. As such, I needed to ensure my time, efforts, resources were similarly divvied up – i.e. into thirds.

The issue was not how much time or energy she could devote to our shared work, but how much I could or should devote – hence no more than a third. However, as the connection was faint, flimsy – floating in and out of consciousness – I missed what our together-work could or would involve. At the same time, it is possible that this meeting was pure 'project-management' rather than content-focused, and there was nothing of import that I missed. In point of fact, it reminded me of an earlier *Malakut* meeting during my winter-dark solstice retreat before I had consciously begun any interaction with the *Card Deck*.

That teaching, some eight weeks prior, had focused on how to work on or engage with projects. It was laid out flat like a board game; I was explaining it to someone else, but learning at the same time. There were three 'partners' on the board, each in a different zone, one of which represented myself. In describing the three zones, it was clear that the final work output (out into the world) had to come from the 'me' zone. The others could only provide input. I had to accept responsibility for what was created, made, shared, communicated, done or completed. This was a very important part of the teaching.

One zone of input was book or text-based knowledge and it flashed golden, rising out of the board like a plateau stacked with wisdom – I understood it to be all the written texts collated or collected from the ancients and handed down. A month later I was to find that Jeremy's painting of the Dancer, *Dragon and Books*, was a direct replica of this plateau of books and scrolls, minus the phoenix. In this context, its immediate self-naming as Scholar should be apparent.

The other zone was called 'Outier'. Directly phonetic, I was to discover when transcribing the teaching, to 'out-here'. I understood it to mean that I move in and through (*Malakut*) spaces which are still 'here' from my perspective, even though perceived as outside or *outwith* (a Scottish word for 'beyond') the material; thus a seamless fit with Mr1300BC's earlier comment re belonging in the beyond. Its focus was input, knowledge, wisdom, assistance from living sentient beings resident in the subtle realms; it fit with my 'beyonding' adventures as a source of wisdom and input for work outputs here.

Nevertheless, the point of the teaching, and where I was rapped over the knuckles by an (unseen) instructor, was that I assumed the Outier zone could be joined, combined with the 'me' zone to create a truly joint output arising from same (backed by the written texts of the ancients). Very strongly, though, I received the message that it did not work like that. The notion of partnerships et al could only function up to a point. Whatever was my project or worldwork still had responsibility resting with me – as in its output or implementation into the material world. Yes, I could integrate the inputs of the Outier voices (as well as the golden wisdom teachings) but it still had to come back to the 'me' zone for finalisation. It couldn't be a truly team effort, with all of us equal 'shareholders' (if you like).

Receiving this teaching made me think I had potentially misunderstood what David had described as being invited to partnerships and collaborations with the Sidhe: 'Reconciliation and partnership, the collaborative engagement of our two peoples is the theme that runs through all these *Conversations*,' he writes in closing *Conversations* (p.171). So too Mariel talks of sharing the mantle as she invites us to step into the Circle; at another point she says: 'Come to us in the fullness of your Light and presence, aware of your gifts, your presence; then we can be aware of you. Then we can be partners' (p.147).

Meanwhile, David writes about what such joint undertakings are capable of manifesting: 'I have over sixty years of experience working with subtle beings of one kind or another, and I know pretty well how to engage with them. I know what collaboration and partnership with a non-physical, spiritual being is like and what it can accomplish' (p.168).

Was my understanding of what a partnership entailed different to theirs? Or was I simply demonstrating my ignorance about how it worked between material and *Malakut* partnerships? I read further in *Conversations*, where David considers the ins-and-outs of what is possible: 'The Sidhe have asked us to invite them into our lives to help and to ask for their assistance. There is no guarantee that they can help with what we want, but if we are specific in our request, it gives them something more concrete to work with, as well as making us more present and visible to them' (p.169). This quote seemed to put the teachings I received into perspective and settled my concerns.

To summarise what I had learnt in the two *Malakut* encounters, therefore: There was a project to be managed, in which each party would bring what they could to the table, but as it needed to be 'seeded' in the material world, responsibility for implementation would rest with the entity who could best see it through to fruition – me. Recognised, however, was the fact I had other priorities and should or could only devote a third of my time and resources to this particular project.

It may seem incongruent with the comments made earlier about my reticence to don the mantle, to share stewardship of the Stone Circle as Mariel had outlined, but paradoxically this clarification, which intimated that the ball was fairly and squarely in my court, had the opposite effect. I felt ready to pursue an invitation to participation now that responsibilities for what, where and for whom had been forthcoming – my unseen instructor had been quite forthright in both communications which suited the practical side of my nature. Simply put, the directness and (dare I say?) professionalism of the approach helped solidify my resolve with respect to Mariel's request.

Meanwhile, the less practical side of my nature was bouncing about like a puppy ready to go for a walk: 'I think I'm quite ready for another adventure,' it said with Bilbo-like glee. It was time to step into the Circle and say 'yes' to I knew not what ...

Donning the Mantle

When Mariel attunes to David, she describes the resonance that draws them together: 'Like all affinities, it is based in love but also in an act of will grounded in understanding. You have a saying about standing and walking in another's shoes. This creates affinity ... I have said that I have an altar that I dedicate to our contact. It is a place – a condition – in which I may attune to you ... it is a place in which I hold the qualities that make up your "shoes"' (*Conversations*, p.145-6).

At this point I need to provide a specific chronology of the several days between when I consciously 'thought the thought' to don the mantle and the opportunity to actually do so. The easiest way is by reproducing my journal entries describing same. But first another quote from Mariel which followed her "shoes" analogy: 'Once you set forth your intent, we can blend with the field you create and enhance its capacities to connect and to manifest' (p.147).

1 March: ('We are pe-ee-eace, lo-o-o-ove ...') Sunday midday, just me and animals. There's a tune in my head and I don't know where it's from; a simple tune that I discovered floating around in there as I was making the bed (i.e. I was in the grail space of the ten-foot-square hut) with the middle bits clearly involving voice but I didn't know what. It's as if I have heard it somewhere, sometime but I can't tell (anymore) if it's here or *Malakut*, present or memory. It's an innocent ditty, but in repeating it (or having it repeated over and over in my mind, *inner*-hummed), 'peace' and 'love' keep popping into the voiced parts and from there I populate it with the rest of my usual mantra (see Glossary). The imagery which accompanied its arising was of young maids holding hands, dressed in flowing white, hair streaming behind and flower-filled, dancing round a maypole sort of structure in a well-lit meadow. Simple innocent joy to dance and sing of how we *hold* and flow the Sacred into the world, skipping around with ribbons and flowers, pastel colours and rippling laughter. Is this the work

of Faerie, planting tune and image in my mind? Are these literally dancers from the *Card Deck*? Such sweet imagery and music, as if written for pipe or flute; such whimsy!

<u>2 March</u>: Last night to bed and reading through my marked notes in the Sidhe book, I came to the Guardian of the Grail ritual and felt: Yes, it's time; this morning post-YMM (see Glossary), it would be time. Yet overnight, a lucid encounter. I was in an (internal) amphitheatre-type setting, people arriving – a proper *circle* with seating stepped up around, maybe two to three rows high, the seating (benches, nothing fancy) divided into sections with entrances at several points.

I was chatting with several people waiting for the event to begin. Decided to move with another woman to a section with a single row (i.e. with no stepped-up seating behind, just a wall), space for circa four to five max. We sat and chatted, all around was activity and bustle as people arrived. We were waiting for one more person to come ('Anne'), and then we could start. She was a bit late but finally showed and sat down beside 'me'. Now our complement of *three* was complete. We introduced ourselves; we hadn't met before. We then decided to go and mingle, introduce ourselves to the other groups – it was as if this were the first part of a workshop.

But as I got up I noticed I only had one shoe. I rummaged around under the bench and discovered the other one pushed far back. Each shoe was different – one a hiking boot, the other an old leather sandal from down under days that I barely have a chance to step out in now. On waking, I immediately thought: Is it because I have a foot in each world? (Later I was to have a giggle when I re-found Mariel's comment about walking in each other's shoes, and later still, I would have an 'a-ha' moment about what it really portended but that is for a future chapter.)

Against such a backdrop this morning I stepped into the Stone Circle and said: Yes. I accept the mantle of responsibility, of guardianship. I said: This life, this time, in this skin, I join your lineage, I share your work, harnessing the energies of love for God, for Gaia, for all. As part of the solemnity of the moment I let my arms do what they will, and they gradually widened out from my body as if someone were slipping a cloak on and then came together in front of my chest as my head dropped in prayer. I felt a ball of pulsating energy at my solar plexus as strong as I've ever felt post-chi. That's when I knew that they knew, that we all knew. All together serving the One and it only works if we all work together. Amen.

In the wake of this event, nothing momentous happened. Life went on; it was a matter-of-course to integrate the Circle into daily practice. We would sit together, meditate. It felt like the sweet 'hanging out' time of good friends – you want to go get an ice-cream? Yeah, sure. That sort of thing. They had joined the grail space of the ten-foot-square hut and I had stepped into the grail within a grail. In the end, no big deal.

Yet after several weeks, I had some strange inklings. When sitting with the cards, drawing them at random, listening to their arising voices, I would 'return' from meditation via a different path than usual. Suddenly I would find myself arriving back *in* the hut from the garden, specifically from under the Elder tree in its corner. A strange sensation – neither a before nor after could I graft to the moment of finding myself there, and then suddenly back here. I knew this tree as the overlighting presence of our garden – *TreeMother*, I call her, and have invoked her spirit on various missions over the years; so too have often sat within her space for a chat and cup of tea, even within her branches when the fancy took me. The self-naming of Jeremy's Faerie Gold Dancer is this presence, pure and simple, but until that point I was unaware she was somehow connecting herself with the hut. Hmmm.

Then, one day, around the time of the Spring Equinox, I wrote in my journal:

> I feel vague, washed out and/or through, parts of me want to speak but only with a breeze-blown quality to match the mistiness-of-me which began last night, sitting with the cards awhile. Suddenly I was 'away' and I don't know where. Now, still, it's as if part of me hasn't returned. A voice announced at one point: *We're here at Leaf Green Meadow Devon Glade.* OK, fair enough, but I have no memory of this place or my presence thereat. It's as if a spring-clean is going on inside today; swept through with aether, there's no gravity within. I am awash with the aetheric flow of the universe in and through me … So let's draw a card, ask its opinion. *When Did I Forget the Beauty of the World?* Good point. Who are you, Dancer? From a Devon Glade? Speak – tell what you know:

> *I am the sweet girls dancing the maypole, a song of love in our singing heart*
> *I am the bird you watched from the window just now intent on a worm for tea*
> *I am a shape-shifter of joy between here and there*
> *My joy my task so you may see –*
> *For when you see truly*
> *How can you forget Beauty?*
> *All around, within, beyond and, too, through,*
> *Aethereal-material are one and the same*
> *In my reality …*

Thank you! Yes, I watched the yellow tit at its task, serious its intent to uncover the prize. A big wormy thing too, it was. Beaten against the branch, then tastily enjoyed. Such a delight to observe! To see is to remember. To see is to banish forgetfulness of the beauty in, of, around, through – Gaia flooded, *awash* with Beauty. Aetheric. Material. I think you mean to say that even as I am awash, not 'me', there is yet the seeing, the *being*? What more? I hear you itching to speak further!

You are here, you are there. No matter. Enjoy the state enjoined. It is part of your journey, education, to experience each and every facet of how manifestation and a-manifestation is entertained. The joy to be, to flow, can be quietly spaciously engaged. You are still within the All – what can not be? You know this, now you simply manifest another facet of the jewel in the spaciousness (spaceyness?) without process-of-experience observed, felt. The encounter can thus be this immediate, the state changed as deliberately unerringly as I at a maypole or a bird feasting become. The time-space intersect is no intersect per se. The conundrum of the here and the there is not needed to be solved, explained. You knew intuitively that you were not disturbed by being awash with space, with a-engagement with the world, not even a felt-sense of gliding to hold you to anything. You weren't disturbed and yet you try to explain.

Simply rest in the awayness of the Devon Glade or any other non-place. You see, therefore you remember. And the felt-sense will return as or when needed to flesh out an a-flesh experience (if needed!). You know there is nothing to fear; you know Love is the solidity within aether, that the Ground ever-grounds you. You're being very silly (but a nice silly, like a child – I don't mean to offend, I just mean to tell that you knew this already and that is why you feel the way you non-feel do) but I'm glad we had this chat. It's been silly-fun for me too. That worm was big! Enjoy the state enjoined (did I say that already?). Embrace the state embraced (for it infused you; 'took the you out of you' as you describe). Be the space, the aether as you are the stone, the mountain. You have a saying: Let wind enter, keep mountain still. It's not far from wind, air, to aether. Soon it will feel like home to you too!

It was a lovely experience to stream this Dancer's voice in text, such a buoyant joyous voice, 'dancing' her quality through her words. Also wonderful was to actually hear her perspective on what I felt (which I only really could when reading the text back through; at the time of transcription it was a pure stream, so fast, like quicksilver, needing to be captured on the page). Later I re-read parts of *Conversations* to see if Mariel had something to say on 'being the space, the aether' as *Beauty* counselled. The following seemed relevant:

'This relationship works both ways. For you to truly enter our world you must become the dancers that weave around us as stones. The cards mirror a reality in both worlds, for we are both stones and dancers. You must surrender your fixity and melt into a more fluid part of yourselves, becoming more Sidhe-like in this regard. But this fluidity doesn't define who you are any more than it defines who we are. It is a capacity that we both have that can enable us to melt into each other' (p.51).

I found this interesting because I often experience what I call the 'meltworld' where my felt-sense is of *mergence* with the All. It generally manifests as a feeling of expansion, or extension, of diffusion into and with landscape and all which populates it, seemingly mirroring Mariel's call for us to 'surrender' our fixity. But the feeling of being 'awash' with aether – if, indeed, it is part of the same phenomenon which I intuit as such in the manner of *Beauty's* comment that it manifests 'another facet of the jewel' – I had only experienced rarely till working with the *Card Deck*. A very long time ago, I had described the sensation in a short story, *A Gentler Horizon*. In the moment of denouement, *the protagonist says: I am the vapour, and I am as light as air.* However, at that point, only a glimpse twinned with a barely awakening practice.

My Dancer, *Beauty*, said: *Soon it will feel like home to you too.* And that indeed has proved to be the case. Mariel says: 'This fluid intermediate state is a natural phenomenon brought about by the differences in energy between your state of being and ours' (p.50). In probing the difference between this felt-sense to other expressions of connectivity with the subtle realms, my best description for it now is 'lightness-of-being'. My being (i.e. mountain) is as intact (and still) as it ever was, but the flow of my being into the world has become dense with aether (i.e. light as air). Beauty said: *You know Love is the solidity within aether, that the Ground ever-grounds you.* This clarified how the density of 'lightness' manifests in my experience, and I thank her for compressing this fact into such a simple wisdom!

It may not make sense the way I describe it (just put it down to my strange Huxleyian mode-of-being), but perhaps Mariel's explanation will help: 'In dealing with us, you must strengthen this adaptability ... (It is) your fluid self, but it's a "grounded fluidity" ... When you successfully adapt to and flow with changing circumstances in your life, you are fluid in a grounded, practical way, one that is connected to what is happening and to your environment. You are not simply swept away' (pp.52-3). *The solidity within aether*, the density of lightness-of-being – very difficult, it is, to use language to describe experiences which are *outwith* language; I thank the reader for his/her patience!

Regardless of vocabulary used, however, it was not a conscious decision on my part to strengthen this adaptability, but in noticing how it constellated within me and in the circumstances surrounding my interactions with the *Card Deck*, my descriptor for the felt-sense – *lightness-of-being* – became a quick shorthand reminder to self each time I felt a certain mistiness kick into action. A top-up mindfulness practice, if you like, focused on attuning to those with whom I share a mantle of stewardship, in trust and in hope.

One final anecdote to close this chapter on first forays with companions known and (increasingly) unknown. Early April, a month or so after stepping into the Circle and donning the mantle, I found myself, together with F, at a formal dinner in an elegant salon – candle-lit chandeliers, perhaps a dozen round tables for eight set out across its lovely polished parquetry, white linen, 'silver-service', the full deal.

We sat at table conversing mainly with a woman to my left, discussing the veritable feast set before us. It was extraordinary – left fusion-cooking far in its wake – and all delectably vegetarian to boot! The whole atmosphere was upbeat, festive, joyous. This was a major celebration and we were honoured to be invited. I had no sense of knowing anyone here; all were strangers, but it seemed an ideal opportunity to get to know each other in polite exchanges. Suddenly the woman decided that to ramp up the festive spirit we should have wine. She couldn't believe my glass was empty!

There appeared a decanter of white wine which she poured into a highly unusual (and tall) glass with (solid) silver rings or ribbons encircling it – the silver wasn't adhered to the glass but formed within the glass itself (is that possible?). In any case, it was a huge glass and she just kept pouring; it must have been half-full by the time she laughingly stopped. Then she turned to F and did the same, but this time with red wine. The atmosphere thereafter became increasingly gay – what a party!

It seems another Dancer, *Sharing a Moveable Feast*, had decided to conjure an opportunity to meet. Such a wonderful treat to be part of this broader assembly, and for my symbolic acceptance amongst the ranks of Faerie to be honoured with the serving of (white) wine. Meanwhile, it is clear F is more at home in the material than the *Malakut* – the colour of his wine also fit to purpose. It's not often that I 'gather up' his energy-signature with my own for a *Malakut* adventure, but given his penchant for a good drop it seemed a relevant excursion for us both to engage in the context of our shared commitment to Gaian worldwork.

At this point in proceedings – chronological and chapter-relevant, let me give thanks to the *Card Deck* for facilitating all adventures so far, as well as David, Jeremy and Mariel for laying such sturdy foundations in the first place. Indeed, who could ever have imagined that this was (barely) the beginning?

Chapter 5: Starseeds and Meteorite Showers

**A connective thread between Heaven and Earth
flowing Love out into the world ...**

I found it a revelation to learn the history of the Sidhe; so too to discover our shared ancestry as 'Children of the Stars': 'The simplest metaphor is that our ancestors worked with sound and spoke or sung into being whatever they were seeking to manifest. ... The world itself was like a giant vibrating crystal singing in the vastness of the cosmos, and our ancestors came to sing with it in a choir of unfoldment and evolution. What you must understand is that the capabilities of our ancestor still live within us. You have a word for it: we are *fractals* of that ancient being' (*Conversations*, p.34).

From a (conscious) knowledge bank of nil on that score, I immediately began to tie wisdoms shared by Mariel to multiple strands uplifted from my own subtle realm learnings over the years. For example, once I stood before the 'ancient' (as my mind comprehended this being) and as the image faded, a finger suddenly pointed out of the aether, touched my forehead directly at the third eye, and said: *You.* At the time I wrote in my journal: 'I understood this to mean not "you" (i.e. me) personally but collectively; humanity as the legacy of this ancestry; I understood that there is a need to reclaim our heritage, what it means to be us.'

'The more you attune to your inner legacy, the more you come into resonance with us,' Mariel says (p.156). It seems a process of attunement had already begun without my (conscious) realisation. This chapter, therefore, describes such memory and uplift of our inner legacy to provide context for how the knowledge became amplified in concert with the *Card Deck*. As the reader moves through the chapter, he or she is welcome to cross-reference what I tell with what is told in *Conversations*. At different junctures, I shall be drawn to do the same.

At the outset, though, to clarify the form in which collective memory emerges (from inner to outer), I find tuning the radio to the right frequency is best achieved in the stillness and emptiness of dream- or night-consciousness or, alternately, deep meditation when all thought-processes (as a natural matter-of-course) collapse. For whatever reason, I am acutely sensitive to white noise and others' subtle 'chatter'; accordingly, it can take a while for transmission lines to clear sufficiently to receive a lucid signal; ancillary to this is the potential to pick up 'lint' or other by-products emanating from the collective field.

In translating what is shared by subtle interlocutors, I try to keep the facts spare and relevant, yet at times include sensory details for context, given that what arises is always couched in symbolic image and language. Thus, the caveat communicated in Chapter 1 continues to apply. So too the introductory comment that the reader will find herein threads in the telling crosshatched with others in chapters fore and aft.

Nevertheless, by the conclusion of (the text's) conclusion, I hope all rhizomatic tendrils, lines of flight and ant armies marching between 'thematic plateaus' small and large (see Glossary), can successfully (and succinctly) intersect in the reader's mind to 'spark' a way forward in their own adventures with the Sidhe. For what I relate is simply the *actuality* of interconnectivity – one to the other to the other without end – of all causes and conditions ripened toward an emergent holism in which our beautiful darling Gaia is seen as centre and circumference (as well as all in-between), an orb of wonder in which we are blessed to participate, at *one* with the threads we weave on *her* behalf (for, indeed, it is our own: microcosm-macrocosm refers) within her delicately spun sphere of crystal light.

Cosmic Relations

Up until some years ago, my ignorance of all matters subtly cosmic led me to think that great beings existed anywhere and everywhere, happening to stop by whenever they were in the neighbourhood, given that I assumed their neighbourhood was the entire universe and/or beyond. At one point Mr1300BC told: *The children of Apollo, the sky god, walk among us and do his work.* With no image to accompany these 'words formed', a distinct lack of clarity existed in my brain to contemplate the notion. But that was before a bunch of dudes showed up in my ten-foot-square hut one day and announced they hailed from the Rings of Saturn (RoS). Readers may chortle at my lame surprise at their revelation but all I can do is shrug in response. Until that point no subtle conversationalist had ever thought to share whence they came, and equally I had never thought to ask.

Although hanging out in the same solar system, I found it interesting that these chaps were far from conversant with the ways of humankind. We share a laugh about it now, but their energetic approach at that first meeting was as subtle as a sledgehammer (yes, pun intended) – it was as 'cold' as any person's whose emotional intelligence (i.e. EQ as opposed to IQ) quotient is zip. I have met far more empathetic beings before and since – beings whose radiance of love has eased any discord in vibrational connectivity. These chaps' radiance was overlain by a seriously scientific and business-like bent, not especially sensitive to a writerly-whimsical lass. Fortunately, however, my ability to integrate difficult energetic signatures improved over time. I know it is simply a matter of stepping up or down the energy differential between the two until there is the possibility of meeting on (relatively) similar vibrational terms, thus none of my commentary should be seen as unkind, but in the moment of encounter it *can* feel very confronting, like being hit with a plank of four by two, even if the wielder of said plank has no idea of the intensity of impact!

In an important respect, though, Messrs RoS' arrival and announcement of home turf opened me to great beings' alignment with certain physical manifestations of the cosmic realms, as well as the 'communities' which may (subtly) dwell in these particular spaces. Thus have I had the joy to receive Mars in my parlour and be instructed in knowledge relevant to unfolding the path to be walked, and to intimately know Sun – dear Home Star – as a loving brother whose 'song' is infused with a child's endearing innocence. Moon is a regular mothering conversant, while Jupiter – Lord of Planets – lives up to his regal name by maintaining aloof observance of (this) mere mortal.

Mariel writes that nothing is separate – a fact which manifests for me as an opportunity to enjoin regular *Hello the House* moments with our whole universal family, something which can annoy my (most proximate) family no end. For example: 'Come and say hello to the family!' I cry from the back verandah on a snowy crystal-clear night. 'Hello family!' the youngest yells from the couch. 'Now shut the door, Mum; we're freezing!'

'To (the Sidhe), all these celestial bodies are living beings who form a most intricate and intimate web of connection and influence, of which Gaia is part' (p.55). Hear, hear. However, the encounters I wish to share in the context of this text relate specifically to my relations beyond the immediate 'back yard' of solar system, to relations vested in stellar realms – something which unconsciously accompanied me all my years as an expansiveness of joy to be awash in cosmic presence tempered by an ununderstood ache of being far from home. Brought to surface consciousness (i.e. remembered) in the wake of my RoS visitors, and

47

cryptically suggested by Mr1300BC that the 'beyond' is where I belonged, finally this knowledge was to deliver me back into the *heart* of Gaia's felt world, right here, right now – to the *life* of Dogen's *Mountains and Waters Sutra* dwelling in (and as) my own body and mind. The 'a-ha' moment came when I realised it mirrored Mariel's wisdom: 'By remembering how you are of the stars, you can understand how to be more fully of the earth' (p.111). Let us begin:

> Between the here and the now
> there is then;
> and then is there,
> still waiting.

Words formed in meditation, by whom I know not. Perhaps, out of time, it referred to the Dancer card not yet arrived in my conscious orbit – Stag and Pool. Self-named once seen, its image, like all others, had been twinned with a snatch of text, a placeholder in my consciousness to re-guide entry to a particular *Malakut* scape once visited never forgotten: *Where we drink at the Sacred Pool ...*

I had been on a journey – my guide the Sky Father, a new actor, one whose energy signature I had not before met; very calm, very settled, very ancient. He took form in my imagination as an extremely tall slim being – half-stag, half-human; hooves for feet and hands, deer-head and antlers reaching high above me. There was an extraordinary depth to our connection; a knowing beneath language which required no communication.

I was part of a group he led to an autumn-wintery landscape. We made our way through a grove of skeletal trees above a pond, but while the group followed him toward a clearing beyond the stand of trees, I felt an immediate pull to skip down some wide stone steps to the pond itself, which I named *Sacred Pool*. In the moment, I literally felt like a young child coming home from kindergarten, only recently independent, out in the world, so full of joy to be coming *home*, to have made it back on my own after the big adventure of the day. Nonetheless at the same time the thought arose: Well it's a bit dumb if your joy to skip down these steps suddenly causes you to slip on the moss! (Thus spake the ego-oracle.) Nothing untoward occurred, however. I reached the water's edge without mishap, and knelt down to greet the pool.

Now it might make no sense to greet a pool but I felt an extremely *deep* urge to do so. And as I communed with the pool *itself*, hands started to rise out of the water to greet me in return. This wasn't grotesque in the least. It was nothing like Frodo's experience in *The Lord of the Rings*; neither was it similar to water-police dramas on television replete with decomposing 'floaters'. Intuitively I knew these to be the ancestors who *lived*, eternally, in the pool. A spontaneous action on my part, no thought imposed on 'true nature' (see Glossary) to do as it did. The fact was I was *home*; thus perfectly natural to *greet* home. Both in and out of the space, I felt so blessed, so filled with joy – the ancestors had arisen, touched me, acknowledged my homecoming with love.

At this point, Sky Father and the group returned from the clearing, and we all entered the pool together. Instantly I floated in the water with all others while he and the Elders walked its surface. In the same moment, I had an insight as to lineage. Words formed: *The Mother is the Mother of the Father and the Brother and the Child*. Sky Father's Mother, went the logic, was the *Sacred Pool itself*. As soon as I integrated this wisdom into my own experience, and affirmed its truth, the pool morphed into a cavern deep within the cradle of the Earth replete with amphitheatre.

Here we sat as our 'Creation' story was projected onto the cavern's domed ceiling. Backed by sung commentary, we communed with beautiful calming images of the planet as seen from space. I knew: *We had come from a place beyond the stars to people Earth*. And as the story proceeded, I watched as if time skipped forward to post-date our current 'negligence' in duty of care (the key words here were 'emissions' and 'we have to leave') to a time when the world was gradually absorbed (re-absorbed?) into the stars, with fiery explosions and much light, while we moved further and further away from the harmful belly of impact.

I returned from this space deeply settled; the profound love experienced in the company of our entire 'sky' lineage suffused me. Finally uplifted to consciousness from the depths of soul wisdom was the knowledge of the ancestral star blood flowing through my subtle veins, as with all humanity's, and which the *Card Deck's* Dancer works to keep radiant and proximate in my daily communions: *Where we drink at the Sacred Pool ...*

My 'take-aways' from the encounter, however, may seem incongruous with the theme of humanity's collective forgetfulness and disrespect for our planetary home projected onto the cavern's ceiling. But in remembering our shared story and why we are here, I felt intimately grounded in (and seemingly inducted into) the *courage* needed to challenge the potentiality of such an outcome. Here was confirmation of *why* we needed to stand in the sovereignty of our incarnation – here, now.

It wasn't long before the theme of negligence repeated. I found myself in a space, witness to a team's misuse of ancient knowledge – without context, it was applied inappropriately, to dire consequential ends. Same ol', same ol'. As a result, I was 'going home', wondering what it would take to solve the mess we had created in the world. Suddenly, a female voice spoke loud and clear inside my head, like an aethereal prophecy. Things in the world would only be as they should be, she said, *when the Spirit is once again at One with the Third*. My insight was immediate – this was Gaia's voice; 'I saw' her torn, rent, wrenched from her home, 'third rock from the sun'. To restore balance, she needed to be at One with her Earth.

Meanwhile, on another *Malakut* journey, I joined a 'bus tour' to witness the chaos and destruction caused by the insensitivity of humanity to partner with Earth toward a vision of holism. Yet this time I held a map in my hands of how it 'should' be. I showed it to the extraordinarily huge androgynous presence sitting beside me on the bus, and said, as if making my own prophecy: *One day Moon and Stars will come here to Earth and share with us their fantasies of how life should be too. That will enrich the Whole-of-the-Whole.*

In the moment, 'I saw' living presences in spaces deep within Moon, as well as others of our planetary kin, and indeed further, beyond, in the stellar realms. I saw all life *sustained* in crystal'd membranes, as if in states of suspended animation, all awaiting their time to arise, to *dance* the shared Gaian dream of holism through the cosmos – all this flashed in my mind at the moment of prophecy. I had said 'one day' excitedly to my neighbour, but still I heard the wistfulness in the voice temper the remark. I *yearned* for us to reach a level of consciousness to make the map I held a reality. I *knew* the potentiality existed …

Starseeds

I have since intuited that I needed to see the tragic impact of humanity's actions on the inner worlds at that time in my personal history, even though causing me much despair. A direct thread of searing pain connected my bloodied heart to Gaia's torn spirit; I shared her primal loss; I wailed, I keened.

Till four 'starseeds' were gifted into my care in a ceremony conducted by an unseen source. I considered, thoughtfully, that one should be preserved where (or as) it was for the time being (there was earthen-type imagery, as if it rested in an urn or a cave, not yet 'brought to light') but that the other three were ready to grow into whatever it was they would grow into. I accepted their shining radiance, held their tiny orbs in my cupped hands; they pulsated with light. In the context of the encounter, the concept of starseeds was completely new to 'me-consciousness'. Yet it was as if my soul already knew what to do to nurture and birth these seeds into the world as a natural matter-of-course. This was its job; it seemed quite comfortable with the responsibility; 'my' task simply to allow the process to unfold in whatever way necessary to take root in this skin's life.

'Me-consciousness' was still intrigued, however, so I decided to ask the *I Ching* for assistance to uncloak the mystery. Its response: *Tranquillity – The small goes, the great comes.* This is auspicious, and developmental. Three yangs followed by three yins; no moving lines (the classic mark of ambivalence, and a rarity in my lexicon). Indeed, I felt real strength and determination in the tossed coins.

They had a message and wanted it imparted: 'With yang strong on the inside and yin submissive on the outside, the primordial gradually returns and acquired conditioning gradually melts away; thereby it is possible to reach the realm of pure yang with no yin. It is a 'matter-of-course' then to be fortunate in action, and for activity to develop.' I was no closer to solving the intrigue but at least the toss confirmed what my soul had felt in the encounter – it knew what it was doing by concentrating on the three 'yang' seeds. 'I' should simply rest in tranquillity, just go with the flow. And indeed, this was reinforced some months later in a conversation with Mars about the connection between ego and soul, the twinning of purpose in their (our!) joint task (i.e. this lifetime's incarnational journey). An overwhelmingly lucid encounter, at the same time I felt centrally *calmed* by his presence. While I had integrated this wisdom previously from other sources, to connect with him directly was a wonderful affirmation for which I was deeply grateful (and told him as much).

My encounter with the starseeds occurred in the eastern Alps a week or so after I had set off on the snow-hike as a self-action to contribute to peace-sink energy, which later led to my first correspondence with David in early 2014. Between these two events I had encountered the Gaian Throne of the *Card Deck* Dancer which was to self-name a year later as *Companions of the Way*. Not long after, the *StarGeist* teaching arrived in my orbit. 'Twas a busy *Malakut* month for which detailed records were a necessity – I had no idea how all these threads would intersect, nor at what point. But everything seemed to be pointing toward integrating the twin notions that we are of the stars and of the earth *simultaneously*.

Over and over, my 'home' amongst the stars would constellate with earthen imagery, my incarnation in the world with stellar brilliance. Once I walked in the 'Garden of the Great Mother', in her company, before being assigned to composting duties – the fertility of the *soil* was paramount to grow her rows of *silver* beet, their shiny, waxed and deeply green leaves bursting with health before my mind's eye. In another scenario, I sat with D designing a poster for his 'school project', its image a beautiful nightscape of mountains rising three-dimensionally into the midnight blue of a star-lit sky stretched about the poster's rim. So beautiful and delicate – this our world, our inheritance, our gift to gift on.

Thus did I tell the legend of the 'sky child' to myself in oracular voice, one of the early legends shared by the Sidhe, before I knew about the Sidhe. It told how our relationship with the Earth began with a child's innocence, discovering the glory of the world for the first time. Full of delight and wonder did she stand wide-eyed before the magic of the world; her eyes reflected the stars within the earth, her tiny arms made great arcs, great sweeping sky circles of her joy. It just was and she just was. I am! she cried aloud, over and over. And all life responded – again, and again. Heart to breathing heart, she and the All *one* in, of, through, with (interconnectivity: 'tis a prepositional party!) Gaia's beautiful garden.

At times in meditation, I would experience directly this joy at the heart of the world; for example when a huge flock of birds once appeared in my vision, banking and turning – making their own sweeping circles of pure joy with wings broad and strong; a display of electric blue feathered freedom in which I was embraced, uplifted by the whole. Glory, glory, glory – all cells singing in concert, the chi (see Glossary) of shared circuitry – this gift, gifted on.

Not long following, the starseeds returned in new form:

In a *Malakut* setting, I sat at a kitchen table with a woman; we were discussing interconnectivity over a cup of tea when, suddenly, a richly textured carpet unfurled on the floor beside us. It depicted the inky night sky; a female shape was clearly discernible therein – like a constellation, but with the stars so closely packed together her form could clearly be seen without any imaginative projection. The figure stood, with one arm raised, as if in the midst of a dance. Words formed as we beheld this image: *We come from the stars and we return to the stars*. Something I had learned from other sources but had never encountered in such ornate visual expression before.

I was then handed a small ball, and understood it to be like a starseed. It was warm, glowing, 'alive', but compared to the seed which was an orb of pure light, this was solid, dense, like a ball. I intuited it was our stellar ancestry *within*; it was called our 'Earth-consciousness'. For the stellar realms to connect with us as *intended*, we needed to return this ball to the stars – not as individuals but as a collective. There it would be absorbed by the energies, their reciprocity of which would enable the continued 'evolution' of Earth-consciousness here in material space and time. The 'return' I learnt in two demonstrations – one where I myself rolled the ball directly into the female form in the carpet (who by this stage was called 'Mother'); the other where the ball traversed a difficult maze-like concourse on the table before dropping down into the carpet. Enduringly, throughout, was the constant refrain: *We come from the stars and we return to the stars*.

I returned from the space energised by all experienced and learnt in such a compact demonstration to find myself within earshot of a joyous chorus singing up a storm; unlike angelic choirs encountered on other occasions, these voices presented as a scout troupe – youthful, marching down a path below my house, song uplifted to where I lay. I felt such joy myself that I longed to join their expression of praise and immediately could – not as vocalisation, but waves of energy surging through me and spontaneously radiating out. This would be my song, my expression commensurate with the scouts'; 'praise' the word accompanying each inflowing, inpouring, outpouring, outflowing wave. A *felt*-mantra, a *body*-constituted-mantra shared on and on, my own liquid light – being *and* flowing the world with blessing.

Here was the purpose of humanity's presence writ large; there was a reason I felt the ache of being far from home, yet simultaneously *embedded* in our Earth home. Indeed do we come from the stars and return to the stars. Yet in the *heart* of the felt world – here, now – our presence is needed; a difficult maze-like concourse to be negotiated, granted, but ever with the possibility to stream our joy from the glowing ball of light we carry within. Our inheritance, our gift, to gift on ...

'Twas not the first time I had been flooded with stellar energies. Learning to work this light, through the platform of my own self (light), is the subject of the annexed essay, *Amici della Luce*. Over the years it would emerge in different ways, yet its underlying energetic intent remained ever the same – to stream light into the world through the grail space of our material incarnation, itself the connective thread between 'heaven and earth' (as my symbolically-inclined mind expresses the relationship). The reader can imagine, therefore, my excitement to find synergies revealed between this small self-practice and Mariel's descriptions of the work of the Sidhe as well as the exercises proposed in *Conversations*.

Like most experiential learning opportunities, this was a classic synapse moment when Anne-thinking skipped over from one rhizomatic line of flight to another. Some years past, I had been writing-into-existence (see Glossary) my engagement with mountain sentience, specifically about being a message bearer between 'home' mountains on either side of the world. Walking a songline in the spirit of Aboriginal *tsuringa* tracks which follow the footsteps of the ancestors, I committed to carry a stone of blessing from one *genius loci* to the other, to connect the special place each had in my heart with the other. No more than a small token of community, but one that bespoke their shared *beingness*.

In writing my understanding of this task into existence I saw the micro (personal) reflect the macro (collective); indeed the action engaged a *broader* purpose – to bind (or re-bind – I have no idea how deep or far back such sentient memory reaches in Earth-consciousness) a thread of connectivity between two completely unique geological sites on either end of the world as an act of solidarity *with* and *for* all unique forms of sentience bound each to the other to the other without end. The result is the essay: *Der Ruf der Berge*, and the synapse moment arose, the leap across the void occurring when I recalled an encounter with stellar presence the previous night, when recipient to the (now) familiar 'flood' of white light. Why, I wondered, had energy from *beyond* the physical plane arrived just as I was putting finishing touches to an essay describing the specificities of my engagement with Earth-energies? What synchronicity was I missing? The wondering went further: Was being a font for stellar energies intended as task orientation similarly? To act *between* the planes of existence? And/or in concert with Earth-energies?

The questions raised by the intersect of stellar presence with Earth-oriented task remained as such for the remainder of the year, until a wonderfully synchronistic (follow-up!) opportunity arrived in the letterbox, otherwise known as the package containing Lorian's Sidhe resources; yet at the time with no clue this prequel constituted a type of apprenticeship-practice for the Acts of Awakening to be outlined in Chapter 7. Notwithstanding, I crave the reader's patience while the scene is set ...

Presence Meets the Present

As previously recounted, a spanner in the works meant my plan to begin engagement with the *Card Deck* and associated texts was delayed until the fortnight spent in the eastern Alps in January. Nevertheless I was conscious of Sidhe hovering in the vicinity, and intuited that I had been witness to or participant in several 'excursions' during my winter solstice retreat. Throughout, however, I maintained regular engagement with (known) expressions of sacred presence as this journal entry demonstrates:

> 29 December 11pm. Outside -5C or so, the snow circa 40cm deep. *TreeMother's* Christmas lights throw the most beautiful aura of blessing out into the garden, to kiss her snowy landscape beyond, and I feign to see subtle beings bobbing in and around the snow-covered branches, topiaries and chairs, dancing with unguarded winter-dark delight. The Tibetan flags are rent and stiff with ice, busy transforming what was to what will be. All in all, a spheric shrine is *TreeMother's* own ten-foot-square hut grail space, radiating sacred presence to all her garden children. Snow reclaims the world as her own, all buried, all shrouded, all one-in-white-in-light. Thank you, *TreeMother*, for sharing with us such beauty from the sanctity of a private peace-sink here in the corner of the garden. Indeed, you are a connective thread between heaven and earth simply by being you, by living, as a matter-of-course, the essence of your true nature – here, now. I will try to learn from your guidance, your silent subtle loving guidance.

Here in Switzerland, Christmas lighting is traditionally subtle, subdued, comprising long strands of 'fairy lights', individual pearls of starlight threaded together, and strung along streets, balconies, hedges, as well as strewn through trees. No blinking or flashing, discordant colour or 'noise' to confront the senses, distract from one's contemplation and quiet reverence. Just like the silence of starlight itself, streamed from the heavens to be reflected in the snow blanketing Earth; 'tis a mute backdrop in one respect, a dramatic presence in another. The crystal clarity of a winter's night in an alpine land is extraordinary, the air frozen, Al Burani's comment alive with *bergkristall* sentience. The German expression, *ganz wach,* a perfectly onomatopoeic and monosyllabic construction to convey what it is to be 'totally awake' in the presence of such *seamless* presence – this knit of earth and sky, this play of 'starfield and earthlight' in Mariel's lexicon.

Fast-forward to several weeks hence, on the balcony of a small flat in the eastern Alps after a day's reading in *Conversations* and communing with the *Card Deck* images. I looked into the 'starfield' of night sky, contemplating their majestic beingness and sentience, their simultaneous overlighting and flooding presence. I looked for my Star Man friend from the Orion constellation (Gary Glitter by another name – in a classic non-segue, the reader shall find the story of our meeting several pages further on where it fits more appropriately to what I share in that section of text). But another, brighter star to the south-east distracted me with its insistent winking – 'see me!' its almost audible refrain. Alright, I smiled: 'I see you' (see Glossary). I returned to the warmth of the apartment and prepared to retire. Universal resonance was particularly fulsome this evening; I was alerted to the fact that 'someone' wanted to say something. A Sidhe visitor, perhaps? But in all honesty I was unprepared for the magnitude of the *Malakut* teaching to follow and how it amplified my understanding of the intersect between us and the stars. As with other extraordinarily deep and symbolic encounters, it is best left to the 'raw' text of my journal entry to explain …

17 January: I feel so blessed, honoured, humbled, unworthy to be granted glimpses of the interdimensionality, multiconnectivity of the world, universe; no more than glimpses and with no clue as to what to do with the knowledge but in tears now, still, knowing that some part of me knows and that that part is in concert with universal purpose and my (small) task relative thereto. The fact that these random gems come out of nowhere and return to nowhere but that while witness-surface-me is faced with trying to remember and make sense of the experience and quiet the excitement at having been granted a glimpse in order to better concentrate on the remembering of my witness, participant me is just hanging out, going with it, 'all good', 'all cool', relaxed in and of the matter-of-factual nature of this singular moment lived.

In essence, I was witness to a specific phenomenon in the heavens. A very long time ago, in the far distant past, I stood with three grand scholar-sages of classical antiquity as they busied with their calculations and made their observations. Each's name began with P – they wore long beards, long cloaks. Each researched a specific (particular) phenomenon but together they formed a triumvirate of knowledge when coming together to discuss their work. Nevertheless, in this *Malakut* reconstruction (to all intents and purposes) our place of observation was not on Earth. 'I saw' Earth as if from deep space; it was 'dark as night', a subdued sphere while the heavens were bright lit with 'life'.

Thus did I stand with these three amongst the stars while they discussed things, used an astrolabe etc. Suddenly, because the specificity of the phenomenon for which one P was responsible vanished, so did he from our place of observation. It was communicated that when it returned to the observable heavens, so would he to complete his cycle of work. This apparently did not affect the other 2 Ps who stayed in the past (i.e. amongst the stars).

So it was that 'I saw' this one P fall from the space between the heavens and the dark Earth. At some level I knew that *now* was the future he was waiting to re-enter – I felt this energetically, as light coursing through their interrelation, he and the phenomenon (difficult to explain). The scene shifted, and I stood in an old house, where all was quiet, still, till a boy (whom I know in another stellar context) came in through the back door and said to me eagerly: *Is he here yet? Where shall I look for him? Is he up on the roof?* (as if his 'hero' were already setting up and making observations). But I knew he was not yet at that stage. He was still preparing to re-connect with the phenomenon from a cellar or bunker within the Earth ...

What a mystery! Is this simply a case of demonstrating how wisdom can disappear to re-surface at a time in history when it can be continued, expedited most effectively? Or is it to communicate a specific (human) relationship with a specific (stellar) phenomenon? In the context of the teaching, I understood P's connection went beyond simple observation and scholarship. A living, energetic thread bound them and their 'together-manifestation' – what an extraordinary thought to add to a (growing!) reservoir of thought courtesy of the *Card Deck*. At some point, I know this will have the potential to be woven into the becoming myth of my own work, but in the meantime all I can say is: Welcome P. Welcome back.

Another night's communing in the company of stars (and sub-zero temps!) saw the uplift of a personal memory long buried. While all other examples related in this chapter were (deep-sea) trawled up from the *Malakut* drag-nets of journals after-the-fact to start populating the jigsaw puzzle of this book (an awakening in itself!), on the balcony of that small flat in the eastern Alps I spur-of-the-moment remembered an incident involving a star in material space on a midsummer's night in a midnight sky years past.

'Twas a star which grew and grew, *bursting* with love as I spoke aloud my passionate embrace of the one-life-in-the-one-world; 'twas a long speech to dear friends with no 'surface' experience of same. The reason I remembered this moment, my shock in the moment to think: *No, that's not possible, in the material, for my eyes to see what they are seeing,* was that the incident seamlessly thread its way back to one of my favourite stories from childhood, *The Starlight Barking*

(TSB). Dodie Smith's sequel to *The One Hundred and One Dalmatians* (and less well known in the public psyche), it was my preferred tale for it told the story of how Sirius, the Dog Star, was so lonely he invited all dogs to leave Earth and join him in his stellar realm. The specific episode which bound 'my' star to the story was how Sirius grew and grew in the sky, drawing closer and closer to Earth, till plonking itself atop Nelson's column (in Trafalgar Square, London) to speak with all dogs of the world personally.

This story 'spoke' my language as a child (and latterly), of all dogs spellbound by the *radiance* of a star: 'Pongo had never known such happiness. It was like food to the hungry, warmth to the shivering, love to the lonely ... He never knew how long the happiness lasted. Indeed, he soon barely knew who he was or where he was; it was almost as if he stopped being himself and became the happiness' (p.116 in my perennially re-read, thus sticky-taped, dog-eared and -chewed 1970 Puffin edition). My eight-year-old self was enthralled. I made entreats to the Southern Cross – querying that if it felt lonely I'd be happy to come visit. But no, I decided. It was in a specific net, it had a community of friends to talk to (and even two pointers so that others knew the way to their house). So proceeded a child's logic.

But latterly I would re-read TSB at least three times aloud (to three children) and wonder at the author's knowing (beyond the links of Christian allegory) to compose a text so poignant about the interrelations between stellar energies and Earth-bound sentience. Was this another case of direct experience wrapped up in fiction for the public palate – something I knew intimately from penning *The Taste of Translation*? Had she experienced a star growing and growing in plain sight, bursting with love, bursting to *connect* with the 'stars within the earth' as Mariel describes (*Conversations*, p.101)? Was this a simple manifestation of 'pre-existent and unknowable psychoid unity' (in Jungian-speak) split between outer phenomenon and inner psyche?

No answers. But communing with Sidhe energies was certainly responsible for me asking this raft of stellar-linked questions. Meditating with the cards outlaid also led to some interesting experiences. Occasionally, I would find myself back 'home' (*Sacred Pool* refers) in conversation with others at table, or at task in the 'Garden of the Great Mother'. My surprise, sudden and exhilarating, would bring me back to surface consciousness immediately. One day I wrote in my journal: 'I had no idea something like this would manifest via the *Card Deck*. I actually went *through* the *Gate of the Stars*, returned 'home'. Is this the purpose of the Stone Circle? To connect me more solidly or consistently to stellar life?'

Another occasion saw me witness to a specific Sidhe task once 'through' the Gate. The journal entry as follows: 'In meditation this morning I saw lots of golden threads criss-crossing each other, like fine filigree, and the 'words formed': *Threads of happiness.* They were like gossamer light wisps (but sturdy) and no tight pattern or grid I could see, just exuberantly crisscrossing this way and that.' I understood that a beautiful cloak of happiness would be the result. For what or whom or where? No information forthcoming on that front though, interestingly, this journey in regular morning meditation followed my witness of Madam S pre-dawn. Was she involved?

What Keeps Us Rooted?

Earlier in this chapter I commented about my longer-than unconscious connection to the night sky, the ununderstood ache of staring into those starry depths, a longing I did not comprehend until recent years' encounters with subtle beings from those realms. I also quoted Mariel's wisdom: 'By remembering how you are of the stars, you can understand how to be more fully of the earth' (p.111).

A coincidence, perhaps, but my direct communion with the *specificity* of stellar energies, the subtle beings *aligned* with our physically manifest Moon-and-Stars family most observable at night, began when I consciously took *root* in Swiss soil. Having felt the ache of being far from (a down under) home (and understanding same intimately!), I deep-knew there was a need to put down literal roots in this land-locked land as an antidote to same. The place to which I was (unconsciously) called was a high wild valley in the country's south, 'home' a tiny four-hundred-year-old cottage which spoke to me as I walked into her domain. She said: *People have slept well here, at peace.* Indeed, it was all she needed to say.

The bedroom is in the attic; first renovation task involved opening this space to create a proper portal between (Casa) *Marianna* and the spirit of the mountain into whose face she looks, (Pizzo) *Ruscada*; later I was tasked with making a pilgrimage to this 'Cold Mountain' (see Glossary) to complete the thread binding the two. The 'opening' of the portal for their (and my) shared communion was a classic case of (irrational) 'Anne-knowing' or, as I compose the line for many a protagonist in my fictions: 'She didn't know how or why she knew. She just knew'. An unveiled arched glass door to a non-Juliet balcony is the result. What this means is that the night sky, patiently enduringly stitched to *Ruscada*'s ridge, has ample opportunity to commune with the occupant(s) of the bedroom while they lie abed.

So can Moon directly bathe my body as she makes her arc through the sky, as can any planet or star subtly stream into *Marianna's* ten-foot-square hut. While I had written Moon's voice into (fictional) texts over the years (she was the one most completely 'in my face', so to speak), latterly I established lines of connection with other stellar beings. The way one such thread constellated in my symbolic world is best turned over to the 'raw' voice of a journal entry penned some weeks prior to the starseeds arriving in my care (and serves to demonstrate how little I intellectually know about star systems).

31 December 2013: There is a star at Orion's feet (or head – I only know how to find his belt) accompanying me these past nights as we slip through space. My meditations on (and with) this star have followed an interesting trajectory. Noticing the hum of universal resonance loud and fulsome (complete, even, could be the description of this heightened level – a felt-sense of inner fulfilment, of complete connection to the source, the harmony of the spheres), and cells singing at different times as I remark and praise my experience of this phenomenon, I began chatting with the star, and by yester evening was even talking about visiting its space, wondering how it was, how such a meeting could be effected given our connection via the resonant hum. Eventually it was time, as the Earth turned, to also turn over for sleep. The *Malakut* landscape I visited in between this waking inner-thought and the horizon of morning was intriguing and lucid. And it made me wonder if I had indeed met the star after all.

I stood on a terrace above the ocean shore with a group of people, one of whom I had known years prior as an experienced open-ocean sailor. We had been invited to visit a particular space in the back streets of the town. Down some stone steps with a iron railing, the place where I had previously found van Diemen's *Book of Voyage*, we came to a locked door painted deep green. I remember to have stood before this door a very long time ago; I recall pushing against it, really wanting it to open, there was something beyond the door I was very keen to engage, but it wasn't to be. Instead I was lifted away, pulled back by Mr1300BC down a very long wind tunnel till again I stood in my room. 'Not yet,' he had said. Hmmm. But now?

One of the group had a key, inserted it into the lock and slid the door open to reveal a subterranean warehouse set up as a public bathhouse. A huge space, all ceramic-tiled in green – floor, walls, ceiling and baths. Waiting to greet us was the owner of the establishment in a white-sequined suit, which looked straight out of a 1970s Gary Glitter video. He greeted me as if we had known each other before, and for a long time. It was as if our slow dance of 'courtship' could finally be resumed. He showed me around – the only real 'bathing' area was for children, the remainder set up as a club or bar with a mezzanine of café-style tables for two. All very subdued, classy, chic despite his less-than-appropriate attire. I was suitably impressed.

Suddenly coming through the crowd toward us was a woman I instantly knew as his mother with full entourage in tow. Now, if he was Gary Glitter, she was bedazzling bejewelled Rainbow Queen in her sequins, diamonds, colourful cloak and extraordinary headdress. At this point I knew it was her decision whether her son could continue to 'court' me or not. I also sensed that this approval process (i.e. of readiness to connect) had played itself out before; I needed to be able to demonstrate my credentials (?) this time. Gliding over, regally, like the Queen she was, she stretched out a rainbow-jewelled hand and placed it on my head. My task to stay strong, firm; while she continued to glide around the space I needed to prove I could glide at the same pace so that we remained connected for however long the approval process lasted ...

Learning to pace my gliding to hers (or any stellar being's for that matter) is simply a metaphor for reaching a like energetic vibration through which connectivity may be made. In my self-apprenticeship on working with light (the *Amici Files* refer), the idea was presented as akin to weaving energetic threads which could carry a current between the two interlocutors, a means of outreach whenever I (or they) wanted to get in touch.

However, latterly, in company of the *Card Deck*, my Sidhe companions have helped me understand a similarly textural means of coming into resonance with stellar presence. Given that when traversing the *Gate of the Stars*, this is the company in which one generally finds him or herself (whether outreach intended or not), it seems amply more fit to purpose. It means we need not be bedazzled, blinded in sight (or by awe) as the dogs in Trafalgar Square at Sirius' approach, nor 'wooed' by (or bemused at) the 'club-king' attire of the likes of a Gary G. (As an aside, the dudes from the RoS were similarly dressed out-of-time – they wore matching sets of conformist 1950s suits.)

Now as I watch a 'star' approach, it is like a whole pile of glitter is moving toward me; fluid, its 'light-form' seemingly suspended in water or akin to 'glitter-glue'. I hope the reader is conversant with this excellent aid to childhood creativity? Essentially it is glitter suspended in a clear fluid adhesive which, when squeezed out of the tube, can make all manner of paper-based art projects come to life. Thus Gary G's form and movement is transmuted to pure light-infused silver glitter, *very* fluid, but in translating myself to a like form to effect engagement, I find I present as golden glitter – and, rather than being able to match his fluidity, the 'solution' in which I am suspended is much stickier and altogether denser – I can almost hear the blob-blob-blob as I 'blob' around. Thus, it is more difficult to manoeuvre or negotiate my 'stellar' nature in its 'human' form, which of course makes sense but at the time of my induction into the practice, it was a charming revelation!

Nevertheless, what this means is that we share the same 'material' cosmic base in which 'colour' and 'consistency' varies. Interestingly, as I was trying to find a word to describe this alternate visioning of the experience (settling on 'textural' in the first instance), the word 'visceral' suddenly popped into my head (thank you, Sidhe!). And yes, it *is* the most appropriate descriptor for the phenomenon, relating, as it does, to the deep instinctual knowing of how we *differ*, yet what conclusively *binds* us together. 'Tis the primal fact of connectivity, yet one which bespeaks our diversity. And imagine: It all comes down to glitter-glue. Lucky me, that I had the opportunity to 'try it out' (and get sticky!) with 70s crooner Gary G, who, by the way, I now realise is (and always was) Rigel, a blue-white triple star system – Beta Orionis. A dear, dear friend, he shall return, in his own way, in Chapter 8.

Thus do we return to Mariel's comment: 'By remembering how you are of the stars, you can understand how to be more fully of the earth' (p.111); so too her remark: 'Your aetheric bodies contain strands of stellar energy that give you a power of connection to more than just the energies of the earth' (p.100). Moving between the *Gate of the Stars* and the *Gate of the Earth*, and recognising the 'form' I took when engaging stellar energy, I wondered how best to express my connection to Earth-energies. A journal entry following meditation in the company of the *Card Deck* refers:

11 March: My Circle outlaid, the energy swirled within the grail space did not want to end its practice – making great sky circles of its joy here in the ten-foot-square hut as well as elsewhere, a touch-of-love gifted throughout the house. Once returned, I immediately felt the need to sit and meditate. Long, so long. Close to an hour passed before I properly surfaced and in that time the resonance of connection deep, fulsome, the energies *anchored* in the space and radiating out from same as a simple matter of course. It was the word – 'anchor' – which began it all. A self-thought about needing to anchor the stellar energies here in the world, to support the Sidhe (and others) in their Gaian work suddenly rhizome-leaped to Kisha (see Glossary) plunging her hands into the dirt of Samir's grave which itself was written-into-existence based on direct experience of how a dear friend's burial impacted my soul-self (*The Taste of Translation*, p.357):

Atop a knoll where a breeze blows fresh. She has walked up a hill and into air. Lightness-infused, her body lightens, feet lift away from the ground. She hears the cry of an angels' swarm. Is this how it is to cross? Samir? she cries into a sea of silver mist, suddenly afraid. It's not my time, she says. Not yet.

Oh, but a part of her wants to detach. Please! it says, fuzzy-loud in her ear. Let me fly from this earth-bound hell!

No! she cries. It's not possible. The body must detach first, it can't be back to front. Stop!

Like a flag torn from a mast, whipped away she could be. An ephemeral wisp of breeze-borne spirit, a cottonhead setting sail on a summer's day, she could sacrifice her gossamer sleeve, be caught by the current, give herself up to the whim of the wind.

Did she know this would happen? Is this why she wore the hat? She who never wears a hat, a woollen cloche Samir had spotted in the market one day, plopped down on her head and said: It's you, it's just so you, darling! in a silly fashion designer voice. A hat which sat in a cupboard untouched until this day.

She pulls the container down hard round her ears, anchors herself in its bowl, grimaces, struggles, shuts her eyes tight. What keeps us rooted? she wants to know before her soul can have its way.

Come on Ki-. Marko's hand is under her elbow. Samir has been lain in the grave. Was she gone so long? He guides her to the edge of the pit where she sinks to her knees, buries her hands in fresh-dug soil, plunges her fingers into damp living earth. Delivered by the structure of dirt, away from the space of space.

The entire physicality of this scene appeared before my mind's eye as I sat in meditation. *What keeps us rooted?* Kisha wanted to know, answering herself with unconscious, unmediated action, by plunging her fingers into damp living earth. And I cried as the answer, renewed in this context, *poured* similarly out of my heart: *Love, love for you Gaia! We come here for love and we stay for love and it is this profound love we bring to the task of anchoring the energies.*

I cried and cried so much in my *love* for the world. And suddenly realised that the very *fact* of our material rootedness in the Ground of Being, here, now, is what we offer as support to the Sidhe's work, is what we offer in service to Gaian holism. We *are* the connective thread between the Gates of Stars and Earth – even if our work is subtle, it manifests materially ...

Yes, Mariel had said as much to David in their *Conversations*, for example: 'Together we are the complements that create a whole, living matrix, one capable of singing the energies of the earth back into the places of physical matter and into our world as well' (p.38). And later: 'The Stone Circle is a symbol of the portal that links the Stars to Earth; when you stand in it, you stand for the earth in its cosmic environment, mediators between stars and planet and midwives to the fullness of Gaia that emerges from this relationship. We are star people not because we come from the stars; you come form the stars as well. We are star people because we bring the Stars to Earth. But we can only bring them so far; there is a threshold we cannot cross, but you can, if you will dance the stars inward and outward with us' (p.67).

I found (re-found) the relevance of such quotes following this (for all intents and purposes) 'epiphany', but like all things it needed to be brought into the *soil* of my own experience before I could work its energy effectively – my Huxleyian mode-of-being requires the mystic's direct intuition *cleaved* to the scholar's intellectually imparted wisdoms as a natural matter-of-course; so too does it need to write such intuitions into *existence*, on what I call a 'plane of intimate exteriority' (see Glossary) – that is, as a (raw) material manifestation of aetheric engagement. The experience exists in its own way within, yes, and is coupled with a felt-sense that begins to bring the inner knowing *out* to meet the intellect, but *writing* completes the experience – like skin completing the fact of our physical incarnation, the space where we 'touch' the world (and to which a Sidhe legend refers).

Just like a sculptor, artist or artisan of any description lovingly crafts his or her inner visionary experience into a material artefact so do I physically work with words, and to which *MakerMan's* history of human creativity refers. It is the simple expression of my being which helps me understand my own being even more – shaping the inchoate into aesthetic communicable form shapes and moulds my being as well. Its purpose, for me at least, is that once understanding is *effected* via this iterative process, I am able to more consciously gift such knowledge (in company of self) *out* in service to the whole. In other words, the experience of the moment, *together* with its record, lovingly crafted, extends and amplifies the experience, is its own *expression* of the experience, and thereby enables the space of experience to be engaged over, ever over, built upon and extended thereto, like a ramshackle shanty which, by bibs and bobs, evolves into a vast loving mansion of the soul over time. Such is my 'personal' myth, in Jungian-speak. But it also has a collective function once shared, as my dear Sidhe companions prompted with the penning of this particular text.

Meditations on the experience of joy, for example: They occur over, ever over, in different forms, places and times and the record of each *cleaves* to its fellows to deepen my engagement, heighten my attunement thereto. Here an example from a random midwinter half-hour to illustrate same and its seamless connection to Mariel's comments earlier re learning to be 'more fully of the earth':

Today I walked Pabey alone during a blizzard – well, the conditions weren't too bad, but it was snowing heavily and not a soul about. I stood, and he sniffed, and I looked out over the silence of the fields and was *in* the space, completely in *touch* with the natural world and how all was being and flowing in concert with the snow's dance. Joy streamed out from me to connect with the All and I said: *I am so in love with you, world. I am so in love with you!* During snow, cold, frozen lips and dripping nose. Somehow it didn't matter. We were alone, *merged* into this space of and with your sacred creation. I am so in love with You and your world, and a mantra flowed out with each step: *We are joy, we are joy, we are joy, we are joy* ... The hymn sheet sung by all sentience in honour of You, in honour of Gaia – our shared voice in shared space. Mirroring joy, blessing Beauty. And in such crazy appalling conditions from a rational perspective?

Ah, but Beauty has her ways. I was as much a participant in the dance as any other whip-whirled round by Wind. Heading down the creek verge, I *felt* the trees' connection, rootedness to the earth, their physicality wed to the One, their being *in* earth, their extremely powerful and resonant sensitivity the result of *primal* connection; my awareness shifted to all the small birds, sheltered herein yet still going about *life* – being and flowing the world with blessing as a *natural* matter-of-course no matter the conditions. It all *is*. It all just *is*. The sky child took up the chorus and 'We are Joy' flowed free as shared voice. So free, yet so *embedded* in the world, here in the middle of a snowstorm, in the middle of a farmer's field – the incarnational perspective of a living *our* Gaian purpose. Sana!

Yet, 'tis not only I who sees, who uplifts. And, indeed, I cannot claim anything other than wordsmithing felt-sense and embodied expression in the extract above. Thus do I defer to the voice of the Sacred itself to close this section of the chapter. What keeps us rooted? *I*, It whispered, loud in my head, on a day years past:

I am the wind through the trees, I am the mist on the breeze
I am the carpet of colour scuffed beneath your feet.
I am All; I am None; I am everywhere One.
I am who I am. I am Love ...
I am the laugh in your eye! The cockatoo's cry!
The burnt orange bark of Beethoven's Goldammer!
The blossoming pear! The meal that we share!
The flow of the stream over weirs of wood!
I am you! I am he! I am everywhere she!
The sentient cell in each sentient form!
All embraced in the One!! The Many in the None!!
You know who I am: I am Love!!!

That day the words of the Sacred spun and danced, I spun and danced, joy spun and danced (and the plethora of exclamation marks in the song above attests as much). A moment lasting many moments, yet my feet never left Gaia's skin, sniffy dog never stopped his perennial sniffing. Buddha's 'love at the centre of all things and all things are the same thing' was *thick* in the air, all sentience *singing* its joy to be, to be *here* – living *one* life in the *one* world of the *one* divine spirit, Love. How can it *ever* be otherwise?

Planting the Seeds

Earlier in the chapter, I described my encounter with the starseeds. Following this I was inducted into how our Earth-consciousness is a dense form of the original impulse housed within, which needs to be returned for the interconnectivity between stellar home and Earth-rooted home to be enhanced. Later, the *Card Deck* was instrumental in amplifying these lessons with the story of the energetic relation binding P, a scholar of antiquity, with the object of his scholarship. So too, in finding myself journeying *through* the *Gate of the Stars*, I grew increasingly aware of a more *stable* energy of connection.

This culminated in the following event:

> 22 February: Pre-dawn. Three meteorites. Burning – which first I hold in my hands, then place at my third chakra and finally apply to the back of my neck. I return to surface consciousness to find my hands still cupped there as if clutching something; my neck feels very warm ...
>
> Reconstructing how this came about: I found myself in a daylit *Malakut* landscape walking down a wide path toward a village as part of a large group of people. Suddenly the shift to nightscape and I see a shooting star. By the time I've remarked it, the whole sky is an explosion of shooting stars; it's a meteorite shower and they're all coming straight down to earth, directly onto us. They hit the ground hard; I hear their heavy thuds. People scatter, to shelter under awnings and in the lee of buildings to escape injury. On my way to cover, I gather up three meteorites and the *sliver* of a fourth; I'm absolutely fascinated! They're the size of golf balls or eggs. I show them to a male companion in the tunnel in which we find shelter (like the entry to a tube station).
>
> I'm so excited! My hands are *burning* but not enough to make me drop them. The felt-sense is intense but not like real pain. I offer the sliver to my companion – not interested. I am the only one amongst the entire group to stop and collect these beautiful treasures. I feel so energised by their presence! They are hard-solid-dense-black-smooth-polished; they look like lumps of coal and radiate enduring heat. I fuse them to my solar plexus; somehow I know that their energy is also 'absorbed' through the spinal chord, hence applying them to my neck. An intensely physical *Malakut* experience.

The three starseeds had transformed into dense material matter. The fourth, which I had left 'in the earth' for the time being, had (seemingly) of its own accord decided the time was ripe to join its siblings' work crew – only as a sliver, mind. It clearly needed more nurturing. But for three fully formed meteorites, their time had come.

It is difficult to describe the impact this 'event' (see Glossary), in a string of events, had on my psyche. It was as if a swirling vortex of stellar-sourced energy was 'quickening' (see Glossary) as well as drawing closer. My usual experience of how understanding unfolds (as a slow dance of 'courtship') had ramped up in both impulse and intent to a point where it seemed as though the entire universe was involved. I felt buoyed on a plane of energy, like a tiny boat in a vast sea, without knowing where the current would shunt us, on which shore we would eventually wash up, only hoping we would not be swamped by a huge swell in the process. Rarely in my life had I felt similarly; that things were moving so fast, all I could do was *trust*. But the *sense* of it was known territory. Thus I had no desire to retreat from my compact with the Stone Circle. Grounded in love, no matter what *happened*, at some level I knew, like Julian of Norwich, that: 'All is well and all shall be well'.

Concurrent with this event, and perhaps supportive of my trust, I had felt the shift in consciousness described in the last chapter for which I sought the Dancer's counsel. My connection with the night sky now felt different. No longer the paradox of longing to go home to the stars coupled with being at home here, *lightness-of-being* seemed to centre me everywhere and nowhere. I wrote in my journal:

> I am as vaporous as the All. What is it that was overlain that has been shed? So that only the strength, the stillness of mountain remains, so that otherwise 'self' is awash with wind, with aether? I feel neither disconnected from Earth-as-home nor Stars-as-home. It just *is*. It all just *is*. Like the sky child's teaching and I, like the child, suffused with wonder. Everywhere, nowhere – *all* is wonder. Everywhere, nowhere, no matter what *happens* – all is well, and shall be. A (non) felt-sense – vaporous, aetheric, as *light* as air. Is this what enables, facilitates the shapeshifting my Pixie cousin from a Devon Glade described? Because there's no attachment to (inhabiting) a particular state, pulled betwixt and between two particular states simultaneously?

The reader may recall that the Dancer, *Beauty*, had said: *Soon it will feel like home to you too!* This period of much fluidity and seamless 'flow' between head- and heart-space, material and *Malakut*, also saw an epic poetry project thrown into the mix. A vast song of praise in honour of Gaia, celebrating the high wild home of *WolfMother*, resulted in the Ocean and Land Dancer card finally acquire its name, *Homecome to the Sea*, in reference to a line at the end of the first Canto of *Onsernone Long Poem* (hereafter OLP; see Glossary). Even though the image ostensibly had nothing to do with a poem about an alpine watershed, I acceded to its request. It was a sweet reminder of where I had grown up down under, an affirmation of the land- and seascape to which our family returned each year like birds on annual migration between the hemispheres.

Hot on the heels, however, came the Dancer's next request, to *join* the Stone Circle on a permanent basis. I was surprised. Where? I asked. Although it made no sense at the time, it was extraordinarily firm in speaking its placement. It needed to sit with my *Companions of the Way* in the *Kiln Room*, itself positioned on the Howe's *Mountain Above as Mountain Below*. A part of me was sceptical – if this kept going, the Circle was going to get seriously crowded. But – OK, I agreed. We'll see how it goes.

Accordingly, I set out the Stone Circle and felt drawn to verbally re-affirm the commitment to shared guardianship with the Sidhe now with a new permanent voice in the Council. I stepped into the Circle, and suddenly felt *at* home – an extraordinary felt-sense to mirror Beauty's prophecy, it was as if I was *in* and *of* a grail space that was everywhere and nowhere, as much as embodying the grail *itself*. Coupled with this was a sudden desire to 'lift' the stones, to set them enduringly in the very ground of my being. Energy swirled in and about the Circle, I literally lived Mariel's grounded fluidity in the space. 'Arise,' I intoned, and felt their collective lift, the density of aether fully material in the moment.

'Holding' the stones in position, I affirmed what I *felt* in the moment to be my Circle's purpose: *To wear a mantle of starlight here in the world to bring the energy of the stars streaming to Earth.* In a way I knew this affirmation of service went beyond what Mariel had asked; in another I saw it as a natural extension to the original compact, in line with being a connective thread 'between heaven and earth', an *Amici della Montagna della Luce* – what it meant to be *me* as a *living* grail, being *and* flowing the world with blessing.

During the ceremony (which had not consciously begun as a ceremony), I experienced local and non-local visioning. Felt-sense and witness were simultaneous, seamless. 'I saw' myself in the midst of the standing stones as much as felt myself firm within the grail; I felt *grounded* in my sovereignty, at the same time witnessing my solidarity with all members of our Circle of nineteen Councillors. Stones or Dancers, none were 'conditional' or 'visitors' in time, space or intent. All of us together in service to Gaia, a call to partnership answered in shared voice.

Two days later, in deep meditation, I found myself at the 'farm' after having spoken again this affirmation on *behalf* of the Circle. My journal entry refers:

<u>1 April</u>: In a flash, I find myself standing in an open shed, finishing up an interview with the 'farmer', having agreed terms of engagement, and even discussed vacation options based on all other requisite commitments in time and space. We are surrounded by stuff, all 'finished product' here in the place where stellar energies are grown, nurtured and harvested for market, 'distribution' on Earth. Phew! Here is where starseeds are planted, where their transformation into dense matter can occur – my meteorites, material stars to be 'shipped' to Earth in those glorious showers. Previously I was on composting duties but now my apprenticeship has born 'fruit', so to speak. Yay!

'George' (see Glossary) arrives to take me on a tour of the community's holding. As we wander round, I am introduced to other workers, some of whom previously met. It's good to know we'll all be working together on task. I tell George how happy I am to participate, how *warm* it is to be this close to Sun, our home star 'source', how I've forgotten how *burning* his kiss can feel after living in a cold clime for so long. Like being marked by a brand. Wonderful!

He makes a typical George comment (take care!) before offering to drive the route between farm and 'market' with me so I know how it works. George's motorway is a slipstream and he must be the fastest craziest driver on a *Malakut* road. Fortunately this is the first and last time I'll need to be in a 'car' with him. It's clear I will get here on my own by flying, reaching my beautiful mythical homeland through the *Gate of the Stars* ... Thank you for the tour, though. I guess you heard my affirmation and it was time to show how this metamorphoses from affirmed intent into lived practice. Joy!!

I returned to *Conversations* to amplify what had constellated in this journey, about the celestial web of connection of which Gaia is a part, and how the starseeds, planted, could contribute to her evolving consciousness:

> *'(T)he pattern and structure of this "web" is changing. Many of the relationships which Gaia has with its cosmic environment and family are changing, and we – you and I – are part of this change. ... As this web changes, the subtle field changes ... This new subtle body enhances the connectedness and communion Gaia has with her cosmic environment. It means that more energies from the stars will flow into this world, and the living energy of the planet will in turn flow more freely into the cosmos. All the environments of consciousness held within the planetary mix ... are being energetically heightened in one way or another.*
>
> *'(T)he spirit of our ancient, common ancestor already possessed deep connections and attunement to the stellar energies now flowing into the earth. It is a seed for the new subtle bodies that seek emergence in and around us.*

But it is a seed we both carry. It will unfold more easily in each of us if we can help it to unfold together ... the larger wholeness that holds both of us within itself is a resource upon which we can draw if we can connect to each other in partnership' (pp.55-6).

Clearly far better expressed than I could ever attempt (many thanks, Mariel and David!), I had been excited by all things seen and experienced (ostensibly) on my own, yet in company of the *Card Deck*, the energy of revelation and unfoldment – the how and the why – had ramped up exponentially. Some metaphoric high-fives were shared around the Circle; done and dusted, I thought – here was the project I could help nurture and flow into the world.

Ah, but as the *Malakut* operates out of time, I should have been looking for clues along different tendrils (and in tucked-away pockets) of rhizomatic abandon rather than assuming a linear progression with the farm's revelation its culmination. Here I was, by mid-April, ticking boxes, in preparation for our family's annual pilgrimage down under. Bags packed, dog in kennels, plants watered, *Malakut* sorted.

I had even managed to do a last edit on *Spring*, the first Canto of the epic OLP (with Dante as adorable muse). A birthday gift to be read aloud to my darling 93-years-young mother, its final stanza, uplifted and written-into-existence by soul-knowing pure (and to which the Dancer, Ocean and Land, had laid claim in its self-naming), concludes thus:

... One day shall find us
homecome. So-promises the universe
as well as lowly I. One day, it shall be.
One fine fine day. When all the rivers run –
know, that we shall be homecome,
to the sea ...

A warning (from Self) which should have been heeded (by self). I have it on good authority, however, that the latter can be very dim-witted at times.

Thus do we pass the baton to the next chapter ...

Chapter 6: Pilgrimage Down Under

All the way from source to sea, from source to sea to source ...

For the better part of two decades my life has been strung across the world, between a perennially brown and dry ocean-lapped continent, a consequent chunk of vast *Gondwana* Dreaming, and a small damp land-locked pearl dressed alternately in frozen white or luminous green. The contrast between these two homelands could not be starker. Yes, I am a child of southern oceans – salty H_2O runs through my veins and the mere thought of sub-tropical fruit sees this Pavlovian dog drool every time.

But once embedded in the stone sentience of the Alps, I felt equally bound to her soul, honouring *Helvetia*'s sacred heritage no less even if certain of her inhabitants' customs, dialects and sensory delights still tie my little 'But why?' gene in knots. Suffice it to say that it never would have occurred to me that pilgrimage between the two on at least an annual basis would be the sum of my life ever since. 'Tis 20,000 miles (as the Boeing flies), there and back again (in Bilbo-speak), and indeed I know the route so well it is inscribed on the skin of my soul.

There are various levels by which to consider this dual homecoming an act of pilgrimage, each valid. But the one I want to concentrate on, in the context of this chapter, is a continuation of 'what keeps us rooted?' – a theme begun in the last. What is it that *speaks* to the core of our being, lets us know we are on our

71

way home, as well as the intuitive sense that says yes, we have arrived, at that particular patch of dirt in which we have taken root? On the way to attempting to answer these questions, I shall share traces of the past which provide waymarkers in this regard. Less cross-referencing with the *Card Deck* will be the result but the reader may rest assured that certain 'actors' from the Circle (as well as a dancing Grecian chorus beyond) shall be re-introduced to resounding applause from the next chapter onwards.

'Great Southern Land'

Australia is ancient – old, weathered, stoic in her deep silence. 'Hidden in the summer for a million years' as the song lyrics attest, she bears witness to worldly tumults from a patch of wild southern seas far from the madding crowd. Sixty-five million years has she stood her ground after separating from her *Gondwana* mother. Thus has she grown up, grown old – alone; an aloneness, a solitude you can feel rising up from the very bones of her cracked ruddy-brown skin. Indeed has she won her cronedom crown; like any desert ascetic, her skeletal frame is her mantle of honour, her deep wells of subterranean waters the source of an abiding sense of inner peace and nourishment. Sixty-five million years of personal history, the last eighty-odd thousand of which (according to recent archaeological evidence) included human habitation, the last two hundred plus of which introduced European and latterly other, principally Asian, waves of migration.

Aboriginal Dreaming holds the stories of the land – the stories this sunburnt land passed to her first inhabitants for safe-keeping. These myths describe legendary totemic beings singing up country, and all sentience, into existence; wherever they walked their footprints left a trail of song, of life. The result is a labyrinth of invisible pathways crisscrossing the continent, known as songlines or *tsuringa* tracks. In his landmark lyrical text for a Western audience, *The Songlines*, Bruce Chatwin writes that by singing the world into existence the Ancestors had been poets in the original sense of *poesis*, meaning 'creation': 'In theory, at least, the whole of Australia could be read as a musical score. There was hardly a rock or creek in the country that could not or had not been sung. One should perhaps visualise the Songlines as a spaghetti of Iliads and Odysseys, writhing this way and that, in which every 'episode' (i.e. sacred site) was readable in terms of geology' (pp.13-14).

Once, I was blessed to witness the worldwork of the Ancestors during a *Malakut* encounter. D at my side, we watched the crone, the spirit of *Terra Australis*, at task – and my, how aged she constellated compared to *Helvetia*'s maidenly spirit! The only way I could capture the sense of the experience was in poetry, something which stunned me at the time, for it reflected Chatwin's intuition of *poesis*:

twig thin she is
soul full of memory
mind an empty well
she sweeps the garden
any size
with a birch bark broom
big as she
while we
quiet as the grave
watch from behind a knowing tree
complicit in our secrecy
to not disturb
but simply witness
the practice of perfection

The creation myths of many indigenous cultures mirror Aboriginal legend-making, so too mirroring the 'creation story' told by Mariel to David in *Conversations*: 'The simplest metaphor is that our ancestors worked with sound and spoke or sung into being whatever they were seeking to manifest. ... (Like) a living tuning fork, able to produce variable frequencies within itself and in collaboration with others, ... the world itself was like a giant vibrating crystal singing in the vastness of the cosmos, and our ancestors came to sing with it in a choir of unfoldment and evolution' (p.34).

Over long millennia Aboriginal culture learnt to *know* their mother, to *read* her ways, worship her and all her children for who they are, and sing in *concert* with the land as they walked. European settlement brought its own worship traditions, as well as long histories of practice in land management which were not adapted to the land, the climate, the conditions. The results are in plain sight, but it is not the task of this text to critique what has been.

Instead I wish to concentrate on what binds me, and my sensibility, to Aboriginal ancestral stories, and how this intersects with my understanding of stone sentience. Despite being a 'whitey', I have learned much from their way of *being* with the earth, a connection forged, principally, by pilgrimage enacted as a permanent state. Whether the journey be to ceremonial gatherings, following seasonal water or food sources, or indeed the undertaking of initiatory solitary 'walkabouts', such nomadic practices are ingrained with spiritual significance far deeper than simply ensuring the tribe's physical survival. Duty of care was an act of *community* – there was acknowledgement and thanksgiving for what Thomas Berry describes as membership in a 'communion of subjects' rather than as owners of a 'collection of objects' deemed of value only for their utility.

In a world of ongoing recurrence, a web of continual exchange in being and form and position that implied the participation of all sentience in a process of 'interbirth' (see Glossary), the peoples of this ancient land were vested with the responsibility to *sing* as part of the universal choir of continuing 'unfoldment and evolution' as Mariel describes the process. To keep the singing alive down the generations was to keep the land alive. And singing meant *walking*, tracing the path of the Ancestors, in order to *know* the land, in order to *root* themselves in such knowing.

What keeps us rooted, therefore, need not be a sedentary notion, a by-product of the agrarian revolution, bound by hedgerows and, latterly, barbed wire. Instead I feel it to be a profound inheritance from our journeying far-past. A Tuareg lad now living in France writes in his *Chronicles*: 'Nomads always return to their point of departure. (My grandfather used to say that) Tuaregs are like acacia trees: they put down deep roots but their branches can spread far and wide' (from Moussa Ag Assarid's text, *Y a pas d'embouteillage dans le desert*). Likewise, my sense is that when we touch, physically, psychically, into one 'bit' of land, having passed over many bits as part of the journey, we touch into *all* bits. Plunging our hands into the earth, as Kisha did at Samir's grave, *feeling* our way into the rhizome of unending interconnections therein, opens us to the experience of kinship with *all* in Gaia's garden, the lattice of this 'giant vibrating crystal'.

When we understand that our participation in a single community stretches across vast tracts of sentient space, as vast as the Earth (and yes, beyond, as I described in the last chapter), we touch into the glorious web that binds each to the other to the other without end, and all back to the One. This is my lesson from Aboriginal Dreaming, in a similar vein akin to the lesson revealed in the depths of the Sacred Pool: *The Mother is the Mother of the Father and the Brother and the Son* ... While each clanship group may have stewardship or responsibility or guardianship for a particular 'stretch' of ancestral song, their several verses are part of a selfsame unending melody in which *all* Ancestors participated, in which all sentience perennially sings, like Proclus' 'heliotrope' (see Glossary).

Thus have I evolved my own ritual for singing up country as I journey the world. In a way it mirrors what Mariel describes in *Conversations*, though of course I was unaware of it at the time: 'You carried with you the memory of the telluric technology of node, connection and flow, shaped by song and dance and ritual. Guided by this memory, you discovered new ways to tap the sites of power' (p.38). Nevertheless, with such texts to backbone self-practices even after-the-fact, my sense of empowerment to *contribute* to Ancestral song *through* same grows exponentially. And with it, courage!

Whether under self-propulsion (i.e. walking) or letting wheels or wings assist the traverse, my intent is to greet and bless spirits of place in any locale I visit as well as when 'homecome' to the particular 'stretch' of territory for which I share stewardship. 'Tis a ritual which gradually developed from Mr1300BC's instruction years past that I should greet the spirits of the mountains our family climbs, and thank them for the opportunity to visit and honour their existence, the sheer sublime fact of their being. At the time of the teaching, I understood that it wasn't that we weren't instinctively connecting to the mountain spirits of place on our summiting way, but his point was to make the greeting *conscious* – that it would generate a much more powerful resonance of connectivity if loving intent were explicitly expressed.

Over time this evolved into the mantra I dubbed: *Hello the House* in honour of the wonderful scene from the film *Out of Africa* in which neighbour Felicity announces her arrival at Karen's homestead. A slim slice of cinema lasting no more than a few seconds, somehow these three words triggered deep soul memory. Regardless of the mores cited for the founding of the greeting in different cultures, to me it evoked the ritual *purpose* of blessing territory on entry. Either fresh or known, either for the first time or on endless repeat, effecting Nietzsche's *eterno ritorno*, my mantra, in the spirit of singing up country, proceeds:

> *Spirit of the mountains, spirit of the waters,*
> *Spirit of the ancestors, flora and fauna,*
> *Hello the House, Hello the House,*
> *Hello the House, we greet thee!*
> *Hello the House, Hello the House,*
> *We send our blessings to you!*

The mantra centres me, ensures task-orientation on pilgrimage wherever, whenever. If focus slips, or consciousness drifts, the song set to the rhythm of my footfalls always pulls me back, calling on *all* energies of place to witness and share in the blessings offered. As such, the reader should not take 'House' too literally; nor be surprised when said 'House' returns the greeting in its own way.

Ancestral Encounters

Ritual blessings tend to take on a life of their own after a while, with the potential to perpetually sub-text conscious practice. Mindfulness becomes deep-etched like the mark of a permanent tattoo. Thus do I find the connective thread linking me to spirit of place down under remains 'live' in *Malakut* consciousness even here in the modesty of a ten-foot-square hut in *Helvetia's* small damp pearl. Specific visioning, involving Aboriginal energies, began some years past but after a particular western desert painting, chosen at seeming random, joined the symbolic interlocutors of the hut several summers ago, it seemed to open a wider portal to this wisdom tradition – something for which I am eternally grateful as it is the ground where I too was sown.

My intuition is that this opportunity arose not through an alignment with cultural perspective per se, but from a deeper engagement – essentially land-connected or Earth-energies attuned. My respect for the Aboriginal wisdom tradition is undeniable, yet I am more than conscious of the genetic and cultural 'otherness' I bring to this understanding. The way-of-love therefore underscores my dance with diverse wisdom paths, toward the centre of all ways; yet in this specific instance it was as if I had come into resonance with ancestral Dreaming from the 'bottom up' rather than 'top down', seeming to coalesce around my peace-sink insights.

These insights had afforded me the possibility to drill down through differing levels of the Earth, as if on subtle archaeological dig. I could see, therefore, that humanity's contribution (or impact) touched, most keenly, the uppermost layer – topsoil so easily prone to erosion if not managed 'correctly', if not *wedded* to the overarching spirit of place constellating as 'deep-natured' presence (substrata, if you like). At times I plunged to and through the bedrock itself, felt the strength and simple beingness of this space 'at the heart of things', whose 'rhizome' of knowledge clearly intersected with my kiln room understanding of stone sentience. In this place I intuited that embedding our *human* roots deep in the earth via the conscious recognition of the very *miracle* of our material incarnation (rather than floating in existential ambivalence around on the surface of her face) would deliver more *sustainable* joy and peace into our own self-reservoirs while at the same time contributing to the infilling of the Mother's peace-sink at the particular location of our 'rootedness'.

Once, Mr1300BC demonstrated a correlation between these insights and a musical score, such that *each* place was linked to *all* places in a web of song and attunement. 'I saw' the five lines of a stave, how each line of music harmonised with its brothers. Across the five lines, each represented a different dimension, medium and technique; for example some lines represented instruments, others voice, emanating from the material or *Malakut*, Earth-energies or stellar-. Once more, Mariel's comment in *Conversations* (p.34) amplified this lesson. Each line of 'music' presented horizontally – like leylines within and *beyond* the Earthern plane – yet was completely in *tune* with its counterparts above and below.

As a result, I understand that my propensity to latterly connect into Aboriginal ways of seeing (and being) has arisen as a function of plumbing *Gondwana's* heritage – having touched into her bedrock, on my way back 'out' I have managed to pick up (or tune into) Aboriginal resonance 'singing' in the substrata. It has meant that occasionally I meet Aboriginal presences in the *Malakut* who share lessons and insights – one significant encounter involved an Ancestor couple of the W clan who, in charting a way to the future, counselled the benefits of learning from other traditions toward an holistic, inclusive 'world' spirituality. We had sat at a round table – drawing on the energy of other traditions was a path to furthering one's own learning, they felt. Pilgrimage (or 'walkabout') to them meant leaving the fold, the known, to go out into the world, learn and experience the new, and return with fresh perspective, to better serve Gaia. In a later encounter, I was to meet members of the clan who had followed the Ancestors' guidance. They said: *We are from the (new) W, but the (original) W lives on* … I understood that the power of change and transformation lies at the heart of the wisdom tradition, as it does with all in a dynamic living universe. This, of course, is analogous to learning the history and wisdoms of the Sidhe (and vice versa) to follow our common Ancestor's guidance, the 'harmony' of the musical score in Mr1300BC's demonstration.

Nevertheless, my experiences with Aboriginal energy heighten exponentially when I am *in* country itself. Especially during recent years this has included seeming ancestral 'encounters' in the full light of material day. A couple of examples of same will establish context for the connection to stone sentience I shall re-introduce in the following chapter.

Several years past our family traced a path through a *Gondwana* World Heritage Area to a stand of Antarctic beech – *nothofagus moorei* – a relict of the supercontinent from which we were the last to break off in that far-distant past. Shifting north at the stunning rate of five to seven centimetres per year wasn't leisurely enough a traverse, however, for *nothofagus* to adapt to new parameters such as the heat and sparse rainfall that came with it; as such it remains only in small pockets of cool temperate fire-free rainforest at high altitude along the eastern seaboard. That said, it certainly adapted sufficiently to ensure we can witness its beauty at all rather than having to rely on rare fossil pollen records to tell its extraordinary story. For *nothofagus* learnt to reproduce asexually – stubbornly coppicing new trees from the roots of the old when no longer able to produce viable seed in increasingly difficult conditions. As a result, these gentle giants are generally seen in family groups, or so-called 'fairy rings' arising from a single clonal individual, and in the area where I hail from, its northernmost community, some specimens have been dated to 12,000 years.

Armed with this knowledge, it was time to pay our respects, detouring off the main trail to *Tullawallal*, 'place of many trees' in the local Yugambeh language. The entire watershed here had been sung into existence by *Woonoongoora*, Queen of the Mountains, although I had seen no texts describing if this particular part of the plateau (the rim of a caldera formed from a vast shield volcano by the name of *Wollumbin*, whose remnant plug overlit the region to the south) had been used ceremonially. Thus, with *Hello the House* accompanying my footfalls, I decided to try and feel my way into *Woonoongoora's* landscape to *read* any Dreaming stories held therein.

The track spiralled slowly, up and around the hill, and I moved with it – slowly, mindfully, witness to a songline unspooling before my feet. Sharing space and breath, the path and I journeyed back in time and as I approached the summit, 'I saw' them. The elders, the ancestors. Rising up out of non-existent mist, out of the midst of a grove of ancient trees above me, each with a twinkle in his eye and a smile on his lips in welcome. There they sat, a crosslegged collective, a fairy ring, within a fairy ring of trees ... 'Twas a strange feeling, I so small – below, beneath. For a few seconds I wondered how to approach this space; I had lost the path in my surprise; literally!

Eventually I found an appropriate place for the last brief ascent and arriving, discovered my elders had turned to stone. Vast slabs of moss- and lichen-bespeckled igneous rock now formed a fairy ring of shared presence with their *nothofagus* kin. Here, our family rested awhile in silence and awe, *feeling-tree* (see Glossary).

Serenity filled the cocoon brought into being by elders and trees as one, a place of shared beingness we were invited to share, a place of secret worldwork, of the Sacred *sung* into existence aeons past, and continuing as long as this *Gondwana* dreaming voice could *hold* its true note in the musical score of Gaian resonance. A place of ebb and flow between spirit and matter, between material and *Malakut*, my consciousness likewise ebbed and flowed between the spaces – one moment delivering a muesli bar to D, in the next feeling a burble of joy beneath my feet at the elders' witness of a simple act of 21st century mothering; likewise when I produced a camera and began snapping away, I could sense their keen curiosity – what could this one-eyed box actually see?

Before I reluctantly left *Tullawallal*, I placed a hand against an elder tree's clonal trunk, my other rested on a stone elder in service to *Woonoongoora*, and offered a prayer of thanks for their presence, for *holding* this place open and present to all. I felt the thread of their connection pass *through* me and 'returned' from my communion to find we were all bathed in Sun's darkly glowing presence, low in a dust-filled western sky. Yes. From Sun's life – trees' life – our life. All one. All shared. Thanks be.

The following year's pilgrimage saw me introduce the boys to a known locale of ceremonial Aboriginal use; many thousands of years old was the rock art in its National Park 'galleries', a place where different tribes would congregate for sacred ritual in the cool of the gorge, cocooned from the baking western plains surrounding the labyrinthine water-carved network of sandstone. By now I thought I understood stone sentience and hiked happily along one day singing up country on the way to a particular site off the main gorge track which I had visited thirty years prior. Recalling how, at that stage, unconscious 'knowing' had led me into this territory, I shared my joy of return – consciously, mindfully – in the way I 'sung' the self-mantra, and spontaneously outreached in physical space to greet a large boulder 'guarding' the entrance to the area.

My! I have never felt such a charge of electricity shoot up my arm. It literally felt like I had put my hand into a live power socket, such was the surge recoiling into my shoulder. Yet in my shock at this completely unexpected and never before experienced event, the exhilaration accompanying it was extraordinary. I was suddenly completely in touch with the ancestral presence of this place, the magic *held* within its stone silence. It was well and truly alive and had no hesitation in sharing its life with little me.

A week or so later that same pilgrimage year, I walked another *tsuringa*-track with family – this time to the singular mountain which defines my own 'ancestral' ground. As old as time, as deep as memory, *Wollumbin*, the cloud-catcher, is a remnant reminder of the vast shield volcano more than a hundred kilometres wide that once breathed in *Gondwana's* millennial past; its (now) weathered 1200metre-high plug looks far out across the sea – a wide-stretched blue sheet of wild Pacific Ocean to the north, south, and east, while to the west lies the baking heat of the crone's breathing heart.

The previous year our planned ascent could not take place – track closed as a result of the severe cyclonic season just over. But for my part I understood why the journey was delayed. It was so I could understand, in full measure, the task to greet the spirit of the mountain as we began to climb, to sing up this magical country with each step taken, and to give thanks at the top for our safe passage 'home'.

My task went further, however – to be a message-bearer on behalf of *Marianna's* window-framed mountain on the Swiss-Italian border where I had learnt Mr1300BC's original lesson, where I had consciously rooted myself in the heart of the Alps a decade prior. In my hand, therefore, I carried a stone, a single simple stone of blessing to add to *Wollumbin's* summit cairn as a greeting from one Cold Mountain spirit to another, a thread of connectivity binding two completely unique geological sites at either end of the world. No more than a small token of community, but one that bespoke their shared *beingness*, their shared place in my life, this life – strung across the world, yet deeply rooted in each of twin scapes.

The night before the trek, we slept at the foot of the mountain in a small cabin. A blinding presence woke me before dawn and I immediately knew it as *Wollumbin* come to visit. Although I had not consciously begun to *Hello the House* (that was to be reserved for my footfalls come daylight), it was as if he were already aware, and had arrived to energetically acknowledge my pilgrimage, one which again repeated a trek made thirty years prior with no conscious understanding of why I had felt *called* to this place at the time. Profound was my humility in his extraordinary sight, and hours later, arrived at the summit, I closed my eyes in prayer only to be immediately transported to the *heart*. There I felt his peace, his ancient dreaming peace. I could have communed in there a lifetime, such was the resonance of ringing silence and primordial homecoming. Purpose fulfilled, however – to twin his resonance with *Ruscada's* – I retraced my steps down through a bird-songed, sun-dappled, liana-draped forest, face wet with tears of joy.

Well do I know that *Wollumbin* is a sacred site to the local Aboriginal clan, something they respectfully request those with a Western mindset to also honour. This I appreciate and acknowledge. If people today have forgotten or lost their access to the ancient wisdom to approach mountain sentience (or any *genius loci* for that matter) with respect and reverence for the sheer wondrous *fact* of its beingness, then we fall 'foul' of sacredness with each unthinking step taken. My practice of singing up country and undertaking blessing tasks as a matter-of-daily-course seems 'natural' to my Huxleyian mode.

What I learnt from *Wollumbin*, however (in a conversation on the way back down from the summit), is that unconscious 'singing' also seeps joy into his subtle bones, just as birdsong or the forest's breath resonates with his own. So even if *my* preferred way to scale a peak is quiet, contemplative, and consciously prayerful, a child's burble of joy, a climber's concentrated sweat, or the chatter of happy hippy hikers is likewise generative if the underlying spirit, like that of Proclus' heliotrope, emanates from the same 'space' of self-light within. We were all held in the cone of his embrace, likewise contributing to same in our respective ways of expressing joy. A 'mirroring' (see Glossary) moment in miniature, and I shall never forget his insight into how his sink is infilled …

Such it is to participate in singing up country, a ritual which roots us deeper in country, to feel kinship with said country and thus *all* country, likewise. Yet when 'homecome' to my own particular *stretch* of land? One overlit by *Wollumbin*, across which his tendrils of ancient laval flow stretch, smooth black basalt fingers tracing the coastline northwards, while strewing the hinterland with 'glasshouse' volcanic plugs of a different clan's dreaming? One where spirit of place is shared with the rock-solidity of granite spurs and headlands, together with the millennial-smoothed edges of ocean-smashed sandstone cliffs? In this place, *my* place, a final verse is tacked on to *Hello the House* thus:

> *With love in my heart, and blessings on my tongue,*
> *Know that I am homecome to You …*

Chatwin writes that pilgrimage re-establishes the original harmony which once existed between man and the universe and cites the Buddhist principle that in travelling the path, one becomes the Path: 'Arkady, to whom I mentioned this, said it was quite similar to an Aboriginal concept. "Many men afterwards *become* country, in that place, Ancestors." By spending his whole life walking and singing his Ancestor's Songline, a man eventually became the track, the Ancestor and the song' (pp.178-9). So it is.

Homecome to the Sea

Flying is in my blood – subtle and actual. It floods my genetic memory as much as astral heritage imbues our soul's inheritance. The (genetic) thread began with my father, an RAAF pilot during the Second World War. Both my brothers were bitten by the bug to learn, the elder would have me 'co-piloting' from the age of five while he did 'circuits and bumps' in a Piper Cherokee at the local airfield. Most significant family photos and home movies featured a light aircraft as protagonist; we 'co-stars' ready for a jaunt out over the suburbs of Brisbane and Moreton Bay dressed in our Sunday best. I had no desire to pilot aircraft myself, but in all the years since, no matter how many or how long the flights, with face pressed to window glass I am as happy as the proverbial pig in mud.

The (subtle) thread, meanwhile, began similarly but ended traumatically. My earliest recalled experiences of night consciousness involved flying – travelling far and wide (and high) above *Malakut* landscapes, arms outstretched like Peter Pan. I have distinct memories of being buoyed by the wind's breath while in flight; I knew her loving embrace was what 'held' me aloft. It was very sensory, the feel of this cushion of air beneath my belly.

As with most childhood passions, however, the assertion of ego-consciousness in, especially, the teen years, dampened its effect. But a singular event when I was eighteen severed the thread altogether, frightening me away from the adventures 'night-flight' brought. As a result of his war service my father was not a well man and at the age of sixty, his body cried halt. We were separated by a hundred miles of physical space at the moment of his passing, yet he 'flew' to me to say goodbye. Then kept flying while I tumbled back to earth in shock.

Twenty years later (fifteen years ago) I unconsciously repeated this flight to the Otherworld while still anaesthetised following psychically invasive surgery. Soaring over sea-lashed cliffs, the sky stretched taut to the horizon and the sun warm on my skin, I finally felt free again, laughing above the boiling bubbling cream of a passionate ocean. Yet once more I crashed to earth, falling, falling far – down below the beauty of the coast, down deep into the cold sterile world of a hospital recovery ward, where I cried over and over: *I don't know where I am!* I knew I had been flying *home*, but where was I now? Sadness and confusion were all that remained, and a body distraught in its sympathy – my soul's attempt to re-establish astral connectivity had failed.

It was not a conscious act, or intentional, therefore, to re-learn to fly the *Malakut* after these disturbing events. However, a decade or so past, I decided to research my father's war experience, to write the story of his miraculous homecoming to begin a family with my mother in fictional voice. Titled *The Long Way Home*, it rests on the Fiction Shelf in the nestedfishes.org library. In trawling the Australian War Memorial archives, I was to discover the role an Empire C-Class flying boat played in his squadron's rescue, she the 'bright white angel' of their survival.

Once the story was complete, in the catharsis of night-consciousness my father's presence unexpectedly returned, for the first time since his passing, to fill my head with the genetic memory of four determined propellers kicking into action, the roaring and rocking of the angel's struggle to take off, more than two thousand pounds overweight. I felt the combined *will* of plane and pilot to carry each of these hungry, injured, malaria- and dysentery-weakened men to safety. They had trekked for days through jungle swamps to finally reach the rendezvous point, used the last of their non-existent strength to swim out past the coral reef on a moonlit night to reach her. It was still a long way home, but this angel would leave none behind …

Somehow the act of writing Dad's story 'into existence' (he who never spoke of it), and the exhilaration, the catharsis of hearing those engines roar into life, re-opened my psyche to the joy of *Malakut* flight, to its ability to take us far, take us *home*. Still, I needed to re-learn the technique. Firstly Mr1300BC arrived to assist but once given my 'wings', I was on my own. Ever the link seemed to be between sea and sky; a rise above an eastern shoreline would be my point of departure, flying out over the ocean, before turning right to hug a wild cliff-ravaged coastline on my way to a mythical southern land.

On occasion, it was as if the whole land on which I stood 'flew' south to meet its neighbour 'beyond'. At such times I was free to take out my journal in the *Malakut* and write the process up for Van Diemen's *Book of Voyage*, for others who were 'blind' to the phenomenon. This was such an exciting possibility, I would 'hear' Self say to self: *I love to watch the world come up! I love to watch it as it happens! And this time I'm going to write it as it happens, so we can keep it, for always!* An extraordinary joyfulness infused these moments together with the excitement of always inching closer to this mythical scape – *Terra Australis Incognita*.

All this could have been purely a function of genetic heritage – prior to flight entering the family equation, migration from the North Sea-hugged Scottish coast to Australia's eastern seaboard had involved ocean-faring in the 19th century, and there was talk of a sea captain amongst the ranks of forebears plying the trade route to and from China. Yet in the *Malakut*, ever the same flight path, ever the same destination. And I knew it was 'home'.

Separately, I unconsciously *extended* the link between sea and sky in my psyche to include stellar realms as this excerpt from *The Taste of Translation* reveals (p.400-1):

Crete, yes. ... Yes, she remembered it all. They spent nights beneath a sky awash with stars reflected in the mirror of the sea. Clear nights, where the moon, once risen, plumbed ocean depths to emerge atop the crest of shore-bound waves.

What if we've got it wrong, she said during a late night walk to the lip of rock above the cove. What if it's all back to front and the universe is actually the sea and the sea up there in space? So that each day we're going for a swim in space.

She worked through the proposition and said: I float, I'm weightless in the water, gravity doesn't bear me to the ocean floor. Beneath the surface there's no air to breathe. I could just as easily be out there, a speck in the universe, rather than a speck here. So perhaps here is really there, and there is really here! She nuzzled into his shoulder.

Or there's no here or there, Samir pointed out. Only is. He stretched out on the grass and sighed. In the end does it matter?

No, she laughed ...

The above riffs on the same melody described in the previous chapter in which Kisha feels herself detach from the world at Samir's graveside. This, in turn, riffs on my 'fear of flying' (with apologies to Ms Jong) described above. Eventually, however, these disparate contemplations were to come together when I intuited that flying brought me home to our stellar heritage. That it constellated in my psyche as a land 'beyond' the sea was a classic case of Jungian psychoid unity in action, a mirror to the outer pilgrimage between homes strung across my known 'material' world. However, at the time of my first solo flight 'home' several years past, I was too exhausted to put any pieces of the puzzle together beyond the sheer relief of having arrived at said destination after a long, arduous and concentrated adventure. I had returned to the place where we learnt to be 'animal', to inhabit and live the *form* needed to come into *this* world, to serve Gaian purpose ...

The fact that the arrival of the *Card Deck* into my orbit would ramp up (so to speak) this point of intersect between sea and sky, earth and stars, should not be surprising to the reader. Rather than sporadically engaged as previously, in company of the cards astral journeys became quite regular, and I realised they manifested through the *Gate of the Stars* (which is logical, of course).

One flight was intriguing, in that it took me to a new 'home'-abode. Apparently F and I were moving and I walked through an empty space which needed cosmetic work as well as furnishing. In my journal I described being fairly noncommittal about the move; understanding it was expected of us to undertake this responsibility, however, I did not question its necessity – an unusual outcome in matters of the *Malakut*, for often my 'self' can become quite argumentative with 'Self' when it doesn't have a clear (rational) understanding of the need for some particular direction to be followed. The back garden was very Oz-childhood-like, and with a tropical fruit tree ...

Regardless of destination, the most precious part of each flight (and therefore the most memorable) would be rolling over to float on my back. Not only did this suggest I was becoming more adept in practice, 'inversion' always tended to shift the scape from day to night. Looking up to the stars, I would feel such peace and love it was extraordinary; I can only liken it to communing with pictures of 'family' – a bit nostalgic, a bit whimsical, coupled with a sense of tranquillity rather than loss or longing, aching or yearning. Perhaps because flying brought me into persistent contact with 'home-turf' I felt more settled?

Later I would twin the insights provided during the conversation with Beauty with my felt-sense during flight and floating. No longer buoyed by the wind's breath, a lightness-of-being seemed to self-generate these episodes in the spirit of: *I am the vapour, said the snow atop Schiesshorn, and I am as light as air*. It literally felt like being in the ocean, but the ocean being space; like the time I 'stood' in space with the three scholars of antiquity named P, the sense of the aetheric felt akin to being in the ocean – surrounding, but also penetrating – awash, the membrane of 'me' as porous in either dimension. My first unconscious glimpse of same had been in writing the fictitious sequence reproduced above. In a complementary episode in the same text, my felt-sense was that it was akin to dust modes afloat in the air – caught by the sun's gaze, they would become 'enlightened' which led to the following whimsical contemplation (p.426):

> *Afternoon sun bathed the bed and spotlit a column of dust in suspended nonchalance. Dust. After all her cleaning, dust!*
>
> *Plain to the eye in the shaft of light but no doubt, at sun-shift, new dust would be revealed, and she sat on the bed, wrapped in sunlight and dust, tiny specks bobbing about her with the random delight of a bottle floating at sea, adrift, with no thought of destination. Yet arriving somewhere, eventually, to tell stories of the journey, of life itself as a speck of dust.*
>
> *She sat and wondered: What's the difference between me and a speck of dust?*
>
> *Is that a trick question? asked Samir.*

So many waymarkers I had not tied together until *MakerMan* from the *Card Deck* began to swirl her creative energy into the whole, and a last piece of the puzzle delivered itself into the Circle – the Dancer, *Homecome to the Sea*, adding its energy to the mix of the inner sanctum. Genetic heritage had delivered me to a sunburnt life on a southern Pacific shore, and the card spoke at some level, so why not? Our annual pilgrimage down under was always to the same core coastal locale and 2015 was to prove no different. As I wrote in closing the previous chapter, once more we were boarding a plane to bring us *homecome to the sea*. I could hear, at some level, the 'singing' of the grail space we had created together, Sidhe and I, but decided to leave the *Card Deck* at home. Singing up country down under did not involve them …

A Pilgrim's Progress

My family upbringing was a modest one – holidays involved piling everyone into the car and taking off to 'home-beach' north of the city to bush-camp. By the time I – last in the brood – arrived on the scene, Mum had had enough of sand and flies and canvas tarps and we graduated to renting a small fibro shack along the foreshore beside a long-declared National Park, a granite headland of quietly dramatic beauty jutting north, to look out over an eastern sea wild to her right and a secluded bay to her left. A tiny tucked-away cove between headland and bay became our preferred rental heaven for a few weeks each year and, later, a regular daytripping location for my group of uni mates.

It makes perfect sense, therefore, that when latterly flanked by a Swiss-infused family, here is where we homecome, its proximity to our hinterland forest (Maleny) a requisite advantage. The peace-sink-pure energy of this place is also clearly present – a spirit which veritably purrs in the sea, the sand, the wind, the waves. From a journal notation years past:

> This morning, down at the National Park with a coffee on the rocks and then later getting bread down at Hastings Street, I had the felt-sense of this place, this spirit of place, once more as a peace-sink. People just happy here, plain peacefully happy, any orneryness dissipating, dissolving as a simple matter-of-course in the face of the latent joy seeping up through the sand. You can't stay angry for long here. Here, the energy of the whole seems balanced, its spirit acting to calm all stresses – naturally, of itself.

Of course one could put this down to the 'holiday' atmosphere that pervades the locale. But there are as many residents in this village as intermittent holidaymakers – drawn to put down roots in its (sandy) soil, I would suggest, by these selfsame energetic qualities. And, given our hemispheric pilgrimage each year, we never tended to be down under during holiday season. Thus did I feel my readings were sound.

I know little of the longer-than history of the region but the *fact* of the preservation of a key tract of prime coastal real estate from the late 19th century has certainly contributed to the purity of the sink. And once I took *VanDiemen'sMan* to this place in the *Malakut*, as if we were there at a time before white settlement, as well as at a time in our personal pre-history before the *Book of Voyage* entered my conscious lexicon. At the 'entrance' to National Park we had stood atop a huge upturned dugout canoe, looking north to whence we came. It brought me such joy to share this pristine scape, this murmuring place where the forest meets the sea, with him.

As I recounted at the end of the previous chapter, our 2015 journey home was a brief family spring-break to celebrate my mother's 93rd birthday. I had completed the first Canto of an epic poem dedicated to our alpine high wild, my gift to read it aloud in her (failing) sight. Its closing line, invoking the energies of homecoming 'to the sea', riffed on humanity's perennial return to the sea of Being coupled with my experience of working with light 'from source to sea to source' as a 'connective thread between heaven and earth' (which I document in the Annexed essays). The Dancer, self-naming as *Homecome to the Sea* at the time and requesting 'pole position' in the Circle, I thought, extended the theme – especially given my astral destinations-of-choice – rather than any literal reference to home-beach down under.

We arrived at this time's rental heaven to which all family were invited from near and far for several days of shared camaraderie. The day chosen for Mum's celebration had coincident significance – 'twas the hundredth anniversary of ANZAC Day, the fateful dawn of Australian and New Zealand troops' harsh initiation onto the world stage during the Gallipoli campaign, and the commemorative day for all war servicemen and women since. Down on the beach, in front of the surf lifesaving clubhouse, a re-enactment would be staged, pre-dawn. Mum was too frail to attend but we would be there for her, and Dad, in spirit, together with more than ten thousand others who crammed the tiny foreshore to hear the *Last Post* bugled as the skiffs pulled ashore, as Apollo daubed the sky in muted tones ...

A moving occasion. We wandered back up to the house, the children headed back to bed, F and I chose instead to walk the headland track five kilometres around to the eastern sea wild, to watch the sun fully wake and flood the world with light. Silent, each of us in reverie – I was somehow drawn to repeat the line 'homecome to the sea' during our steady hike there and back again. But at one point I stopped short – there was the Dancer's image plumb bang in my sight. I 'knew' this stretch of track well, *and* this particular view, but had not directly equated it with the image. Was I missing something in its self-naming, as well as self-positioning?

On the homeward stretch we took a small detour courtesy of a sign pointing the way to a townhouse for sale in the street behind. F noted down the time for 'open door' next day. I demurred. It did not look so special from the outside. If it fitted into the program, well and good. If not, so be it. Next day duly arrived. I woke 'buzzing' but could not put the energy down to anything specific, apart from the fact I had a great desire to read the first part of the epic to the children before we all went our separate ways for the next several months (such it is with the older two at university in Melbourne). Poetry is meant to be read aloud – 'tis a spoken art (bardic) and one I love to engage as it brings self and Self into creative touch in the here and now. Hence, by the Canto's concluding line, 'homecome to the sea', my felt-sense of being 'aether-infused' had reached a prophetic height.

The boys were not interested in looking at another boring house for sale, but daughter-dearest came with us. We wandered round the corner and found many others had the same holiday-weekend idea in between trips to the beach or local café. Name noted on the agent's clipboard, he invited us to enter. Strangely, given the quantum of humanity circulating, I stepped across the threshold and straight into a cone of silence.

It took a moment to recognise what I was experiencing and to let 'soul' do what it will. I felt the tug of the 'unseen hand' hook into my heart, pull me straight through the living space – out, into the courtyard beyond. There was the familiar felt-sense of gliding in the liminal space betwixt and between, and I knew a subtle presence was attempting to make contact. I stood still in the 'cone'. *Hello*, said a voice. And I turned to find an avocado tree welcoming me to her domain.

The intuition was immediate, rhizomatic interconnections synapsed all over my known and unknown world, firefly sparks burst to energetic life as I walked across and placed a hand against her trunk. Together our *chi* sang, and I promised I would try. Within three minutes of entering the house I was back out front with the agent to inform him of our 'serious interest', then rushed back around the corner to rally the boys. 'Why this place, Mum?' asked the elder. The only response which Self *knew* self could communicate in a moment of soul-knowing pure (i.e. for which there are no words) were: Because it feels like it could be home, a home for us *all* to come home to …

Ah, but things are never as simple as a knowing soul would expect. Or a Sidhe chorus, for that matter. Latterly, in preparing this text, I re-found Mariel's comment in *Conversations*: 'In this partnership, be aware that we may ask help of you and of the energies you can invoke' (p.147). Hmmm … Are contracts and mortgages in their lexicon, I wonder? At this juncture, I shall turn the next days' rollercoaster – both material and *Malakut* – over to the 'raw' voice of the scribe on her plane of intimate exteriority as she tries to make sense of the signs.

27 April: So, spirit of the mountains, waters, ancestors, flora and fauna – what do you want me to do? You know that I have homecome, that when all rivers run to the sea, I will have homecome. Is that now? Is that here? That you want me *rooted* in this place, this headland, that this is a 'right' way forward toward greater mergence of heaven and earth here? Now? It seems *so* silly but it was so spontaneous, heart-led, -tugged *through*, to be greeted by a sweet spirit of fruitful longevity! Can I fruit and flourish here with as much serenity as I felt in her beautiful bones? *So* silly – this instantaneous knowing; explaining to B I could imagine it as 'home'; that it had a feel of 'home', not the typical glitzy holiday or touristy stuff.

In *Malakut* wanders overnight, I was being covered in fine filigree starlit webbing – it spread so fast over my arms and body. I assumed a spider had crawled over me and created a web in her wake but was she now camouflaged? Mergent with her creation in beautiful fine-laced patterns? So glorious a design and inherent its shimmered light but I had work to do in the garden (forest) – weeding or planting, grubby work so E helped me peel it off. It really wasn't 'practical' in the circumstances; I didn't want it damaged.

Still, I wonder at its message – is it that a fine-silvered 'fairy' web is enfolding me more and more in the space I inhabit, which *Beauty* said would soon feel like home too? Are these the threads of happiness I saw woven into a beautiful cloak after my encounter with Madam S? If so, what does it portend for the transaction? For later, in a half-space when I *specifically* asked for guidance, I suddenly found F and myself at table in the courtyard overlit by *AvocadoTree* with an 'Ancestor Couple' who smiled in shiny starlit welcome. At some level I understood *they* were the guardian spirits of place, its memory *and* potential. When I became aware of this, suddenly we were 'inverted' to float in the 'aether' of the courtyard; table upturned, no longer needed. I was reminded of the time I floated in the sea of stars – homecome. I seemed to sense their message but was it real or self-conjured hopefulness that this is the right path?

28 April: When life dwells in the realm of possibility, the feeling is light, expansive, fleet of foot, soaring. And then, reluctantly pulled back to the solidity, materiality, banality of 'normalcy' (contractual processes, financing et al) and I lose *all* interest, passion. As if the senses have been deadened by humanity placing strictures and structures on the *joy*, the *passion* of life – lived!

I collected, on the beach yesterday at Peregian (see Glossary) and on the rocks yester-morning here at Little Cove (ah, but can I call her 'home' yet?), keepsakes and touchstones to bind me to place, *this* place. But shall it only be lived, enjoyed, embraced in the context of *Malakut* realms? Where are the great sky circles of joy in the all-too-human approaches to 'binding' self to place, this all-too-profane external coupling that a contract and potential purchase would enjoin?

I felt so flat yesterday during our 'chat' with the agent. The details and tasks and 'best offer needed' because of 'other interested parties'. Blah, blah, blah. Just *so* flat that joy can be *so* reduced, boiled down to a point where its essence just floats away ... F tried to buck me up, said: Let's go have a beer on the beach and watch the sunset. There, ridiculously, the epiphany happened. F discovered the stubbies weren't twist ones and went off to find someone with a bottle opener, and while I sat, flat, the peace-sink's spirit gave me a hug, and setting Sun a peck on the forehead. A classic case of needing a shoulder to cry on, and in their compassion, they spoke ...

Meanwhile, all around was happy chatter, people hanging on the beach on a glorious eve. Suddenly F was back with open beers and the funny story of the father at the next picnic table who had a technique for knocking the lids off with his fist against the edge of the bench (don't try this at home, kids!). A regular weekday after school, his family had come for fish and chips as the daughter's birthday treat. They hailed from only a few miles inland, but this was their chosen perfect spot on a perfect day.

Something snapped in my brain. At Peregian I had tossed small stones into the waves, found a scallop shell with a conveniently-sized hole to thread onto my silver chain as a symbolic interlocutor of intent, and spoken aloud my hope: *Help me to homecome, all thee spirits of place.* But now, instantly, I realised the intent was far more inclusive: *Help me to help others to homecome.* 'She didn't know how or why she knew, she just knew' – this time a knowing brought into play by the memory of *AncestorCouple*'s smiling welcome less than 12 hours ago; as they had welcomed me, so too my task to welcome others 'home'.

This is what the *energy* of partnership actually *feels* like – it's the vision of *twinning* my/our purpose with the peace-sink's purpose: *Help me to help others* ... Oh, what a revelation! Now I know the task, why we have been called – to provide a home to which *others* may homecome, to connect with Spirit rooted here in the land, deep-sunk in the sand-soil of an oxygen-rich peace-sink-pure headland ecosystem. *Help me to help others.* All flatness banished in the twinkling of an eye! Oh, blessed day! And with such intent firmly expressed, I now detach from the outcome.

<u>1 May</u>: I am fully lucidly awake. It is 5:30am. We are being lashed by a 'Great Eastern Low' and I have returned from the *Malakut* my heart thumping and leaping as three women present me three cushions. They were 'guests' here; it was time to return their cushions; it was time for the mantle to pass to our family. Immediately, in the space, I burst into tears of gratitude and joy at

their gift, their welcome, their *honouring* of our pledge – tears which returned to the material with me. For yesterday I signed the contract of offer using the numbers I 'knew' were right in the three minutes it took between entering the house and statement of intent to the agent. Yesterday he said: 'You're up against another offer. They are local, have easier and shorter-term access to finance than foreign bankers. Are you sure it's your best offer?' Yesterday I shrugged and said: 'What will be will be. We're on a plane back to the other side of the world tomorrow ...'

But now? Is it already known in the *Malakut* what will be? For earlier, in this 'very lit' space, we were out in the garden; all friends and family sitting around, the agent there as well, lots of people coming to his 'open door' while I (teasingly) dug him in the ribs and said: *Yes, but we followed through in the end* ... It was at this point that someone came and said: *Anne, there are women here who want to meet, say something to you*, and I turned to find the three women with their three cushions. Oh, what an encounter!

A Great Eastern Low (pressure system): We drove south to the city later in the morning through torrential downpours, flooding; vehicles aquaplaned but somehow our little rental car stayed *cleaved* to the bitumen. The entire stretch of highway, I slipped between *Malakut* memories from the previous winter's dark, the last stanza of OLP's first Canto (especially the phrase 'when all the rivers run'), keeping my concentration on a barely visible white line, and F saying: 'How strange. We're going home to reports of torrential downpours and flooding back in Switzerland today too!'

The word 'convergence' illuminated in my mind's eye. What is pre-cognitive? What is unconscious invocation? What is soul knowing pure which contains in itself the event, the actualisation of its own 'thought' as Emerson intuits? Four months prior, in a winter's dark *Malakut*, I had been part of an excursion to witness the phenomena of two landmasses coming together – 'Pacific' and 'North-West'. A line of mountains formed the boundary or border where these two would meet. When they finally connected, it caused an extraordinary meeting-of-the-waters phenomenon called 'convergence'. 'I saw' driving monsoonal-type rain; it was as if this was something very important and in the moment of their connection, I felt uplifted, filled with 'their' energy likewise.

We arrived safely at Mum's for our last night on Oz soil, unaware that our own 'convergence' was about to turn to manifest reality. For, as the sky split open with electrical energy, it seems the agent was trying to call – but who could hear the phone over the sound of rain and thunder? The text message I discovered several hours later, however, was clear: *Congratulations. You're in.* 'In where?' said Mum.

90

But by that point I was already beyond, thinking through next steps of a partnership unfolding before my feet, and an intuition already present that once the 'profane' had been sorted, we needed to return down under again post-haste to greet the soul of the house, thank it for its faith and trust in our stewardship, and formally: *Create the 'home' to which others may homecome* – in the spirit of Mr1300BC's longer-than counsel: *We all breathe life into what we love.* Suffice it to say it was turning into a very expensive year.

A 'new Maleny'

The reader will, I hope, recall that in Chapter 2 I described a *Malakut* encounter during the winter-dark cycle preceding active attunement with the energy of the *Card Deck* with a locale described as 'new Maleny'. Coincidentally (or not), the 'convergence' encounter documented above post-dated new Maleny's 'discovery' by the exact same six days as in the material.

Therefore, to close this chapter, and ring in the next (with GreenMan-like glee), where a raft of partnership tasks shall be fully outed onto a plane of *manifest* exteriority, let me close with some cogent quotes from *Conversations* into which I was to (re-) dive as soon as returned to my ten-foot-square hut (jetlag notwithstanding):

> The earth is still a planetary crystal with energies vibrating and coursing along a vast latticework of connections. The phenomena you call the 'ley lines' are only an outer representation of this, the manifestation upon the physical of these deeper lines of living energy and consciousness. ... Perhaps the image of the crystal with its latticework of nodes and connections is a way to illustrate our differences. You took from our common ancestor the capacity to be a node in the lattice, while we took the capacity to form connections (p.35).
>
> Together we are the complements that create a whole, living matrix, one capable of singing the energies of the earth back into the places of physical matter and into our world as well (p.38).
>
> Stones have long been used to anchor the star-forces into the earth, making them available to the living world. The Stone Circle is not just a portal to our realm, a connection with us, but also an organ of respiration that connects the life breath of the stars with the lungs and body of the earth (p.93).

These thought-starters backboned my contemplations on hooking new Maleny into a 'home-grid' (for want of a better word) of stone-centred energies with which I could connect from afar, as well as extending the notion of 'home' itself to include others beyond our immediate circle of intimates invited to 'share' our living spaces, with the potential to be 'touched' by its overlighting spirit of place, to connect with the peace sunk deep in its subtle bones. Further, the crystal mountain I had seen in the *Malakut* encounter at new Maleny I assumed was symbolic of the planetary crystal rising up to 'touch' stellar energies.

Yet what was our purpose here? I trawled other pre-Sidhe winter-dark encounters for clues and re-found the teaching (described in Chapter 4) on how to work on projects together – how each party brought what they could to the table, but its seeding in the material world meant responsibility for implementation would rest with the entity who could best see it through to fruition (i.e. me). Beyond that, everything seemed quiet (on the Western front) apart from a ring (described in Chapter 2) to which I was attracted in the *Malakut* as a 'connective thread' to I knew not what.

As Mariel says: 'Once you set forth your intent, we can blend with the field you create and enhance its capacities to connect and to manifest' (p.147). It was time to set out 'my' Stone Circle once more – the (now) nineteen cards of the permanent Council, the fourteen dancers (as witnesses) offering input as and when appropriate – and continue the adventure in full knowledge of the part I had been asked to play ...

Chapter 7: Acts of Awakening

'**By spending his whole life walking and singing his Ancestor's Songline, a man eventually becomes the track, the Ancestor and the song**': Bruce Chatwin, *The Songlines*.

This chapter specifically engages Mariel's description of telluric technology to tap the sites of power. The reader may wonder how I *knew* that my shared task with Sidhe companions involved awakening (or re-awakening) the energy housed in stone in order to establish a connection between Pacific and North-West, to engage the forces I had observed in the *Malakut* experience of convergence during last winter's dark, to contribute to a shared vision of Gaian holism.

Indeed David's comment in the companion text to the *Card Deck* refers in this context: 'At heart the *Card Deck of the Sidhe* is about incarnation: the incarnation of the Earth and the incarnation of a partnership between Faerie and human that can serve the planet at a time of need' (p.169). Yet I understood my task, in company with Sidhe, concentrated specifically on the potential to add new sites of *conscious* power to the planetary grid in the spirit of Mariel's comment in *Conversations* (p.67) thus:

> *The stone circle is a symbol of the portal that links the stars to earth; when you stand in it, you stand for the earth in its cosmic environment, mediators between stars and planet and midwives to the fullness of Gaia that emerges from*

this relationship. We are star people not because we come from the stars; you come from the stars as well. We are star people because we bring the stars to earth. But we can only bring them so far; there is a threshold we cannot cross, but you can, if you will dance the stars inward and outward with us.

I had stepped into the Stone Circle and donned the mantle, saying yes to I knew not what less than two months prior to 'convergence' occurring on the *physical* plane. I understood this was a serious undertaking, one which would require consideration, dedication and spirit. Donning the mantle, therefore, had only been a first step. The energy with which I now engaged spoke to David's sober assessment in the companion text to the *Card Deck*: 'This partnership expresses what in Incarnational Spirituality we call a "Gaian Consciousness". The motto for such a consciousness is "to think like a planet", that is, holistically, systemically, in terms of connectedness, ecology, and fostering life and its development. In a human being, this kind of awareness most often manifests as love' (p.167).

Yes, love – soul-knowing pure – had brought me this far on the path, had *uplifted* the intent I expressed on the beach that sunset eve of peace-sink serenity: *Help me to help others* … Yet I knew this intent needed more focus, more concretisation for the partnership field to begin to form. In point of fact, more focus would also help bring my felt-sense of deeper purpose into sharper relief, which seemed to hover around the *Malakut* vision of the *StarGeist* some eighteen months earlier. Using all waymarkers described in previous chapters, allowing them to sit and foment in my mind, for the threads of cognition to make their rhizomatic leaps, synapse between seeming disparate lines of flight toward an holistic unfolding of task, I crafted my intent as follows: *Help me to help others homecome to the One through the connections I forge with these spirits of place.*

The 'One' is the Sacred, the sole Ground of Being (see Glossary) – in the context of planetary consciousness, it is the expression of the Sacred by Gaia herself as well as any/all sentience within her field. As I have been blessed to homecome to the One, to experience the joy of *service* to Gaia through my connection to spirits of place, I wished to *share* this connection with others; perhaps they too would feel the burble of the peace-sink beneath their feet, perhaps likewise have their consciousness tugged by the 'unseen hand' along a homecome path.

Thus did the *specificity* of intent start to coalesce in my mind: I had deep and rich relations with home 'territory' in several *genii locorum*; I had been invited to steward a new space, however my vision on the beach had confirmed it was not intended simply for our family's benefit. Rather, it offered an opportunity for outreach on behalf of (*AncestorCouple's*) spirit of place to *all* who engaged (their) spirit of place. I understood this home needed to be returned to the pool of the peace-sink itself, so that all who *entered* the pool had the opportunity to homecome to the (Sacred) Pool as described in Chapter 5. The interlinkages between telluric and stellar energies, Sidhe and human ancestry, alliance, and the particularity of this partnership project were becoming clearer all the time.

To be frank, however, this introduced a completely new dynamic into my way of 'being-with' spirit of place in said home territories – *Hello the House* a body-mind-soul practice of engagement and (intensely physical) presence. David's 'awareness that manifests as love' (quoted above) ever-guided my (homecoming) way, underpinning the cultivation of a shared space of co-belonging, of 'being-with' once reciprocal recognition enacted, the way-of-love consciously invoked. It simply could not be otherwise than love as the irreducible core, an *embodiment* of the landscape; thus was love the *opening* itself, the conduit to *becoming* the landscape, as well as the *object* of union – nestedfishes each hosting a spot of the other's colour to enable their communion, their *oneness*.

But now I was being asked to establish a connection to spirit of place, before stepping back to enable others to experience the connection. Instead of being present, physically, to host family and friends and *mediate* their engagement with 'home', I was being asked to *trust* that spirit of place *itself* (in which dwelt the soul of this new 'home') would undertake task on my behalf for people I would never meet – hence the emphasis on connection, establishing *enduring* connectivity with a locale far-distant in physical space, in my formulation of intent. 'Twas this I specifically asked Sidhe companions to help bring to manifestation, to support my intuition that to achieve same, I would need to enter a *compact* with stone sentience in the spirit of Mariel's commentary in *Conversations* (pp.37-38):

> *The crystal matrix of planetary forces is still as available to you as it is to us. As we who became Sidhe retreated, and you who became human expanded upon the world, you carried with you the memory of the telluric technology of node, connection, and flow, shaped by song and dance and ritual. Guided by this memory, you discovered new ways to tap the sites of power. The practice of building stone circles and erecting standing stones began. What once was done by a person became embodied in stone. This worked as long as the stones were alive, but as the descent into matter continued, and much more importantly, as you lost the ability to form connections with the livingness of matter, the stones have become just what you see today, dormant and in some cases truly dead to the ancient powers.*

So began a project to help me awaken stone sentience, to ask its permission to form a compact to facilitate intent – a partnership within a partnership as I was to discover.

Defining Tasks

In closing the previous chapter, I alerted the reader to the raft of tasks awaiting my return to Swiss soil in order to manifest the partnership's 'field' of energy. Like other aspects of being, my approach to task-orientation is a particularity of Huxleyian mode. Thus I crave patience while I outline a process model which seemed to evolve in this regard, to help quiet and focus the heightened energetic state that had accompanied the 'convergence' event – a relevant objective in order to guide intent through all potential hazards in the stream over the coming (all too brief) six weeks.

Given that I dwell in multiple spaces as multiple 'faces' (as do we all), the requisite faces (i.e. aspects of consciousness) identified in the wake of our pilgrimage down under were three-fold in said project's 'management':

- Procedural Anne (PA) ticking all boxes to (hopefully) turn a legal contract into formal 'ownership' (involving a significant financial investment that had not been anticipated or planned for, this was far from a *fait accompli* and resulted in many tension-riven days as well as sleepless nights along the way);
- Mantle Anne (MA) continuing to commune with and uplift insights from the *Card Deck* to *externalise* the various facets of my intent; and
- Scholar Anne (SA) diving into research on how to establish *enduring* connectivity to achieve same.

Clearly all tasks interlinked, like a Venn diagram with common central themes. 'Twas to the centre of 'layered' labyrinths each Anne traversed, whence the crystal mountain overlighting new Maleny stretched skyward. But it still meant I needed to be aware of the different 'hats' I wore at different times on these different paths, so that I would not go 'off the deep end' (for example) with subtle *Companions* when a very physical bank manager was proving intransigent. This involved SA taking on a type of mediation role within my tripartite 'circle-of-self', a buffer zone, if you like, between the different roles PA and MA undertook so that their time-space intersect was limited to times of (relative) calm in this foaming sea.

Further, SA needed to wear two complementary hats. Self-scholar (s-SA) was involved in extensive review of the reams of documentation I had (fortunately) retained of all *Malakut* encounters and instructions leading up to this point. The principal reason I retain such reams is two-fold (yet, like all else, interconnected): Writing *Malakut* encounters 'into existence' help me *translate* immediate (and potentially transitory) felt-sense into more enduring textual imagery for working with further down the track and/or re-guiding my entry to such spaces; likewise they serve as *external* memory to connect seeming disparate encounters along different lines of flight (such as with the energy-signatures of certain interlocutors) on a single rhizomatic plane of consistency across which synapses of 'enlightenment' occur (i.e. 'firefly sparks of meaning').

Research-scholar (r-SA), meanwhile, was involved in re-visiting a plethora of texts by 'conversation partners' (see Glossary) which could prove relevant to task. Having SA 'stand-in-sovereignty' within the circle (of self) was a critical strategy, I found, and one to which I always returned (retreated) to (critically) think things through. At times, when even the Stone Circle was far from an oasis of calm (opinions and suggestions flying left, right and centre!), SA needed to wield a metaphoric gavel to call all to order and on occasion even shut down the assembly altogether because of the clamour!

The seeming organic flow of what this chapter describes, therefore, should not be considered smooth sailing by any stretch of the imagination; the perennial counsel of Gary Snyder was invaluable to SA in this regard: '(Notes are) mnemonic aids, like signals to open up the inner world ... trail-markers. It's like finding your way back to the beginning of the right path that you were on before, then you can go into it again. ... (They provide) access to the territories of my mind – and a capacity for re-experience – for recalling and revisualising things with almost living accuracy' (from *Look Out: A Selection of Writings*, p.131). Such support from a conversation partner was a godsend in terms of evolving process toward awakening stone sentience as well as developing the acts (or rituals thereto) themselves.

A flow-chart of shared work appeared in my mind's eye replete with arrows hence and forth between the SAs, PA and MA; iterative feedback loops were a necessary adjunct to the model, especially when various Stone Circle Council members (as well as *Card Deck* Dancers) offered specific suggestions for follow-up. Mind-mapping is difficult enough when one mind is involved – the potential for the process to become unwieldy and seriously derailed with this many voices ever-niggled, especially given the time constraints. Mariel may have said: 'Once you set forth your intent, we can blend with the field you create and enhance its capacities to connect and to manifest' (p.147), but my chief difficulty was slowing down the energy and hiving it off into bite-sized chunks. I remembered the project management counsel of the female Sidhe presence during my early forays with the cards and sighed – would things 'fall off the table' if I could not maintain her principle of the 'thirds'?

Yet persistently Beauty's voice arose to settle my nerves (*you know Love is the solidity within aether, that the Ground ever-grounds you*) and I revisited Mariel's explanation of how best to engage Sidhe energy (toward shared outcomes): 'In dealing with us, you must strengthen this (fluid) adaptability ... it's a "grounded fluidity" ... When you successfully adapt to and flow with changing circumstances in your life, you are fluid in a grounded, practical way, one that is connected to what is happening and to your environment. You are not simply swept away' (pp.52-3).

Throughout, my felt-sense was that all *Companions of the Way* were eager and committed to helping this project succeed; I felt the energy of their support, a 'we'll hold your back' sort-of energy regardless of which Anne was at her particular tasks – SAs, PA or MA. Sidhe presence, therefore, was not confined to Stone Circle Council meetings themselves, nor to my regular meditations in the ten-foot-square hut. Various presences would glide at my side on a continuous basis, observing, inputting and (at times) even prodding me along some tack which my usual reticence and shyness would have denied (the production of this text a classic case in point).

Three in particular were implicated in seeding this energy, and acted to bind themselves to the various faces of Anne accordingly. One should be clear to the reader – it is the Dancer who named itself: *Yes I am a scholar*, a direct reference to the image which had appeared during last winter's dark board game encounter (described in Chapter 4) prior to the *Card Deck* entering my conscious orbit. The zone of input representing wisdom and knowledge, it had risen out of the board like a plateau stacked with books and scrolls with a golden flash (which I now realise was Jeremy's phoenix not yet fully manifest). This Dancer accompanied SA in her work.

Regarding the other two, which were to align with PA and MA respectively, I remind the reader of the two heart stones from the Gates of Earth and Stars who had named themselves *MagicMan* and *MossMan* when the Stone Circle was first laid out, but had remained stoic in their silence ever since.

Along the axis of connection between stellar energies and the 'stars within the earth' as Mariel describes in *Conversations* (p.101), and likewise representative of the connectivity I engage in my own practice of 'threading light', suddenly these two bounced into action with my statement of intent – *MagicMan* to apply his earthy 'magic' to legal and financial procedures (amusing in its own way), as well as to provide a link to the Sidhe 'on the ground' down under; *MossMan* eventually to find himself centre-stage in MA's work to uplift insights from the *Card Deck*.

The fact that this also mirrored *MakerMan's* counsel in the board game I have only consciously realised in developing the text herein. In the end the three entities on the board were actually my three 'faces' working with three different streams of Sidhe energy – MA's work to input from the 'Outier' zone, SA's from the domain of wisdom and knowledge, while the Anne I thought the only 'me' at the time was little miss procedural tap-dancing with the Heart Stone at the *Gate of the Earth*.

Yes, it *would* need to come back to this zone for finalisation – without the property there could be no physical manifestation of intent. And yes, I did need to respect the principle of the thirds. If I spent too much time with the cards, where would that have left the solicitor?

To Hit The Ground Running ...

A brief six weeks to achieve intent, all notes and comments above coalescing in spontaneous uprisings, each Anne busy with task; MA's *Malakut* wanders, moreover, kicked off an intriguing correlational string three days after returning to Swiss soil:

6 May: I am at the house down under; all very white, 'lit', and I'm going around trying to figure out which switches turn on which lights. Out back the garden is very muddy, crisscrossed with planks after all the rain ('convergence' refers) to not chew up the lawn. The 'agent' is there, just leaving. He's been cleaning. We briefly discuss aspects of the contract. Apparently I will 'inherit' a particular freestanding cabinet in the middle of the living room beside a huge tree. It is a cabinet of much beauty and very old and unusual. I've never seen anything like it – a polished wooden surround with sliding doors in patterned glass, star-etched, the glass a lovely muted green, the pattern embossed to catch the light. Really, really beautiful!

I crouch down to slide open the doors, one to either side on a grooved rail, slowly and carefully as the cabinet is so fragile. Inside is a doll's house of tiny figures and furniture – upstairs and downstairs. Breathtaking. The figures are made of unbleached linen, and wear beautiful 19th-century style clothes. A woman comes up beside me as I reach my hand in to examine and admire a doll more closely. She says: *Are they filled with rag?* I press and squeeze and say: *No, sand.* She comments that this means they are very precious. I am so in awe of the whole ensemble – cabinet, sand dolls, doll's house. And this I will receive as part of the contract of sale?

I returned from the *Malakut* and immediately intuited the rhizomatic connections, how this insight lyrically followed from the women returning to me their guest cushions some days prior, as well as *AncestorCouple*'s 'welcome to country' (see Glossary) earlier the same week. The 'agent' I realised was *MagicMan* – an interesting development as I suddenly remembered having met him in the *Malakut* way earlier, in a companion scenario to 'new Maleny' some days following, when shown around a housing development by a typically upbeat salesman-type with really unusual eyes. This, of course, only synapse-fired when F said to me following contract signing with the 'real' agent: Did you notice how he has different-coloured eyes? The point is, I didn't. Einstein's 'spooky action at a distance' can be quite literal on occasion, and was typical of the 'fun' *MagicMan* conjured while supporting the project (and not out surfing with his mates).

Meanwhile, the precious cabinet rimmed in wood I knew to be the forest of the National Park at the back door which, when 'opened', transformed into the 'house' of the *SandPeople*, their energy-signature 'Faerie' from the depths of the peace-sink. Preserved in a state of suspended animation like 'dolls', their 'dress' (Victorian), pointed to the time they felt the need to go to ground, to retreat from the world like the *Wildmännli* folk of the Alps. But what could bring their energy back to 'life' in the here and now? Simply my inheritance of knowledge of their presence, or?

10 May: A very vivid *Malakut* sequence, a landscape extraordinaire! Huge ten-metre high waves crashing, surging along our stretch of Pacific coastline, even swamping the land on occasion, and I witness to the *ShiningOnesoftheSea* (self-named in the space) surfing these intense conditions. This the Peregian shore where I had tossed small shells and stones of blessing into the waves, calling on all spirits of place to help me homecome two weeks past. Now I have returned in the *Malakut* to see its civilisation revealed – a civilisation of Sidhe at home *in* the sea. So *enspirited* are they to enjoin the *life* of the swell, and I likewise uplifted, exhilarated by my witness.

Yet I know these conditions are too intense to fulfil intent; our home, fittingly, lies on the lee side of *Mother'sHead* (see Glossary); this the access point to the 'settled' energies of the peace-sink, she the Ancestral protective force from the unpredictability and intensity of the elements, the wildness and exposure to the full brunt of ocean to the east. Thus do I begin to walk home from Peregian, north along a high path up and around the headland, the way 'marked' for me with runes painted on the stone slabs I traverse, broad as breaching whales. All the while I watch the surfers. These shining sylvan cousins – so effortless their manoeuvres; each spectacular heart-in-the-mouth 'wipeout' clearly orchestrated, consciously engaged, successfully negotiated.

A wonderful insight to follow on from the *SandPeople*. I 'knew' this stretch of coastline so well in the material – consciously, since toddlerhood – but now to finally witness its *Malakut* existence? Such a revelation! I felt so blessed by the trust these encounters affirmed; that, in bearing witness to the overall *constellation* of the landscape, its different energies and presences, I could begin to actively engage its subtle life, specifically the space deep-sunk in settled stone. I had returned from down under with several symbolic treasures to act as 'connector-threads' to terrain, introducing them to the grail space of the ten-foot-square hut, to be present whenever the energy of the Stone Circle was invoked:

- Two sea-smoothed stones from the cove's shore – one granite from *Mother'sHead*, the other basalt, streamed from the volcano heart of *Wollumbin* far to the south;
- Two scallop shells from the eastern sea wild – one worn since the day of *AncestorCouple*'s welcome, the other resting in a symbolic (wicker) representation of the Sacred Pool together with other longer-than symbolic interlocutors of my *Companions of the Way*; and
- A tiny silver-lit stone upifted from the same Pacific beach, which I dubbed *StarlightSeed* – for some reason it seemed to 'carry' the energy of the starseeds gifted into my care; no bigger than a pea, it lay cradled in the scallop shell, a linking stone, a stepping stone; from here it seemed only a short hop to a mantle of starlight perpetually donned.

During this time, an idea had begun to emerge that I needed to write a conscious ritual of invocation in which to embed my intent; it would be a way in which the swirl of energies in which the three 'faces', their three handholding 'muses', together with a chorus of advisors and extras approaching Grecian proportions, could engage, to funnel our aetheric (and aesthetic) engagement into a more compact, dense and pliable form. I would guess this suggestion arose from *MakerMan*, my 'theatre director' of longer-than standing. But how it presented in my psyche is best left to the raw notes of my journal:

20 May: An extraordinary felt-sense overnight of bringing the whole of Little Cove home and headland (sea, forest, house itself) *into* my body. This was all entirely conscious. I was aware of lying face down, on my stomach, when suddenly an entire 'presence' infused my body. It literally felt as if I *carried* all of 'it' and all of 'me' *equally* in the moment; and in fully absorbing the entirety of presence I *felt* how we became fully mergent, one. The whole ritual (phenomenon?) was preceded by 'thinking, reviewing' procedural events – incl. agent, solicitor, cash transfers, key handovers – and in this phase I literally *felt* all these items (even signed papers!) *flowing* through me, as if I were a feeder between A&B, X&Y. All smooth, nothing 'stuck' anywhere in the circulatory system (of 'me', I assume) and everyone happy, active, *doing*, in their roles (there were other actors but none specifically recalled). It was the most super-crazy felt-sense; quite extraordinary.

Once this energy 'settled' (which, I am sure, is as metaphoric as it is pre-cognitive of literal settlement on 15 June several weeks hence) came a final phase which clearly needs to be built into the Summer Solstice ceremony – no longer a 'flowing' energy, but simply an absorbing, holding, carrying energy. Yet I didn't feel any 'weight' to this presence; nothing heavy or cumbersome or distended, distorted. I understood the *whole* of place was *in* me, would *stay* in me. Such was my commitment, such was the trust *vested* in my stewardship. All of it so sensory; I felt my body to an incubatory womb for its potentialities in time. We are bound, we are *one*; this is how my prayer is/shall be answered: All homecome *into* me, therefore into the *One*. Sana!

There was much to contemplate in the wake of this event. At some level, it felt as if this 'state' or dimension constituted an 'intervention' *beyond* my intent as expressed, of how *future* engagement *could* unfold its potentiality in shared beingness and worldwork on behalf of evolving Gaian consciousness. As such, my immediate sense was to retain focus in the space of *current* engagement, on developing a ritual to connect myself to 'home' from afar, and dubbed 'prepping for a nodal connection'. Interestingly the ritual began to 'write itself into existence' as song, a love song in a bard's (i.e. poet's) voice.

In the *Card Deck of the Sidhe*, David writes: 'In Celtic society, the Bard was the one who knew the history of the clan ... all the relationships and connections that made up that history. The bard was the keeper of the collective memory which he or she could share through his or her songs and narratives. The bard was the keeper of vision ... (and) connected the clan with the world around them, with each other, with their own past and with the vision of their possible future' (p.48).

It seemed fitting, therefore, that this first 'song' (in what was to become a string) carried in its bones such interconnectivity between past, present, future; between personal and collective; between physical and non-. It also seemed fitting that the 'song' constellated around and arose *through* the energy of *MossMan*, 'my' bard and 'muse' to MA who, each day, more and more, lived Beauty's observation: *Aethereal-material are one and the same in my reality ...*

By the end of May, activities were beginning to coalesce around the prepping notes I made for the 'grounding' ceremony on the Solstice, its purpose to *ground* the energy of my connection to spirit of place here in our garden, for outreach to 'home' on the other side of the world. My felt-sense was that the nodal point should be connected to the physical earth; while symbolic interlocutors in the ten-foot-square hut in my home (such as the *Card Deck* and other, longer-than companions) were *my* means of connection to the subtle realms, the *Malakut* experience of bringing the all of Little Cove into my body which I described above seemed too 'big' (and potentially unwieldy) an undertaking on the physical plane. Bite-sized chunks were required, and I had an inkling (no doubt Sidhe-supported) that an earth-to-earth connection *outside* the hut offered the best opportunity to 'ground' and 'hold' the energies required to establish an enduring nodal thread.

There is a beautiful old crone of a tree in the back corner of our garden. Long have I called her *TreeMother* and from the earliest days, a Dancer from the *Card Deck* aligned herself with this meditative presence accordingly. I went out for a chat in the wake of these thoughts and the words formed: *Grail Space.* I was reminded of my self-naming of her as such at last winter's-dark, my comment being that she offered the sanctity of a private peace-sink in the corner of the garden. A 'knowing' at the time that I did not know was 'knowing'. But now it leapt out through skin – this would be the place for the 'inner to come out', the place to root my connection in the earth.

It had been a delightful Spring and shaping up as a warm Summer – the space beneath her canopy was filled with my foster family of oaklings and a bevy of brightly blooming pot plants, while in amongst her leaves burst delicate fragrant blossoms. I knew her as *Holunder*, but discovered her name in English to be *Elder* (the reader must excuse my ignorance, but a knowledge of Northern Hemispheric tree species is far from given for a down under girl). Over time I had strung prayer flags to her branches, looped and twined various whimsical items around her gnarled skin, but now I got busy, bringing different symbols out from the *inner* ten-foot-square hut grail space, to populate the *outer* 'grail'.

Meanwhile, SA began research to learn all about her own symbolic nature, and discovered how the Elder is sacred in Celtic lore (amongst others) – the Lady's tree and a passage to the realms of Faerie. Indeed, on Midsummer's Eve, it seemed, a portal would be well and truly opened amongst her roots to the Howe. I began to put pieces of the puzzle together – how, at times, while meditating in the Stone Circle, I would seem to return to the hut via the garden. Had she always been so-connected to Sidhe energies? Suffice it to say, it seemed 'fairies' had been hanging out at the bottom of the garden (literally!) and finally I had been invited to join (or rather 'host') the party.

Sunk Sentience

A favoured dog-walking route of mine leads out of our village past farmers' fields to a creek which wends its way through a copse of trees. When I first came to live here, F described how an environmental project of the local council had recently 're-opened' the creek, to let it flow naturally rather than funnelled through a pipe beneath the fields. In the process, earthmoving equipment had unearthed quite a few *Findlinge* (glacier erratics) and had assembled them as a collective, replete with plaques as to their provenance, beside the creek.

I have always found the German word for such boulders uncovered far from home sweetly poignant – the literal translation is to the English 'foundling'. Conjured in my mind's eye each time I walked this path, therefore, was the image of abandoned infants discovered on people's doorsteps to be taken in, given shelter, a warm and loving home 'found' with a mother, cuddling, cooing: 'Oh, the poor wee bairn …'.

By chance we have one in our garden, unearthed in the process of the house being built more than fifty years prior. When the Elder was planted, it was apparently shifted into the back corner with her. Strangled by ivy (both of them) when we came to live here fifteen years past, a slow process of developing the area into a nice sitting nook beneath her branches involved my stripping the massive green 'lump' which foregrounded the tree. When I first saw that within was a boulder, I had my first lesson in *Findling 101* – another new experience for an antipodean lass.

On this particular day's dog-walk beside the creek, I was in a meditative space courtesy of the notes for the 'grounding' ceremony being penned all morning. Making my way past the collective of boulders nestled in the copse along the bank (which I had, at some point, affectionately dubbed the *FindlingForest*), I felt drawn to reach out and touch *JollyGiant* (the largest in the family). Suddenly, words formed: *Slow to wake.*

This stopped me and dog in our tracks. What? Was he suggesting I needed to weave the *Findling* in *TreeMother*'s grail space *specifically* into the mix? That it was not enough just to make notes, intellectualise what I had read in *Conversations* about what occurred *within* the grail space of the Stone Circle, but to bind such energy to an *actual* stone itself? At this stage the reader is quite within his or her rights to conclude that I am especially dim-witted for not having made these connections myself. Clearly my Sidhe colleagues did, which is why words needed to be formed at the *FindlingForest* before I headed too far 'off-track'.

In trawling notes from last winter-dark's Sidhe overtures to flesh out this text, for example, I found the following clue overlooked in my excitement post-'convergence' event: 'Conversation with a woman about connecting glacial erratics (which I told her were called "*Findlings*" here) and quoted to her a *haiku* I'd written way back about a grey heron in the stream being like a "silent *Findling* at my step"'. The benefits of documentation, indeed!

Yes, Mariel had described the background to the stones as living forces: 'Together, the singers, the dancers, and the holders turned the raw power of planetary energy into energies we could use to (for example) transport ourselves instantly from one node to another … and (ditto) to bring vitality to the surface to enhance the life of everything in the region of the node, working with the devic forces in that area' (p.36-38). Yes, I understood this essentially described a task commensurate with my intent – to connect nodes across the world and enhance life in the region of said nodes.

But when I read the following words, somehow I missed the connection to anything specifically physical in my own home environment, and therefore my (and its) role thereto: 'As you lost the ability to form connections with the *livingness* of matter, the stones have become just what you see today, dormant and in some cases truly dead to the ancient powers' (ibid.). Was *JollyGiant* intimating that the living sentience in my *Findling* could be woken to enact tasks on my behalf?

Given that the dear soul had never before been used ceremonially, I imagined – in the moment – it would be nigh-on impossible if Mariel cautioned that even previously used stones in *existing* circles were now dormant or dead to the 'ancient powers'. Yet I was reminded of my experience the previous summer down under, when zapped (literally) by the energy of a guardian stone at an Aboriginal ceremonial site. The connection must have been intense between these folks and their inner elders for its sentience to still be so 'present' all these years down the track. Was I capable, in this trial-and-error way of working with Sidhe companions, of bringing a new node into the living grid of earth energies? *JollyGiant* had left the door open to manifesting such a reality with the word: 'slow'. I needed to get on my bike with this experiment, and quick!

With dog in tow, I rushed home to the garden, shared the news with *TreeMother*, asked for her assistance. Then a first touch-of-love to *Findling* with some words of introduction about what we would or *could* do (together) and that I understood perfectly it would be 'slow to wake'. I crouched before it, connected with its skin, the moss growing on its smooth hide and intoned: *You shall be my MossMan, my Standing Stone in space-time.* Suddenly revealed was the connection to the Bard in the *Card Deck*, now 'present' in physical form! In my joy I instinctively hugged him – the touch-of-love transforming from first 'overture' to known 'return'; in the spirit of reciprocal recognition's 'slow dance of courtship', I was being very forward! Yet to think this dear friend had aligned with *Findling*! The process would be slow, yes, but this gave a wonderful boost to my confidence. Our *joint* efforts would bring much more resonance to the task, an energy which the following *Malakut* experience delightfully had a hand in shaping.

7 June: I was in a complex of offices after hours, all white, lots of corridors and doors, no one about. I had been 'offered' this space to retreat to for several days, to work in silence on the project, but at one point was drawn to go 'out' to watch a band play at a summertime 'open-air' concert because I was very aligned with their 'lead' singer. He had a completely bald pate, was bright-eyed and charming, performed a specific song – a new wave number from the 80s by the Scottish band Simple Minds – Don't You (Forget About Me), signature song for the film The Breakfast Club. The line: 'Rain keeps falling, rain keeps falling down down down ...' repeated ad nauseum in my mind, an effortless segue to the 'convergence' event.

Here he was with 'backing band' and dancers – much choreography was involved. It seems it was pretty special that he had the chance to perform at this event because he was usually 'restricted' to a particular space; the 'authorities' had given him a leave-pass, but were waiting offstage to take him back again. Hence, after the performance, there was little time for us to be truly 'together'. Yet he accepted his fate, even to the extent of having his own 'gilded chains' (handcuffs in gold) ready to offer the guards. I rubbed his completely smooth head affectionately in farewell. *MossMan* – my 'knowing' was immediate as soon as I returned from the space. Yet wondered why he presented, energetically, as a force which is mostly 'locked' away but can have 'day-release' for special occasions?

When I went back 'in' to the *Malakut*, I discovered myself at the place he had been returned to, as if now I knew it existed I could visit anytime. It had the same energy as the space I had been at the start, but now I saw it externally – an institution or facility with lots of people on various floors. It was as if my 'retreat' were over and all back at their workstations. This I could see because the whole building was glass. I arrived as it began to rain and started to sing: *Rain keeps falling, rain keeps falling down down*, then continued the whole song once inside: *Don't you forget about me* etc; the acoustics in this space were just too good! I explained to someone that it was just so appropriate to the mood of my arrival as well as my intent being there – to visit. I hoped he hadn't forgotten me; as he walked on by would he call my name? So that's where it ended, channelling Simple Minds (which, when I was talking to the person, I couldn't remember the name of ...).

The humour underlying this event, a specific song 'uplifted' for my 'simple' mind was one amongst many examples during this project of encountering the playfulness of Sidhe energy. David writes in the *Card Deck* text: 'There was a deep seriousness about this project and yet there was playfulness, fun and delight as well' (p.177), something to which I can most emphatically attest. On one occasion, while 'cleaning' in the *Malakut*, a bright-eyed tousle-haired merry 'energy' arrived to help and I asked his name. He told me several times without me 'getting' it, so I said: Can you spell it? Slowly (for dim-witted Anne), he spelt: E-L-F ... we both laughed. And, in the tension-racked days leading up to PA's settlement of contract (would everything work out OK?), in meditation 'I saw' a being covered in soap suds as if enjoying a bubble bath – head fully immersed then lifted with a grin. Each time the bubbles dripped down, he would slap another handful on his face. A voice chastised: *You're not taking this seriously enough!* And I surfaced, smiling. Thank you *MagicMan*!

Following the particular encounter with *MossMan* (and band), I was drawn to write more 'songs' to add to the ritual's *Poems of Place*. The *Malakut* 'link' to the band Simple Minds offered another classic rhizomatic segue to one of their latter-day compositions once returned to the material – *Home* (2005) which had accompanied me (with its *VanDiemen'sMan*-like poetic counsel) the past decade since consciously taking root in Swiss soil. Suffice it to say, this song's text also wove seamlessly into *MossMan's* intended 'performance' of task.

Further, I set in train a process of regularly offering a token, a gift of love to the shrine (or altar) of *TreeMother's* grail, specifically as an 'act' to slowly draw *MossManFindling* (as his energy was now dubbed) from sleep in the lead-up to the formal solstice ritual. These included gifts of words, 'love-letters' to the stone itself – haiku created, penned on small slips of paper, folded and placed into a heart-shaped chalice set on his sturdy back. I was reminded of the *Malakut* experience of the kiln room; indeed it seemed the energy of mountain sentience, in the form of this *Findling*, was perfectly 'me-sized'.

With this I could work; this I felt I could *hold*. And with each new offering, I went out to sit on the gravel at his side and recite the evolving string which, by the time of the solstice, was a ring-song all its own – for haiku are three-lined poems, each of which I would repeat three times before moving on to the next on each third day the ritual engaged:

9 June:
Lightness of being:
this I feel as I sit with you
and think on us

12 June:
MossMan, dear Findling:
so do I name thee my Standing
Stone in space-time

15 June:
This day the deed done,
waiting now for your aetheric
kiss in six more

18 June:
So here we all stand,
and I hear the singing of
light-love stirring you

I called this full period from 9-21 June the 'Twelve Days of Consciousness'. It was a time of intense energetic engagement involving each Heart Stone specifically. Intriguingly it tended to manifest as a continuous felt-sense of physical *warmth*, and glowing presence, centred within my own heart. *VanDiemen'sMan*, longer-than writing muse for the *Book of Voyage*, supported the energy of 'writing' the ritual itself each day. I felt *MossMan* busy coaxing *Findling* awake. And once settlement of the property occurred (i.e. the mantle passing *physically*, finally!, into my loving care) on 15 June, there was an internal 'shift', a clear 'movement' as PA's energy (together with her *MagicMan* muse) relocated (gratefully) from head to heart – to coalesce (or re-integrate, as it were) with her other 'faces'. Earlier, with the completion of prep-notes and research, SA had re-melded with MA, her task-oriented Dancer (Scholar) fading once requirements had been fulfilled.

This re-integration of all faces into a single Anne I can only describe as a wonderful concentration of energy in a central font, heart-commensurate. From this place, my capacity to mould the densifying aetheric energy of engagement into a fully material manifestation of same would be sound, I felt, *grounded* in love. It was no surprise, therefore, that *MakerMan*, my 'theatre director', arrived on centre-stage at this time, to choreograph the production. She would accompany me in this last phase of *translating* the development of a detailed methodology to awaken dormant stone sentience into material and energetic fact.

Two 'performance-dates' were implicated in the 'open-air' program I had conceived: 18 June and 21 June, the texts of which are contained in the Appendix. The earlier date was a necessary pre-ceremony, I decided, in which to formally give thanks for *TreeMother*'s overlighting presence and ask her permission to use the grail space for the purpose of establishing the nodal connection.

Further, it was an opportunity to acknowledge her space as the locus for actively engaging Sidhe energies, for interconnecting horizontally (through the Gates of the *Rising Sun* and *Twilight Zone*) as well as vertically (through the Gates of the *Earth* and *Stars*). Thus, the pre-ceremony was written and designed to formally 'consecrate' the grail as a generative font of blessing as much as a zone of interconnectivity so that the solstice ritual could focus on the specific act of awakening *MossManFindling* to (our) joint task.

At this point I crave the reader's indulgence while I set out the flow of events these last days – whether in material or *Malakut* – in the raw voice of the journaller...

<u>17 June</u>: 6pm. A resonance that presents as the F below middle C, and the song follows in its wake ...

At three of the clock I sat on the verandah at the little tea table set for two to have my 'brekky' this afternoon. Sitting there, finally, after a not-feeling-well

108

sort of day, only finally getting back to 'me' while out Pabey-walking 1ish with Sun in his shining sky and fresh-bloomed cornflowers (after all the rain and storms) for bringing home ... So there I sat, finally fed, and Sun still shining, and feeling warmed, star-kissed and golden, trailing my hand through Willow's hair at my side and my thoughts turned to task – 'immersism' (rather than immersion – there's a difference) in the ceremonies tomorrow and Sunday and the thought of singing with Faerie 'our' peace-love-and-light song, when I was reminded that my 'original' plan had been to 'sing' *MossManFinding* awake by tuning up his *Poem of Place* (who knows where that thought is in my notes now, but the idea was that it would need to be 'low tones', mantra-ish, mann-ish, to 'meet' him in *his* depth-of-space) when **all-of-a-sudden** on the verandah, there and then, a sound, a tone presented and I just went with it as it *projected* from a single note into a 'riff' that sounded very ancient mariner or sea shanty dirge-ish coupled with an indigenous, clannish (runic, even) quality.

Such was the felt-sense as it arose and continued as its own ring song over and over till I thought I'd better return to some sort of surface-conscious space and get it down on piano before 'lost'. A real ceremonial circular narrative feel to its arising, but in the moment I intuited that the original F (below middle C) was *MossManFindling*'s extant or 'signature' note, his *own* resonance (though, most likely, several octaves lower than my female pitch), and that the riff which followed was the *singing* into being of his awakening (as in – bringing his depth *up* and out into the light, like an Aboriginal dreaming, singing *up* country).

So now I've come out here, into *TreeMother*'s grail space, to write, and to sing/hum *his* song to him, over and over. Actually now I think about it some more, it almost has a lullaby quality to it – so shall it sing him back to sleep again? But that's the sea shanty, rowing over a moon-aglow sea quality to it. It also has the feel of an Eastern-Asian (Chinese or Japanese, Taoist or Zen) meditative gong quality to it. Anyhow, whether out of memory or 'created', the original note I *know* is his own and this melody the *string*, the *thread*, to take it on, *weave* the connection into existence, across a shining world between *MossManFindling* and Little Cove's ancestral *ground*.

Here my notes from the moment of its arising: *MossManFindling, your tone is the F below middle C, and your 'song' began there, using the scale of A♭ major as your spun thread stretched out to touch (with love) Little Cove's nodal point of connection. Is this an extant resonance? A hum you can share on my behalf between the two points, back and forth, as the weavers weave this filigree web of evolving consciousness? As these threads of happiness are strung across the world? Thank you for bringing it into my orbit, for now I may sing it to/for you. Sana!*

And like all things, this course set in motion by a bit of random web surfing yesterday, a sound 'therapist' at Maleny working with vibration, tuning it to one's own soul vibration. It reminded me of my connection via the resonant hum and suddenly the firefly sparks in the rhizome took off when you, *MossManFindling*, presented me with your 'chord' of being with which I could connect. Blessed be!

18 June: *Rain keeps falling, rain keeps falling down, down, down ... Sipping from each grail cup — in honour of Faerie, in honour of Humanity, on behalf of Faerie, on behalf of Humanity — and a petal falls from TreeMother into her Humanity tea a moment before I lift the grail to take a first sip on their/our behalf. Whimsy! Joy! Blessed be!*

What a glorious ceremony! I began preparing before 11am, taking out *TreeMotherTea* (TMT — I had made an infusion of Elder-blossom by giving *TreeMother* a haircut; she is an aged crone, with few sprigs within Anne-reach, so some rationing was in order, but there was certainly enough for the 'grails', two goblets in recycled night-sky blue glass, one for Faerie, one for Humanity), lain on the Oz wooden board and with the posy of cornflowers at their centre (which a bumblebee decided to visit once established — sweet!), and had collected nine wild strawberries as the food offering (gifts from the garden) into the circle to go with TMT.

I set out the two candles, the Council of Elders with Dancers besides and the two printed-out Tarot Deck 'blow-ins' which specifically referenced Elder energy. I set a chair beside the Circle, told my story (after greeting *MossManFindling* and gifting him his last haiku) ... The rain began, as a smattering of drops ('just spitting', Mum would say) as I began the story; later the wind blew while I stood in the Circle and I thought it best to 'weigh down', actually anchor (!), the cards with real stone.

Coincidentally all ready for the ceremony just as the clock in the church grounds beside the garden struck 11, And, just as if in church, I waited quietly, sitting in the chair, while the bells did their five-minute tolling bit before beginning to speak; meditatively waiting, like the priest does. The irony of the moment didn't escape me, nor the fact that the ceremony just happened to 'close' on the dot of 12 and I could intone my usual mantra, a seamless (and unconscious) fit to the ceremony.

A full hour, followed by sitting in the picnic circle with all *Companions of the Way* for sips of TMT and melting strawbs in mouth. The rain had set in to a real shower by then — perfectly timed? — and I was able to toss the remainder of TMT back onto her trunk as a gift returned to the source before singing my exit (with the Faerie song) up onto the verandah and in to the house. Blessed, blessed be! The petal in the cup just beautiful. My felt-sense of the specialness of all evidenced in tears. On, on 21 June! (But hopefully rain-free!) Thank you, oh blessed day; thank you TM (and TMT) and all realms of Faerie. Sana!

<u>19 June</u>: 9am. A twig and a snatch of TM bark have found their way into the ten-foot-square hut. Lord knows how, in which fold of scarf or shawl (or notebook or cards pouch) they squirreled their way back into the *heart* of home but all of a sudden announced their presence audibly, spontaneously, a random arrival out of seeming nowhere. All I can do is laugh at the synchronistic incongruity of it all and place them, for safekeeping, in the wicker Sacred Pool till Sunday when we *all* troop outdoors for the ceremony. Much as TM's petal dropped suddenly, deliberately, directly into the cup – no fluttering down, wafting, and then by chance plopping into the grail, this was a perfect plummet, a dive from the ten-metre board, the judges' head-nods of approval in unison for this divinely executed act. No omens, these. Just evidence of Presence. And that makes me happy. Hello family!

Meditations on Trust

Earlier in this chapter, and the last, I commented on the trust I had felt inherent in the invitation from *AncestorCouple* to steward a new 'home' into existence, one to which others could homecome; how this revealed itself in the responsibility to connect nodes across the world, thus setting in train a partnership with Sidhe in order to facilitate same. In acknowledging the risk my subtle companions took in trusting I could or would be up to the task assigned, I also needed to trust that this rollercoaster wouldn't derail, that the energy of collaboration and engagement in this *compact* would lead me (and my long-suffering family) in the right direction.

In this context, I re-visited a specific comment of Mariel's in *Conversations* every now and then to ensure I still felt soundness (or sturdiness, *solidity*) in the energies of 'alignment' relative to our shared task: 'The aetheric planes of the earth are cloudy and polluted; the lens has imperfections in it that can distort the forces that are released. There is much to be done before either of us can safely recapture what once was' (p.38).

This quote gave me regular opportunities to 'stocktake' throughout the process. And each time I arrived at the same answer. Yes, I trusted in my readings of the subtle environs of the peace-sinks I wished to connect, that they were 'pure'; yes I trusted the fidelity of my intent in engaging the forces, that the lens was not distorted by my 'desire' (see Glossary) to act. What I needed to trust, in the end, however, was that my Sidhe companions had not made a mistake in trusting *me* – for all their help and support and 'being-with', I am still just little old Anne. And as the day approached for the awakening, I felt this more and more ...

111

Indeed, prior to writing the rituals of 18 and 21 June, I had asked for a final piece of counsel from the *I Ching*, the hexagram *Fidelity* the result: 'Fidelity means wholehearted sincerity without duplicity. Above is heaven, strong; below is thunder, active. In the hexagram, the action is on the inside; this is setting the will on the Tao. Once the heart is set on the Tao and the living potential is activated, the original creative energy returns. In the hexagram, the strength is on the outside; this is earnestness in practice.'

The sole foundation for trust, in my experience, is love. Perfect love (the Gospel of St John refers): Love without condition, love that casts out fear of any and all 'what ifs' that can hamstring the productive energy of desire. Of course, none of this absolves either side of responsibility – throughout the process we each made our best efforts to see it through to success. Yet what made this possible was our way-of-love, embedded *in* love – specifically our love for Gaia; that this work *may* help her evolution of consciousness, *may* help in weaving more filigree threads into her beautiful becoming cloak, the living matrix of which we are part; *may* enhance, in Mariel's words, 'the connectedness and communion Gaia has with her cosmic environment ... (so) more energies from the stars will flow into this world, and the living energy of the planet will in turn flow more freely into the cosmos' (p.56).

Energised by love, *trusting* to love, we engaged in shared worldwork to 'sing up country', manifest the 'new' in an ever-evolving latticework of nodes and connections on Gaia's behalf. Yet I was still stunned by a final gift received from my Sidhe companions in between consecrating the grail space and the awakening ceremony. For, as the following journal entry outlines, 'twas a gift of love which ultimately confirmed their trust. So too I knew whence the lesson arose – my wonderful 'flying' instructor who had aligned with the (Edge) Dancer as: *Gravity always gets in the way when we don't make a big enough leap ...*

19 June: Wee hours of this morning as I became 'aware' of where I was in the *Malakut*, D&I on ponies coming down a very steeply sloped path. The ponies small, like Welsh pit ponies – my feet could touch the ground, and this I did to support the pony's stability along the way. Others were on the path ahead of us, and many on the way up. Busy! Beside it was a shelter-shed of sorts with picnic benches etc stepped down the hillside, so if anyone tired or wanted a break in either direction, they could pop across. There were some parts where we needed to jump between platforms on the way down but nothing which seemed impossible; there was also a huge drop further along to negotiate, over the edge of a cliff. On the surface it seemed 'dangerous' but I felt it was doable.

On our way to this point, I met a fellow who was hiking up the path – that route joined the main one from a side-track, at the 'junction' with shelter-shed and cliff edge. We greeted each other and he handed me 'his' rope. It was really long – his offer was that I could try his, see how I liked it before getting one of my own. After use, I could leave it for him at an agreed point. He held it out. Massive – a huge coil of relatively thin silvery rope. I thought: Gosh, this will weigh me down! But instead it was extraordinarily light. I thanked him and we each went our respective ways. What a (temporary) gift from the realms of Faerie! Thank you! Do you mean to say that if it 'works' on Sunday, then I'm in a position to 'weave' one of my own? Perhaps. But you guys will have to come back and teach me how to weave!

Sunday 21 June dawned windy, rainy and cold, but by sunset when I stepped from the ten-foot-square hut *out* into *TreeMother*'s grail space – slaked clean, head to shining toe, with 'mantle' donned – the prevailing conditions did not seem to matter a bit. I stepped *into* a cone of blessing, and, in *Beauty*'s words, experienced in full measure aethereal-material as one-and-the-same reality for the duration of our communion. Over and over throughout the ceremony I hummed *MossManFindling* 'F below middle C', continued the melody, singing up country between here and there, wakening the connection.

All energy spent, catharsis in its wake – when suddenly *AncestorCouple* was there amongst the assembly, appearing, presenting in image-thought, smiling, shining … I immediately burst into tears at the revelation. Yes, I had 'written' their energy into the ceremony but had no idea if the thread would be 'live' enough for their literal attendance. Oh, the joy, surprise! *Gravity*'s Elven-rope had enabled their traverse! Unexpected outcomes, indeed – in meditation with the Council earlier in the month, these were the words which formed, accompanied by an image of unbaked bread twists on trays ready for the oven. My 'skill' in baking would be key. And now including a hungry slug that decided to slope over and nibble the food offerings in the midst of proceedings? Fun!

Time to relax, one would think. It was done. I shook my head at the wonder of it all, the *fact* of deep magic to which Mariel alerts the reader of *Conversations*: 'Deep magic is a blending of ourselves, our life energies, our will, and the energies and life of the world. What results … is something created in concert and harmony with the life within the world. It is a joint creation. Understanding magic as a form of communion and engagement with the world, born of honouring and loving the world, means that we can live in magic' (p.105).

Deep magic which, in the wake of my assumption that 'it was done' reminded me that things are never done, that only one small step had been taken along a path unfurling beneath my feet …

<u>24 June</u>: A ring song – a song of power, resonance, affirmation, awakening…
All this while ironing in the ten-foot-square hut this afternoon. It just flowed
out of me …

this is who you are
shining shining star
living in the earth so far
standing still in peace
rivers run so deep
you the thread no more to sleep

Context: I had been humming *MossManFindling*'s 'song' while ironing,
drifting in the half-space between the hut and *TreeMother*'s grail, remembering
(fondly) all that had taken place there three days prior. All of a sudden, words
began to populate the lines of the song. As written – 'it just *flowed* out of me' – so
it happened; deep magic at work. Each word arose seamlessly to join its brothers
on a blank slate in my mind's eye.

Still, I wondered how the line about a 'star' deep *within* the earth had arisen
as relevant to *MossManFindling*'s being *and* awakening, when a synapse to 'the
fourth starseed' leapt into action; as well Mariel's comment in *Conversations* thus:
'The (purpose of the change in the earth's aetheric structure) is not to enable you
to hear star-songs more fully but to hear the star song within the earth more fully
… while this change will make it easier for you to connect with stellar energies,
(its purpose is) … to enable you to blend more fully with it … to see and hear and
be part of the 'stars within the earth' (p.105). 'Tis the subject of the next chapter,
in point of fact.

Tears of recognition: Was this too lain down in tablets of *stone* long past?
What work had been done on the *inner* planes to ensure vibrational attunement
between my (*MossMan*) partner and me – for the connection to be made, for the
melody to arise, and now for the lyric to present? Our shared song 'sung' into
being, the inner fully 'outed' – my realisation of what this could imply was very
exciting. Did the process we had developed, Sidhe companions and I, constitute a
replicable methodology – to awaken *fresh* stone sentience, to establish *further* nodal
connections, to thread *more* starsongs through the earth via our helpmates' extant
notes? Was it to this unknown outcome that *trust* had led us?

I sensed a desire within the Stone Circle to *strengthen* the bond freshly laid
out in *TreeMother*'s grail space. I felt *called* to be a weaver of new threads in the
becoming cloak of Gaia's aetheric structure; not to simply 'charge' a home-node
and leave it at that, but share responsibility to *form* connections with my Sidhe
cousins. Here, Mariel's comment refers: 'Perhaps the image of the crystal with its

latticework of nodes and connections is a way to illustrate our differences. You took from our common ancestor the capacity to be a node in the lattice, while we took the capacity to form connections' (p.35).

Was this song, therefore, *my* particular length of Elven-rope after *Gravity's* temporary loan? I re-found his teaching from many years past, how it formed part of a string with others, of learning to 'spin' wool by hand. A partner was always involved; none of this could be achieved alone – the energy of the relation, of 'being-with' (see Glossary) required to manifest such potentialities.

Yes, we had 'anchored' the energies here, strung it out across the world to another nodal point; yes I had 'breathed life' into what I love as Mr1300BC had counselled on another occasion – equally relevant here as love the foundation (stone) on which each 'act of awakening' based. But what would it be to *become* the songline itself, to walk *together* the footsteps of our *common* Ancestor – threading a trail of 'awakening' song across the land like Aboriginal Dreaming attests, but from deep *within* her subtle bones, from *within* her sentience cloaked in stone, to summon more 'stars within the earth' *out*, to contribute to Mariel's call to service?

She says: 'The phenomena you call the "ley lines" are only an outer representation of this, the manifestation upon the physical of these deeper lines of living energy and consciousness' (p.35); so too: 'We are star people because we bring the stars to earth. But we can only bring them so far; there is a threshold we cannot cross, but you can, if you will dance the stars inward and outward with us' (p.67).

Thoughts swirled but I still needed to finish the ironing. Beyond that, family had descended for a summer of hiking Heidiland – the house and garden would be abuzz with humanity over the coming two months. I would return to these considerations in the quiet of their departure.

Or so 'I' thought …

Chapter 8: Creating the Home to which ...

**Rumbling, the ships steamroll the sky;
following night, chased by dawn ...**

This chapter's purpose is to draw together several lines of flight occurring concurrently in the wake of *MossManFindling's* 'awakening' to purpose, their coalescence especially supporting my intent to return down under to 'create the home to which others may homecome' as soon as possible, a next step in the overall partnership project as conceived. Formally welcoming the spirit of Little Cove to 'family', I felt, was central to the equation of helping others to homecome thereafter; this entailed being physically present to its energies and 'creating' a loving home space in communion with same with my immediate family likewise fully in attendance. My own ideas as well as perennial influences from Sidhe companions of the way during the intervening several months between the solstice ritual and returning down under post-equinox may seem to have arisen from disparate sources on first glance, but their coming together at this time was instrumental to the pursuance of task. And, as outlined at the end of the last chapter, I inherently *trusted* the logic of seemingly illogical interconnections, intuiting that their relevance would be revealed in due course.

To begin with the most chronologically proximate of the lines of flight, the reader is reminded that throughout the text, but principally in the earlier chapters, I described my connection to mountain sentience, to feeling at 'home' in the heart of the Alps. The thought, therefore, of spending summer in the high wild with my nearest and dearest, introducing them to places which sing in tune with my soul, had me in raptures. I could barely contain my excitement to don hiking boots and backpack; indeed I was like a horse champing at the bit, impatiently awaiting their recovery from jetlag, the somnambulant delight of easing (back) into the everyday of home life, desperate to tug them off on fresh adventures.

First port-of-call was *Silberen* at the beginning of July, a repeat of my birthday hike of the previous year. The mountain's name means 'silvery', thus describing her broad smooth limestone mantle. During the climb nine months prior, I had mused on her name, invoking as it did a notion of starlight, and how this, in turn, surfaced a memory of the *StarGeist* I had seen in the *Malakut* at the start of that year. At the time, however, I took the thought no further, intrigued instead at the variety of different karst formations and crevasses we crossed on this high wild plateau. Within the depths of the mountain were systems into which only experienced cavers ventured. For my part, I had read the legends of the region, their connection to Faerie, 'wee folk' hereabouts called *Wildmännli*. As a result, these were the thoughts which kept time with my footfalls during 2014's outing.

At the summit, a widespread sheet of foil reflecting Sun's glory back to the face of the sky, we picnicked in full sight of a chain of snowy peaks to the south, and I asked for a photo of self to record the minuteness of my being, no more than a pinprick in a sea of majesty, evoking, as it did, the beauty of Suzuki's 'nothing special' (see Glossary) on this, my special day. No explicit connection to *genius loci* did I make, but felt the peace of sunk sentience in *Silberen's* subtle bones and how it expanded out beyond (far beyond) the boundaries of her silvered skin. I felt this, because I felt swept *up* in it – words formed: *Im Einklang mit dem Universum* (see Glossary). 'I saw' the mirror at work – mirroring joy, its shining shone-through reflection was pure light, and instantly I felt drawn to contribute in song.

In a way my joy was comparable to the occasion when a Sidhe scout troupe's song of praise had me longing to join in. On that occasion, 'song' did not present in voice, but as waves of energy surging through me and spontaneously radiating out (as recounted in Chapter 5). Now, however, real song burst from my lips – in the form of a particular yodelling cry, a 'women's one'. I had heard it the first time (as a documentary's signature theme) the previous year and immediately connected to its evocation of the *strength* of female energies encountered in the high wild, as if representing a specific Alpine *vocalisation* of same. This strength is something I describe in detail in *Der Ruf der Berge*.

Hiking *Silberen* that day, I heard 'her' call from deep *within* the mountain as an outward *surge* of joy to meet the sky, and instinctively wanted to join the soundwave. My arms flung wide in the same moment as a first note rushed out to share this group hug with all sentience – the extraordinary simplicity and magical wonder of existence *in* and contribution *to* the World Soul's expression

118

of self. 'Twas a soundwave I knew to come from the 'kiln room' at the heart of the mountain – the sense of inner and outer mirroring, centre and circumference 'im Einklang', was keen.

As a result of this experience, is it any surprise I wanted to introduce such a special place to family? Off we trooped on a day of high summer, together with friends. The others moved ahead gaily as a pack; I trailed behind to *Hello the House*. I recalled my previous insights, yet on this occasion was not led 'out' but *in*. Words formed: *The Sinkholes of Peace*, and I feigned to see the entry to Faerie amongst the deeply-scored and aeons-long water-eroded limestone slabs, the hidden passageways hairy-footed *Wildmännli* took to scurry out of sight of our heavy boots. The connective thread to Presence grew stronger all the way. I touched a boulder – reciprocal recognition begun and maintained – and a stone on the path, silver-infused, outreached to be seen, noticed, uplifted. I put it in my pocket; a 'brother' beside I gifted to the summit cairn on arrival.

Later, on the return stretch – down the 'back' way where *Silberen* cradles an *Urwald* (a stand of primeval forest) in her skirts – I came to a place where the resonant hum was particularly strong. The path veered left across a 'land-bridge' between two grotto'd cave entrances but I felt a tug into the earth straight ahead, into the 'hollowed' hill itself. Fresh words formed: *The Magic of the Mantle*. I stopped for a moment to consider this, 'heard' nothing more and continued walking. But now arisen was a simple verse invocation, as if on behalf of the spirit of *Silberen*, set to the steady beat of my boots: *May the magic of your mantle bring the energy of stars streaming here to Earth* ... Somehow 'I' had made a connection between the commitment made upon stepping into the Stone Circle with my affirmation to 'wear a mantle of starlight here in the world to bring the energy of the stars streaming to Earth' and the words formed above. Quarter of an hour later or so, a voice suddenly jumped 'into' the midst of the verse and said: *Shall we work together?*

Understandably this stopped me in my tracks. The voice sounded 'Faerie'-pure – the sing-songy lilt of a female voice 'bouncing' on air. Alright, I agreed, as the memory of the *StarGeist* surfaced afresh, as the voice gave me that little zing of Bilbo-ish energy to set off on a new adventure. I picked up another hunk of limestone – this one 'threaded' with light, seamed with other sedimentary material, as if connected, fused in shared *compact*. This would seal a fresh partnership precipitated by her offer. The spirit in which the year was unfolding in company of Sidhe meant I had no second thoughts on this occasion to instinctively honour the *Alliance between Humanity and Faerie* (as a permanent Council member of my Stone Circle had self-named) although I had no idea where this particular 'alliance' would lead nor how it could or *would* intersect with existing commitments.

Ripples in the Pool

The greater part of our summer in the Alps was spent communing from the stone silence of *Marianna's* 400-year-old cottage in the country's south, venturing out mainly on day hikes or looking into the face of beauty from her pocket handkerchief-sized garden. In between, I madly scribbled notes for the next Canto of the epic long poem dedicated to the valley's divine high wild. Weather-dependent, our main foray during this time would be a three-day wilderness trek across the border into Italy to the end of the valley where our river has its headwaters. The previous year I had undertaken a blessing task in the area, an act of pilgrimage to its source, a 'sacred pool' in its own right; here was an opportunity to introduce a wondrous landscape to the children as well as further explore this seriously magical *Amici* territory.

A window of several fine days in a row opened. All proceeding to plan, camping gear packed and ready to go the night before, I felt a buzz of excitement extend past the boundaries of me and cottage to mountains and sky. Whimsical reverie pre- and post-dated slumber and I woke at dawn to the following encounter, whose magic only a bard's voice can capture:

> *What would you do if the wind*
> *offered to take your hand, show*
> *you things beyond your ken?*
> *For my part, a reply sought swift*
> *to split these lips, but ere-before*
> *gravity could take its chance,*
> *I felt a soft brush of this writing paw,*
> *as here-now sought she to catch*
> *same in firm embrace. Shared smile,*
> *updraft lifted, we were off, and away …*

Wind's offer and generosity of spirit was something I was to remember and give thanks for each of the three days. At the time of the encounter, I 'flew' at her side. It sounds strange, I know, yet constituted an experience of 'beyonding' pure, and had the effect of settling any nerves I may have had about the adventure. 'Twould be a new experience to add to the annals of family history and despite there being plenty of grumbles, my felt-sense of 'no mishaps' was borne out in truth. Wind had arrived as an emissary of *WolfMother*, in whose territory we would trek, to grant safe passage; Wind had alerted the subtle *Amici* to our visit (the human *Amici* we had ourselves notified to seek permission to camp in their *rifugio* – a disused goat barn by another name). Suffice it to say, deep magic flowed in the veins of this watershed and my joy of return, to *homecome* to the place I had engaged in blessing, could hardly have been greater.

While the details of this repeat pilgrimage form part of the essay, *Amici della Luce*, its relevance in the context of this chapter can be summed up in a single monosyllabic word: Stone. Nothing fancy or beautiful, a precious gem or jewel liberated from deep in the earth and crafted to perfection by human hand; instead a small modest stone plucked from a dry down under riverbed had become the carrier of my blessings into this perennially flowing watershed. All the way from source to sea, from source to sea to source: 'Nothing special,' Suzuki would say and I agree each time. 'Tis the ordinary which is extraordinary, each 'thing' in creation infused with the selfsame divine spark of love at its core, each with a role to play in unfolding the *consciousness* of interconnectivity in our grand Gaian experiment.

Such is my (after-the-fact) reasoning why small humble anonymous and seemingly invisible members of our Gaian community should have as much opportunity to contribute as the grand and the great. My meditations on a speck of dust refer, as well as my understanding (with profound thanks to Mr1300BC) that: *We all breathe life into what we love.* Any material 'thing' can thus be a container for our blessing, when *vested* with our love, when its beingness is further *enlivened* with blessing, to carry *shared* blessing on. For some reason stones outreach to me in the context of blessing tasks, and vice versa. Yes, it began with stone 'giants', with the majesty of mountain sentience pure, but each tiny chip off the (old) block carries the same spirit. Without realising, therefore, by 'charging' simple gifts of the earth with love and blessing as connector threads between spirits of place during my years of 'self-apprenticeship' as physical message-bearers of blessing, I had seemingly seeded the plan to 'waken' stone sentience in company of Sidhe.

So it was that during our pilgrimage down under the year before, I had collected two small red-river-rocks (R3s) from a dry and dusty watercourse to bring back to this side of the world, with no conscious thought at the time as to their task. Yet now one R3 lay in the (outer) 'sacred pool', my contribution to the liquid light of this watershed, while his 'brother-bear' (as a Dancer self-named to capture the spirit of these sweet kids, their expression of 'grounded fluidity') rested in the wicker 'pool' in the ten-foot-square hut of home as gateway to the inner. The entire process of growing my understanding of how to *work* with light had been a self-apprenticeship, but by *repeating* the trek toward the source in company of family now, I saw how this work segued seamlessly to the desire I felt within the Stone Circle (following our shared 'success' to waken *MossManFindling*) to *strengthen* the bond so-established.

I realised that to achieve same, each home-node must not only be charged with love, discretely, to anchor the energies of my love to spirits of place, but be *bound* together in a web of shared light in the same way I had seen the Sidhe weave 'threads of happiness' into existence, in the same way I had been covered in Madam S's fine filigree web of starlight. This would be my length of Elven-rope, my contribution *beyond* a contribution, the calling I had felt to be a weaver of new threads in Gaia's becoming cloak now approaching a next level of commitment. In the moment I felt a rush of energy to find R3 in the pool. I wanted to *physically* connect with him, in the spirit of *extending* his remit; as well as continuing to carry my blessings out into the world from his adopted 'home' territory, it was time to hook him into the becoming grid of other 'home-nodes'. Would it be possible?

The one thing about a red-river-rock from a baked desert heart transplanted to a silver-skinned granite alpine scape is that it stands out (like a sore toe) in the crystal clear waters of their relatively shallow lakes. The other thing about such crystal clear waters, even at the height of summer, is that they are bone-numbingly cold. A final observation: I'm no baseball pitcher, hence R3 (fortunately) lay circa three metres or so from shore, at the depth of around a metre. I stripped; the family looked the other way. It was now or never …

There he was! I lifted him up with my toes, laughed to see his funny moon-child-Miyazaki-tree-spirit face again, kissed him in joy over and over, felt exhilaration *rush* my veins, brought him back to shore, renewed the vow, tossed him in again, this time for all time. And watched, waited, till the ripples in the pool stretched all the way to shore to kiss my frozen toes. Blessed be!

That night, curled up in a sleeping bag on the dusty attic floor of the *Amici's* simple stone shelter, I crossed the veil to its *Malakut* scape, climbed down the ladder to sit at table beside the hearth with, amongst others, a giant and a dwarf. I felt to be in company of *Amici* of every colour and creed; there was such simple ease in each other's presence; 'twas nothing other than familial. Compared to the previous year when, as described at the start of this text, I had had contact with the Sidhe in *WolfMother's* territory during which they had acknowledged my presence and intent, it was as if this return pilgrimage, and extension of R3's task, energised our connection at a sincere level. The irony, that I had originally ordered Lorian's Sidhe resources in the hope it would bring me into deeper resonance with this particular group, was not lost on me. Yes, the conduit first opened was now strengthened, but only in the wake of all that had gone before. Clearly no complaints, but I did find it humorous in the context of all adventures proceeding over the past half-year which led to this unprecedented point.

The ripples in the pool did not end here, however. A week or so later, returned from the wilderness, returned from the south to the sanctity of the ten-foot-square hut, *TreeMother's* grail space and dear sweet humming *MossManFindling*, I received the most thrilling affirmation of the thread being 'live' between these two nodal connections; although in the midst of the experience it was quite disorienting:

<u>22 July</u>: Monday night we returned from Ticino. In the middle of the night I woke and sat bolt upright in bed. Something was different, hugely different. The bed and I were in a different space – literally *not here*. This was no usual *Malakut* night wander where I leave and then return to the hut, quite 'aware' of whichever space I am in. A *Malakut* landscape had come *back* with me into waking consciousness and 'I' didn't know how to get down and out of it, my mind incapable of reconciling what I 'saw' with where I 'was supposed to be'. I knew I was in bed but it was as if the whole ten-foot-square hut had transformed into a Ticinese-Italian high alpine landscape – the space very lit, shimmery; all aglow, glittering in luminous golden-green. The sound of running water filled my ears.

Here, in bed, I was high above the pools – like mini-versions of the lakes, source, pale blue and starlit. Here I was above, trying to figure out how to get down from and over the bottom of the bed across a huge pile of strewn boulders (so silvered in their granite cloaks!) to reach the pools. How to negotiate from bed to boulders, and then on? I was barefoot and in PJs, for heaven's sake! Everything seemed so close to the eye, yet I knew it was a huge leap from where I was, down. I *knew* it to be the place above the pools on the way to the Pass – but compressed, steeper, closer ... David's description of the 'Sidheverse', as well as Mariel's commentary refers: 'In one way, our world would look familiar to you, with landscapes filled with beauty ... Or more precisely, we live in a world that is the thought of matter that precedes the dense manifestation of matter into the substance you know. Our wavelength is "upstream" from you' (p.24-25), demonstrated to stunning (and literal) effect in my vision.

'I' was split – part wanting to negotiate the non-path down to the pools (i.e. continue the *Malakut* journey) and part knowing: This is ridiculous, I'm already back here! It took *ages* in earth-minutes to bring *enough* of me back to 're-assemble' consciousness in the here-and-now, and 'retreat'. I clambered back up from the end of the bed, turned and put my feet to the ground on 'my' side. 'Twas then the setting faded. Yet the experience still so vivid in my mind. So lit, so beautiful, so home, so at peace. And I understood that the 'threads of happiness' woven between R3 and *MossManFindling* in company of all *Amici* had brought this into being; such joy!

My length of Elven-rope had had a real workout with this experience but had come through unscathed. I felt the capacity to form connections and contribute to the work of my Sidhe cousins developing – in effect, as the nodes woke more to task, so the threads between them tended to strengthen, become more durable. The rope itself I visualised as a stretch of 'song', in the spirit of Aboriginal dreaming – what I walked and sang into being mirrored the songline itself. A case of *Malakut* and material increasingly attuned, it seemed that whether I worked in physical or non-physical scapes, I could trace the 'deeper lines of living energy and consciousness' which Mariel describes as the work of our common ancestors' 'choir of unfoldment and evolution' (p.34-5) on behalf of Gaia. As such, I visualised how I could use my song, my rope, to energise and *refresh* the manifest 'footprints' of the Ancestors with my love for and connection to (and between) specific *genii locorum*.

Not long following came the next ripple in the pool, yet this centred purely on a *Malakut* instruction (as ever, symbolically delivered).

31 July: A stone, like sandstone, lighter-coloured than *MossManFindling*, more shaped, cut like a block but of similar size. I needed to re-enter the space over and over for the full instruction to be revealed. At one point, the stone morphed into a cardboard box which, when opened, hosted 'treasures' inside, artefacts, icons of a particular ancient civilisation. At another, I 'entered' the box which was now as large as a room and witnessed these artefacts in a ceremony involving robed priests. All very interesting but where was it going?

Next, when I went back into the space, I witnessed a man and his family in a stone hut or chamber looking out onto a medieval castle keep. It seems he was tasked with doing something with these artefacts when it was 'time' for them to be revealed in/to the world; he wasn't kingly or so, simply an anonymous worker or servant within the great machine. Nevertheless he had received this task from someone or something and would know its timing because (and at this I witnessed what would occur) a point of light would reveal itself from within the earth on one side of the keep (as if hollowed out by the light, a golden 'melting' of the earth from beneath) and then burn as a line *through* the earth over to the other side of the keep to join with another hollow point of light which had spontaneously appeared at the surface there.

In seeing this played out, I immediately thought: Aha – connective threads ... Meanwhile, in the space the man became super-excited, woke his slumbering family and basically said: *We have to start digging!* It was as if a trench were needed along this line in order to *facilitate* the flow of molten gold or 'liquid light' (?) between the two points; somehow, out of this, the 'artefacts' would manifest anew in the world. Hmmm – a sandstone block, hewn, morphing into a box of ancient treasures; the timing of its release determined by the 'melting' of the earth at two 'distant' points across the 'keep' (of the human world) and then a river of molten light joining them? Somehow I think there's a particular stone to find at Little Cove ...

The next ripple beckoned. The reader may recall George, the driver from the 'farm' community where previously I was on composting duties in the garden of the 'Great (or Earth) Mother', but now tasked with distribution between (stellar) farm and (Earth) market. In that encounter, I thought I had been assigned my project in partnership with Sidhe, only to have Little Cove plonk down in its midst with sandy salty abandon. Now, however, it seemed – like the *Amici* from the south – that the different rhizomatic threads were coalescing into a more concentrated and focused form. In short, the weaving work itself acted to densify our energy of engagement. Here, a string of three *Malakut* encounters refers:

> With the Earth Mother (EM) in the back of a huge mobile home-type van (replete with garden and gate); George up front past a vast cockpit door, driving. EM has some thick twine or slim rope – she opens the side door of the van (oncoming traffic, the whole bit), leans out and starts 'measuring' its length against the height of trees beside the highway; I'm worried she'll fall out but she says: *It's OK; I just wanted to check if we need to buy some more.* She then toddles up front, throws open the cockpit door; George says: *What are you doing here? Go back to your seat!* But in she comes for a chat, and tunes the radio to a country music station. It seems we're off to Amberley (an airforce base) for a big festival.

> In meditation, I am on my way to the 'kiln room' when I encounter EM. I had been holding another elder's hand when she passed by, 'outreached' to me with a perky smile (red-lipsticked to boot!) and I reciprocated. Suddenly I am 'away', gone, and when I return I know it is from somewhere very deep.

> Again I meet EM in meditation. This time I am standing on the bridge beside the motorway entrance when a hippie-style Kombie drives toward me and then turns left onto the motorway, direction east; maybe she doesn't trust George anymore, but here she is driving, with her red-lipsticked smile from yester morn. Just delightful! The van is full of joyful souls, all heading off to their day's worldwork, and with my light added to the cargo to take where they will it needed. Sana!

Simultaneous with these encounters, during evening meditations – where my focus is simply on being-with – I would find myself 'breathing' through the third eye (sixth chakra). Sporadic in the past, most often associated with an energetic connection to a subtle being, now it seemed to enduringly ebb and flow, as a matter-of-course, with my physical breath. Each in-breath I felt as an expanding or garnering of energy which, on the out-breath, contracted into a direct point of light or 'consciousness' out to *TreeMother*'s grail space – like a 'whoosh' of energy sent out to greet her and all within her field. I intuited that such concentrated 'light-breath' could be my point of connectivity between the nodes, but I found it very tiring. Still, I set myself a practice to train up this freshly-discovered 'muscle'.

So many ripples in the pool! Nevertheless I consciously asked all companions of the way to slow down while I sifted and sorted the different signs. I wanted to design a follow-up ritual to conduct on the approaching Equinox, to 'alert' all in the Circle, formally, to our intent to head down under again and physically welcome Little Cove to the family. Yet my own buzziness kept me from task. I had a strong desire to climb some more mountains …

The Quarry and the Stars

Summer holidays had passed. It was a solid two months since we had breathed the air atop *Silberen*. I kept returning to the Sidhe's offer: *Shall we work together?* Unsure where to go with it, the only clue I had was the presence who had self-named as *MakerMan* – her original instruction from close to two years prior had described the particular line of mountains where she 'hooked up' with her *StarGeist* to work together. I knew this range as part of the *Alpstein* in Switzerland's north-east, a particular peak of which I had always admired on our motorway drives along its southern flank. I asked F if its name, *Leist(-)chamm*, 'meant' anything. He shook his head; not that he knew of. Yet it rang a bell in my memory.

I looked up the dictionary. The verb means 'to achieve something'; its noun *Leistung* translates as power, performance, the *strength* to achieve same. Had it been recognised as an energy conduit previously perhaps? Or did it intimate I would achieve something by connecting with it? It wasn't a difficult hill by any stretch of the imagination but there had never been an opportunity for a daytrip in the family calendar. Till now. I decided to trust to the psychoid unity of replicating a *Malakut* lesson in the material, something which has stood me in good stead over long years. As well, I was reminded (again) of Mariel's counsel to 'see and hear and be part of the "stars within the earth" (p.101). If this region constellated similarly to *MakerMan's* world, maybe I would learn something by trekking the path to a summit I had long admired from afar.

Pre-dawn, on the day of our ascent, I woke to the following words formed: *Love wants to come with today.* A delightful uplifting whimsy to the words, and how they presented, stayed with me as I rose, abluted et al. Returning to the room, to make the bed, to leave the ten-foot-square hut in a serene mood, I felt my consciousness tugged to the wicker 'sacred pool'. The words repeated. I gaily began an internal conversation, along the lines of: 'Well, Love always comes with me wherever I go, because love is within, the core of the self, the centre of being in the Buddha's words; blah, blah, blah.'

Again, the words repeated and this time I saw they specifically emanated from the tiny silver pebble I had collected from the shoreline of the eastern sea wild as a talisman for the Little Cove rollercoaster earlier in the year. It's *our* love, the pebble specified – *our* love wants to come too. I had to laugh; unbeknown to me, the *ShiningOnesoftheSea* had aligned with this tiny sea-pummelled stone (in the moment, it self-named *StarlightSeed*). Words spontaneously spilled from my lips: *You really want to come too?* before giving it a kiss and popping it in my pocket. I feigned to see their excitement at this adventure, to bring home tales of what it's like to journey to the top of a mountain rather than be roiled in the washing machine of an endless ocean, sandpapered to smoothness, and washed onto a Pacific shoreline ...

On the climb, greeting spirit of place with *Hello the House,* I discovered this to be limestone country. Walking the trail, I now understood *why* it had been shown me as a locus of connectivity between the energy of the stars and earth; and definitely more physically proximate to boot! Perhaps because I had never acted on the original instruction, drawn instead to *Silberen,* twice, 'forcing' family to do something off-the-beaten-track rather than just down the road, the energy had shifted when I intuited the 'magic of the mantle' there?

I picked up a sliver of stone to add to the summit cairn in honour of my better-late-than-never realisation and another shard to bring home to add to the sacred pool. We picnicked on top, high above a fjord-thin turquoise lake, with the three 'kids' – *Leistchamm's* two plus *StarlightSeed* – and entered communion with these magic-mantled-mountains while other hikers came and went. I felt *StarlightSeed's* tiny energy burst through its skin. Was it trying to outreach to the spirits of place here on its own behalf for the *ShiningOnes*? Indeed, love – in the form of these three stones had 'come with', stayed, and returned this day. 'Nothing special', yet so, *so* special – all one and the same, in the end.

In the wake of the hike, I formally welcomed the limestone shard (LCS) to the circle of companions in the ten-foot-square hut. Although silver-toned, its shape, size and smoothness was highly reminiscent of the fourth meteorite I had collected – the 'sliver' I had offered to my *Malakut* companion. I outlaid all members of the permanent Council, named all Dancers; *StarlightSeed* rested on *Homecome to the Sea* to tell tales of this great adventure; LCS nestled into the *Gate of the Stars* in honour of its potentiality, with the two *Silberen* stones flanking same to hone the energy of intent. Together we all simply sat, 'being-with'; a collective meditation, generating a spirit of togetherness – of shared purpose – was engaged there in the grail space. No need for me to hold the energies; of their own accord, in this safe and loving space, they coalesced around love – the felt-sense, the principle, the intent, the underlying Ground of Being. Love drew all energies to itself. Love ... pure ...

Over the following days, I felt a small 'buzz' of resonance at LCS's inclusion in the group, but no specific messaging to accompany. Something more was needed, something more than just a gradual growing of energetic fit with existing interlocutors. I went dog-walking to the *FindlingForest* and there discovered one of their number is limestone. While *MossManFindling*, *JollyGiant* and many others in our area, are Verrucano, until the *Silberen* adventure limestone had not been top-of-mind and I had never looked closely at the others' provenance. Most definitely a 'chip off the old block', its plaque noted the lakeside village below *Leistchamm's* overlighting peak. Carried here by the same glacial tongue, its energy *was* literally just down the road.

At the same time on this walk, I mused on which stone should be 'charged' at the equinox ritual to carry blessings to Little Cove. One of the *Silberen* stones or LCS? No. I felt-sensed they were needed here to 'root' the connection to whatever *StarGeist* tasks I would be asked to assist. *Silberen's* two hunks of limestone had rested permanently on *MossManFindling's* mossy hide beside the heart-shaped chalice since the pact was made in July, thus effecting (to my way of thinking) a gradual cleaving of longer-than intent and partnership to the physicality of *TreeMother's* grail space.

The dog stopped to roll in some muck, and in watching, sighing, knowing this would mean yet *another* bath, a small stone 'leapt' into my field of vision. Dark as night but threaded with silver bands – the synchronicity of linking spirits of place via a gift from *this* specific place could not be faulted. Thank you *FindlingForest* (and grotty dog)! I returned home, thinking things would now settle, but still a restlessness to seek out more interconnections niggled. Whether it was my restlessness or the Council's I could not tell, but it manifested as a strong need to climb another mountain in the *Alpstein*.

A fortnight later, the opportunity presented. I had researched each of the peaks – which ones had too strong a human impact (ski lifts etc); what was doable from a capability perspective. The one settled upon was broad-backed, squared-off, 'hewn' almost, and centred in the line-up amongst sisters fore and aft. Her name, *Brisi* (pronounced breezy), also evoked *Wind's* offer from earlier in the summer to take my hand. From here it was a short rhizomatic hop, skip and jump in my mind to *MakerMan* taking flight with her *StarGeist* as it rose up out of the mountain. *Brisi* would solidify intent – with LCS in my pocket this time, I set out to walk 'her' songline.

Maintaining a mantra each step of the way, the words chosen were my usual 'peace, love and light' invocation to, for, and on behalf of all spirits of place. About halfway up, though, suddenly tripping over the top of the mantra, *MossManFindling's* 'song' presented. It stopped me short. Why? This was *his* song, *our* song. Ah, said a voice. But listen to the words which populate your 'shared'

128

song. Isn't it something which could draw *any* star within the earth from sleep?

This took me aback. I had felt-sensed that the words could also apply to (i.e. mirror) my soul-self's 'awakening', drawing more of the 'me' out of 'me' (the *Inner Coming Out* as a Transition Stone had self-named). In *concert* with *MossManFindling*'s awakening I had certainly *felt* how I had grown into the role of 'Standing Stone', anchor to the energies within my remit. But now for the song to spontaneously morph into an opportunity to draw out the spirit of *this* place? That by likewise *singing* the relation into being, the means of connection to its *StarGeist* could energetically manifest as a complement to consciously walking the songline?

Of course, in the moment, Mariel's commentary was far from my head, but several threads in *Conversations* were my saving grace upon returning home that it was OK to consider taking my engagement further in this direction. For example when she says: '(A mountain) is a principal ally upon whose energy I particularly draw as it is a major conduit through which the energies of stars and earth meet' (p.130). So too: 'In you, stars and earth meet' (p.141). Was it possible to 'waken' a mountain to shared purpose as if a 'giant' standing stone? Could its *StarGeist* be opened to the possibility of partnership? I had seen *MakerMan* 'hook up' with her 'partner', and 'take flight' together. But what did their relation actually entail?

Again, I was reminded: 'We bring the stars to earth. But we can only bring them so far; there is a threshold we cannot cross, but you can, if you will dance the stars inward and outward with us' (p.67). Later she says: 'In this partnership, be aware that we may ask help of you and of the energies you can invoke' (p.147). I had read these words earlier in the year and giggled at the implication of legal contracts and mortgages on this side of the veil. But was singing up a connection to mountain sentience using a song of love *crafted* from my attunement to *MossManFindling* now the energy stream I could invoke to help the Sidhe's own work? Was this why I had been shown what could or would transpire from *MakerMan's* 'crafting', the history of *human* creativity we had discussed – she the 'theatre director', but my role potentially as 'lead-singer' in an altogether larger performance?

Suffice it to say, I went with the intuition (which the preceding after-the-fact quotes and self-queries put into perspective), and 'sung' the connection into being for at least an hour of solid climb thereafter followed by walking and singing it aloud atop her solid spine a short while before meditating and giving thanks, LCS cradled in my lap.

Serious fatigue in its wake; but my Sidhe companions were not about to let me off lightly. In a *Malakut* scape that same night, I was part of a small group discussion. It centred on our role within the 'quarry' of the Earth, on behalf of the *collective*, encompassing the whole of Gaian life itself – a notion akin to David's 'thinking like a planet' but as always my insights present in symbols which 'speak' to my Huxleyan mode. In this instance, F piped up and said: *We need to be the* *quarry and the stars. Yes*, I agreed, repeating: *We need to be the quarry and the stones,* at which point I had a vision of each of us holding *both* within our being – the individual and the collective. 'Stars' was the right expression in the context of the discussion – the stars *within* the earth were 'stone' to all intents and purposes, the whole of Gaia's extant form the 'quarry' of sentience, of *shared* existence.

Thus did I see all stars, starseeds, light beings existent *here* in the quarry of the earth, all ready to be 'excavated', brought to light, to participate in drawing the energy from stellar realms *into* Gaia. For example, 'I saw' little *golden-people* asleep in garden beds – the size of dolls, naked, chubby, Renaissance-cherubic even. Certainly Children of Gaia, I thought. But the lesson was that none of this could be 'forced'; all were 'ready', yes, but it could not be humanity calling the shots (as we more often than not – dare I say pretty much exclusively? – do). We needed to respect 'rules of engagement' in working the interconnective plane, as *true* partners. Thus the lesson proceeded that when they *chose* to wake, we could offer 'moon-cake' in blessing. Otherwise to be let be – the flow of engagement only functioned when true-nature-inspired and as loving matter-of-course.

In the moment I was reminded of Madam S's testimony, as well as instruction. The point being that none of us stone 'stars' can exist separately from the *whole* of Gaian consciousness – thus our work, individually and collectively, needs to ensure we hold *both* manifestations of presence within our field of blessing, honouring the individual and the collective beingness in the same moment, encompassing each perspective, *holding* the whole and the fractal simultaneously. In this way we would reflect the true spirit of partnership.

I returned to the words of 'our' song, words which had arisen of their own accord to 'populate' the melody uplifted in the wake of intuiting *MossManFindling*'s extant tone: *This is who you are, shining shining star, living in the earth so far* ... Here, I was presented with another facet of the jewel, the prism, the *life* of the crystal peak; here I would leave my meditations and contemplations to dissolve into the aether of deep magic. No more scholarly *thought*; all grains settled in the pool, I gave myself up to simply trust in *their* trust – that I had a role to play, as mediator between the energies, as facilitator and helpmate to Sidhe who cannot cross a certain threshold in the 'dance', to support the quarry *and* the stars; a role where 'I' too *the thread no more to sleep*.

The Prequel of Creation

As described above, the different lines of flight were beginning to coalesce. My focus, in the approach to the autumnal equinox, however, returned me to *TreeMother*'s grail space, to re-energising the nodal connection and stating my formal intent to return down under, to 'create the home to which ...'. At this time, the following *Malakut* insight appeared in meditation:

Streaming between here and the garden as usual; suddenly unbeknown and/or unremarked, I showed up in Little Cove – in the bathroom of the April unit and thought: That's not right, I should be in my 'own' (to come) bathroom and 'moved' (literally) to its 'latent' look and feel, my imaginal concept once home 'created'. At this point, I let myself relax into the vision, and felt my consciousness *flow* back out of the bathroom into my room, to stand at the verandah door and greet Noosa Hill, the *Mother'sHead*. Hands brought together in blessing, I intoned: *Namaste* (all of this was intriguingly organic, fluid; no *mind* intruding on such heart-centred acts; only witness with a little 'wow' of surprise at what it saw transpire). All of a sudden (a-ha!) I knew where the stone would be I needed to find – on Noosa Hill itself, in direct sight of home. At that, mind kicked in with a remembered journey up this track one of the past years and yes, there were hewn stones in that space and I pictured the finding of whichever one 'speaks' as well as offering the *FindlingForest* gift in return.

I began to pen a specific ritual of invocation; the solstice ceremony I used as template, given the effectiveness demonstrated. This included giving thanks for the summer just been (replete with fresh bardic *Poems of Place* to offer) and honouring and welcoming the *StarGeist* energies' support of, and strengthening of task-orientation. As ever, I felt the need to formally speak aloud the connections I wished to invoke, as well as seek permission for same. Nevertheless, I felt strong, buoyed by spirit, more 'self-sovereign' (if that is possible) in skill and focused intent; equal amongst equals, I engaged our *shared* strength knowing it all came down to a simple fact – love; the love I generated for all in our shared energetic field, the love I felt streaming back to me in the selfsame moment which the following journal entry on the morning of the ritual sums up perfectly:

A shame I feel so ill, like throwing up, on such a beautiful morning, such a beautiful perfect clear day to welcome autumn – day of equal night, night of equal day. Much of the night I tossed and turned till the alarm sounded. As soon as downstairs, I opened the verandah door for Pabey and stepped out myself into the freshness and clarity of pre-dawn, hoping to clear this poor old head. There in the east rising beside the church tower was a very bright (and near) planetary presence: Venus. I looked into her face and she into mine. I cried aloud: *I feel so loved!* And burst into tears with this knowledge as much as my feeling of illness. It was like in the *instant* of her outreach, and my recognition of same, I knew her to be an emissary on behalf of *all* universal consciousness to anoint my burning forehead with love. *I feel so loved!* the only thing I could say, think, feel to express the enormity, the sanctity, the overwhelming spontaneity of the moment. It is this I shall remember, ever, to bolster inner strength even while outer is depleted – love, pure, elemental, real ...

The point was I didn't need to *remember* it because love literally *infused* me, brought me *back* to 'health' during the course of the day, such that all preparations *flowed*, all energies aligned. Because of love, I could fulfil intent that, at three of the clock, we *all* stood together in the grail space for the ceremony. And, in the collective *presence* of love, I felt well enough to perform the ritual in the cone of joy *formed* in the space, well enough to ingest the morsels, 'gifts of the garden', thanks given for summer's bounty, on behalf of all – the fresh and fermented, together with a cup of *TreeMotherTea* on this, the International Day of Peace.

In the process, I realised that flow enacts itself, naturally, as a matter-of-course, because of the love *vested* in the undertaking – love vested is 'reaped' in the flow of how events unfold and manifest themselves out of all potential possibilities. Love, it is, which gathers the creative energies to itself, of the right causes and conditions to manifest intent. And with *all* our love vested in this space, in *shared* intent? Ah, the beauty of partnership engaged with Sidhe companions of the way ...

A short fifteen days stood between the equinox event and my being *homecome to the sea*. I had closed the ceremony with a prayer, one I would repeat on the shores of a southern ocean a few weeks later. A prayer offered on behalf of self, on behalf of all – the quarry *and* the stars:

> *Dear Gaia ... All this love we have brought into being in this space through our ritual, all our intent, by connecting our sacred places, letting the threads of light and love flow between the nodes in our care, all this we dedicate to you, offer into the collective font of your intent. Dear Gaia ... Please take this love; this wave of love flowing along lines of flight, threads of joy, through your world to use as you will. May Love touch every heart in creation; may Love bring Peace into the core of each self; may the Light of Grace support each own to burn brighter ... All this we offer from our Garden Grail of Beauty ... May it be so, may it ever be so ... Amen ...*

I watched for signs from the *Malakut* – in night-vision and day-meditation. Was there anything more I needed to integrate in advance of our departure for down under? I re-found in my journal the following note from 5 May: 'I consciously invoke my *desire* to homecome in October, to greet the soul of the house, thank it for its trust and faith in our stewardship; the intuition of what I must do during that brief window of nine days to fulfil intent – to create the 'home' by which others may homecome to the One ...'.

This, of course, reminded me that I would not only welcome 'new Maleny' to the family but as well celebrate and invoke the energies of Maleny itself in a ceremony on the shores of her 'sacred pool', to formally bind her soul to the network of nodes. In all practicality, this would be conducted post-Little Cove; an image popped into my mind that the link would be granite head to granite head – the *Mother'sHead* to Gaia's granite mantled hinterland – whereby a single simple stone of blessing would evoke the synchronistic connection between this (not so) high wild sacred pool and her eastern sea wild cousin, each bubbling forth from a pure wellspring of the earth.

I sat with the Stone Circle outlaid, asked if there be any guidance, last insights: *Speak now.* As well as reminding me to pack the *Card Deck* for the rituals, words formed: *Clearly state what it is that is needed this time to fulfil intent this time.* An image-memory accompanied it – of the tumult of the rollercoaster (inner as well as outer), weather as much as the energy of creation, from earlier in the year. The image was followed by a single word: *Flow.* Yes, this time the flow needed *moderation* so I may concentrate on task, to not be swamped by the energy of convergence. I prepared the following centring invocation, accordingly:

May the flow of my love and the light of Your grace
come into this home to create
May the flow of my love and the light of Your grace
connect with this spirit of place
May the flow be calm steady gentle peaceful joyous
all rolled into one
May the flow be calm steady gentle peaceful joyous
all rolled into one
(oh, and warm) Thank you!

So too, resting a final time in communion with dear *MossManFindling*, a poetic offering arose from the bard's tongue in support of task:

At five of the clock
I sit with you, Sun,
and some TreeMotherTea
in this sacred grail space
this 'home' nodal place
and ask all for your
blessings, your loving support
this pilgrimage quest
to fulfil ...

133

The morning of our departure, I sat briefly in meditation, and discovered myself 'washing' hats before setting them out to dry. I wear so many hats, it seems, but now they were all readied anew. I sat some more, and a wondrous 'triple star' appeared in my vision (thank you, Rigel!). So bright and beautiful, a good omen I hoped, and began my *Hello the House* greeting to country, 'announcing' my homecome way to all spirits of place, that the journey was about to begin.

Safely arrived, finally 'home'. Yet so many acts to create a home! One physical manifestation of same was central to all symbolic manifesations, however. To bring the *spirit* of place into the house, a spirit which *blends* the forest of the headland with the sea lapping her shores, to root, *anchor* the soul of the house in both, the living room wall needed painting. The colour chosen to bring the green and blue together as one was called 'Wishlist' (in artists'-speak, a 'fresh mid-toned aquamarine blue; in warm light showing its sheer green base note'). After my first giggle at the Faerie-like whimsy this name suggested, I gave thanks – that Little Cove was no longer on an (unconscious) family wishlist but fully texturally and spiritually present as our 'new Maleny' home, one to which others may homecome.

The Magic of the Mantle

Nine days. Nine brief days of creation. A busy time – of family and joyous celebration – the energy engaged around a communal table an integral part of same. Love *always* the third who sat at my elbow while the ritual of homecome creation continued apace – unexpectedly, magically – with long, open, sharing, joyous, peaceful, calm, steady (and warm) camaraderie. I said thank you into the belly of the house over and over as I watched from the kitchen one particular day the delight of *all* at table in the courtyard, this wonderful *Innenhof* its own container of peace-sink energy pure, where I myself had been welcomed by *AncestorCouple* some six months prior, where I now sensed the wide smile of *AvocadoTree* to preside over a scene in space and, now too, time – one where the magic of the Dancers, *Moveable Feast* and *Joy to the World*, were very much present.

Yet when would I find space-time in the slim schedule to be alone, the solitary ritual of thanksgiving and blessing to perform? The issue had already been recognised by Sidhe companions of the way, I was grateful to note. In the wee hours of our first night, a night when I had consciously donned the mantle to bring the energy of the stars streaming to earth in this place, I received a shining visitor. A 'fresh' presence to the Circle, she described herself as a 'designer' or outfitter of space. She had travelled very far for this ritual, from very far 'north' which, in the context of the *Card Deck*, means through the *Gate of the Stars* (see David's comments, pp.30-31). Specifically I knew her to be the Dancer, *Stairway to Heaven*, from 'Mother's' community, a crystal'd membrane within the Moon I had had the opportunity to visit early in my work with the cards. We discussed our respective commitments and agreed a time to celebrate 'Mother's Day' together. I knew this meant engaging the energy of *Mother'sHead*, at Noosa Hill. She confirmed it wouldn't take too long; she would 'have me back in a couple of hours'. I agreed.

Allowing 'flow' to work its magic, a small window opened to propose a walk up said hill, a reconnaissance prequel to 'creation', and neither boy-child objected. Out the back door from home we went, crossed the garden to the National Park, headed along the silent sandy forested trail which wound round and about, spiralling up her bushy bird-songed crown. There I found a local version of a stone cairn, this *Steinmännli* no more than a rough heap of rocks, domed, midden-like. We all shared a laugh at Oz-chaos versus Swiss-order; I circled it a couple of times as the boys headed off, intuited that a small stone from here would be the 'return' blessing stone up over and plucked one from the pile. It was squared off, hewn, young and 'edgy' in its energy. It would buoy up the thread with its youth and scout-like song.

Meanwhile, tracing the path down from *Mother'sHead* out to the sea itself revealed the 'hewn' version of *MossManFindling* plumb bang beside the main walking track at the park entrance. Hmmm. Its location rang a bell for another reason – 'twas here that I and *VanDiemen'sMan* had stood on an upturned dugout canoe in the *Malakut* 'looking north to whence we came'. The threads were coming together of their own accord. From source to sea to source, we walked home via the coastal path.

Next was the need to replicate in the material my *Malakut* journey home along the eastern sea wild from Peregian along the shoreline from which I had watched the *ShiningOnes* surfing. This date had been set in stone in the itinerary – come hell or high water etc. All causes and conditions conspired, fortunately, for it to be low tide, for the day to enact itself as perfectly as all others – smooth the flow; calm, steady, peaceful, joyous, warm all rolled into one. Somehow 'gentle' had dropped off the radar of invocation, but never mind, we were coping. I maintained mantras the entire fifteen kilometre stretch, stones of blessing snug in my pockets, singing up country each step of the sandy shore. All ripe, the 'way' cleared. Now I simply awaited the return of *Stairway to Heaven*.

Tuesday, 13 October, dawn; 'twas New Moon and here she was, returned, with an image of a linking thread, repeating over and over like a wave in space, a 'sideways 8' or infinity symbol and its energy of binding, between self and spirit of place was profound. I immediately rose and set out on the verandah in sight of *Mother'sHead* the candles, cards, incense and stones (each a link in the infinite chain, on and on without end). *AvocadoTree's* lushly leafed canopy softly rustled in the (ah, gentle!) breeze at my side, and *Nachwuchs-Kookaburra* (see Glossary) sat in attendance – emissary of Ancestral dreaming, he had perched in her branches or on the railing each day since our arrival, listening to each conversation with a keen eye.

As ever, I began the ritual with an energy-cleansing and 'freeing-of-field' – this my next 'new' ten-foot-square hut – in order to bless the space as a container charged with sacred purpose. I thanked the soul of the house for welcoming us, established our intent to 'create the home to which ...' to receive, hold and *flow* our love on to any and all who spend time within her cone of peace and joy, as a *contribution* to their own homecoming way to the One. Thus stripped of all extraneous self-accoutrements, I intoned: *May your light, dear home, shine unhindered. Amen ...*

Following the ceremony I traced the path again up Noosa Hill, left *FindlingForest*'s gift in the cairn, threaded the path on down to the sea. In the moment I found myself 'wake' (or was it their stirring from sleep I sensed? Chicken-and-egg like, perhaps, but in the moment I recalled the *SandPeople*'dolls') to the energy of the trees on the lee side of the headland. It felt as if an ancestral elder presence were held there; fronting the sea north, 'twas an old man Dreaming I sensed, they the guardian spirits of the 'Mother'.

Interestingly, I also 'woke' to why *Shaping Man* had self-named and self-chosen his place in the 'string' of Dancers' summoning. His whole bearing said 'Aboriginal' but now, post-ritual and with *whom*, I recognised the link between his card and *Stairway's* in the wisdom bones of these gnarled *shaped* 'man' trees. On my next return down under, I decided, they would be formally included in blessing work and outreach.

For now, however, it was time to bid farewell. My final *Malakut* wander on our last morning was poignant; I traversed 'Wishlist'-coloured hardened basalt flows down along the beach – so smooth and *lush*, so voluptuous and sensuous their curves, spewed forth aeons past from *Wollumbin's* core. In the space, I engaged deep-time, forest and sea meeting on the living room wall *our* contribution to the flow from the heart of (now) home. And so left 'new Maleny', drove the hinterland road home to true Maleny, gift to Gaia as a nature refuge in perpetuity, where the simplicity of coming home to this original home (in all senses of the word) needed no formal uplift or enactment of task.

Walking the tranquillity, the *peace* of the sink, greeting the Bunyas in their Dreaming, being greeted by *SacredKingfisher* (see Glossary), gifting Little Cove's granite brother-of-blessing to the pool, thanking the pool's spirit for outreaching to me in the first place oh-so long ago. A sacred pool of life burbling to the surface, right-here-right-now, on a granite outcrop at the end of an unending ridge, 'twas a no-brainer (literally). Heart-felt, heart-led, heart-knowing said: Yes. And yes it was, this day as every other day: I simply *walked* home, tossed home *into* home, waited till the ripples reached all the way to shore; source to sea to source now fully completely *bound*. All ye gods – how better could you have possibly answered my homecome prayer? Thank you! On and on – thank you!

The morning of our departure, return journey to the far side of the world. Pre-dawn the *Malakut* beckoned wherein I participated in a ceremony, a 'Farewell-Thanksgiving-to-Country'. *Stairway to Heaven* had returned to conduct proceedings, and I was *so* grateful that she took on this responsibility to complete the circle, to weave the flow between homes (and worlds) as I slipped in and out of the space, so utterly exhausted by all felt and experienced and engaged during this too-brief time of communion that consciousness was close to meltdown. Nevertheless I knew the ceremony to be a heightened 'repeat' of the one in which I had felt the flow of Little Cove through me; this ceremony a conscious integration of same, of affirmation, commitment, gratitude – a way in which to backfill any gaps in the script that I had not been able to act upon, given the full-on 'outer' task list. Yet such a necessary close-out to the entire process and my *relief* in the space, that she had set this in train. Oh, the benefits of partnership! Otherwise, how remiss would I have been, failing to honour the forces, the energies of the *ShiningOnes*, emissaries come, all support gladly selflessly gifted!

'Know the Way'

It is time to set out in text the extraordinary culmination to this pilgrimage songline on the (long) flight back to up over. The experience does not give itself up easily to text; I can only (attempt to) describe it as an induction into a practice of 'linking the lattice' in another form – yet a form which built on all that had proceeded till then.

In hindsight, it was possibly set in train by my finding of the 'ring of glacial blue' in actuality, my connective thread to 'fly', *homecome to the sea*. Given the string of events in which this ring had been implicated, somehow I thought at the latest it would cross my path in the material down under, during our nine short days. So it was to be, and I wore it permanently thereafter, thus involving it – together with all other rings, symbolic interlocutors donned as part of the mantle each day – in 'creating the home to which …'. Each has a name in a thread of song as popped on to its relevant finger; this one self-named accordingly as: *All the way from source to sea, from source to sea to source …*

A further remark before launching: I have since intuited that the experience represented a deepening of the farewell ceremony *Stairway* conducted on the morning of our departure, as well as seeming to herald a next (potential) incarnation of how my ritual undertaking could unfold. Neither intuition has been confirmed by Sidhe companions; likewise, nor has it been denied. However, once returned to the sanctity of the ten-foot-square hut post-pilgrimage, words formed: *It is done*. And I could not disagree. Thus, during my first meditation, did

I find myself 'back' in the kitchen at Little Cove where a 'sisterly' voice called out from beyond the front screen door: *Hello, are you home?*

When I went to let her in, though, I was seriously taken aback. This was no 'sister', but a brand new energy signature, a real 'I mean business' presence ready to blow in like a stiff wind; all in white, briefcase-inclusive. I backed away, saying: *I don't know you; I don't think you should come in.* And immediately 'surfaced'. The voice had been friendly enough and I hadn't been scared by the energy, just confronted in the moment; while perhaps I could engage it on neutral ground, it seemed too unknown a force to invite into 'home'. Clearly it was ready for the next dimension of 'work' but heck, me? With jetlag? I went back 'in' and apologised; intimated that I wasn't yet ready to engage. There was plenty to sift and sort on my own for now.

So to the experience ... the leg Singapore-Zurich, 13-hour long haul leaving at 1am local to arrive 8am local, the entire way spent following night, chased by dawn. As is my usual practice, I spent much of the stretch in meditation, 'exiting' the *space* of time, *outwith*. Yet the visioning I experienced was entirely outwith *all* previous experience. It enacted, after a fashion, my physical walking of a homecome *thread* across the world. And indeed how fortunate I had my notebook in the seat pocket to record briefly the felt-sense of these astonishing hyper-conscious episodes as I flowed in and out of the space of encounter over *hours* before finally coming back *into* myself, and thinking: Wow ...

I was literally out-of-body, I was the *space* of engagement, I was actually outside the plane, atop the craft, and I flew (I *knew* I flew) at the same velocity, with the same directional intent, as the craft as if we were companion 'entities' sharing a common flight path. I remembered how tired I had been to fly 'home' solo; was this like hitching a (subtle) ride to perform task? In a (brief) moment of 'witness', I *knew* it was 'Love' riding the sky waves (and then suddenly I was back to *being* the space of engagement; thus I *was* Love), weaving the thread across the world between 'homes'.

Now, the thread was silver, and presented as a silvered line strung out behind me and craft, our *joint* task to fly it on. All Love was *in* me (like all Little Cove in me); Love therefore the silver thread trailed out *from* me. In going in and out of the space of encounter, this was a real surprise. I remembered how my energy had previously presented as more 'sticky', like golden glitter glue compared to stars' energy signatures, but definitely 'saw' and likewise 'experienced' the thread as silver, filigreed, not sticky at all. It wafted, *flowed* like water, wind, behind me. Neither taut nor tight-strung, it was languid, joyous, *wei wu wei*-ish in construction as opposed to being facilitated by a deliberate 'striving' energy. It just was, and I just was, and the plane just was – all 'true-natured' and matter-of-course describes the felt-sense of the experience.

Thus did I *live* how flow was enlivened, envisioned, enacted in material and subtle dimensions *simultaneously*. I engaged the *spirit* of the A380. I know it sounds completely hallucinatory but I was as lucid as can be, hugging it, calling it my Divine Omnibus – and then giggling. Had Sidhe energy connected with the plane to facilitate this alternate manifestation of 'linking the lattice'? My notes describe the life-exuding qualities of flying *and* plane, how uplifting it was to *share* time together weaving what I knew to be 'sky-threads', so-named in the space. Is this why they presented as silvered? Would earth or sea 'threads' connecting home-to-home maybe look more golden in form? Is it possible that I was in the space of what Mariel describes as 'only being able to come so far' before the Sidhe's threshold is reached? That I inhabited, engaged, an intertidal zone *between* the two where our shared tasks may align? A zone exhilarating in intent yet extraordinarily calming, peaceful in execution; no feeling of 'effort', just the joy of service in its ability to flow?

Interestingly I tried (when attached to the outer skin of the plane) to connect with the star energies of the night. I consciously 'called' Rigel who had sent me on my way down under with the triple-star vision, but 'heard' nothing. It was just me and plane doing our stuff, which was affirming in a way. Indeed: *It is done.* May this work, like all work, help you, Gaia, in your healing and evolution. May we all come along with you for the ride of our lives *in*, *with* and *to* the Divine.

When I returned from the 'act', and had penned my notes, I meditated again but it seemed the 'work' itself was at end. For now I stood face-to-face with a huge tree – tall, straight, its branches so high, so *beyond*, I could not see them from where I stood. My only space of engagement its mammoth trunk right before my nose, its bark hide fully mantled in *moss*. I grinned. Hello *MossMan*, thanks for the induction. Afterwards, I wandered a garden centre; I felt it to be attached to the farm community, that here all starseeds grown 'big enough' to be flown to the world, for distribution to market, awaited (my) delivery. Here I connected with a tiny wizened Chinese fellow, one of the original market gardeners of this place, yet dressed in alpine *lederhosen* (?), watering and tending the stock. He grinned as I passed and then turned back to task; but I noted the book in the gardener's belt on his hip. It referenced a particular pilgrimage destination, and was titled: *Know the Way*.

Layers of meaning, as with all symbolic references. Nevertheless I knew the specific layer to which he referred – 'twas the commitment, the new adventure, to which I returned. Yet the reader must wait till the next – and final – chapter for *StarGeist's* call to partnership to be revealed …

Chapter 9: The Path Itself

This the Way, the only Way, the Way of Love our Home ...

We all need a ten-foot-square hut, a temple, a grail space in which to host our conversations and contemplations, to which all companions of the way may be invited, all welcome to sit at our fireside at the foot of Gaia's throne, in a fellowship of joy and service. An outer space to mirror the inner kiln room of the heart, it need not be great or grand; it is woven from love and, like Mariel's, 'a blend of energy and substance ... (that) reflects the true altar which is in my heart' (p.119). I have had, and continue to have, the extraordinary good fortune to create and now steward four such temples of the heart in the world. Each is home, a nodal point within the material, a hub of connectivity to the *Malakut*, our home amongst the stellar realms to which one day we shall return, we children of the stars, when our loving weaving work to sing up the stars within Gaia's glorious earth is done.

In formalising the connection to each of the nodes, however, I understood that the thread strung *between* each is also home, the path itself; by sharing with Sidhe the task to *form* connections, to weave new threads of light and love in the becoming cloak of Gaian consciousness, I understood that more spider-spun filigree threads in the web, in the lattice of her crystalline evolution, could manifest. '*Creating* the home to which ...', therefore, was an altogether more inclusive and holistic proposition as a partnership opportunity than I had at first envisaged.

Further, in the extraordinary experience I recounted at the close of the last chapter, flying the string across the world as 'sky-threads' together with my *MossMan* bard, I lived the horizontal and vertical 'dancing' of the stars – inward, outward, across and through – like a carpet loom on overdrive. This I understood in the context of Mr1300BC's musical score, described earlier, whereby each line of 'music' presented like leylines within and *beyond* the Earthern plane, yet was completely in *tune* with its vertically-positioned counterparts above and below.

Now, 'unattached' to or between any specific 'home'-node, a fresh connection discovered when spontaneously constellated in space, this experience delivered me an insight of further opportunities to probe, to which to apply my *length* of Elven-rope in this ever-evolving alliance. Indeed, in the way the thread wafted and flowed during the flight, I recalled Beauty's counsel: *Aethereal-material are one and the same in my reality ... Soon it will feel like home to you too!* I also recalled: *You know Love is the solidity within aether, that the Ground ever-grounds you.* Yes, I had felt-sensed during the experience that the *All* of Love was within me, therefore that the silver thread trailing out from me was Love, *flowing* like water, wind, behind – a whole new dimension to Mariel's 'grounded fluidity'.

'Home,' Beauty had said. 'Love the solidity within aether,' she had said. Now the firefly sparks in the rhizome took over. I understood that 'home' related not only to the state of love experienced in connection *to* place, but to the length of Elven-rope *itself*; whatever my 'stretch' of Ancestral song (in Aboriginal-speak) constituted a stewardship of territory in, for and by love: 'In Aboriginal belief, an unsung land is a dead land ... if the songs are forgotten, the land itself will die;' 'Song (is) both map and direction-finder. Providing you knew the song, you could always find your way across country' (Chatwin, pp. 52 & 13 respectively).

Love the original song which sang the world into being; love working its magic to uplift the song which 'awoke' *MossManFindling* (and me!) to task. *Know the Way* the book on the Chinese gardener's hip – is to *know* the way to *be* the way? The path *itself*? Where the song of love acts as both map and direction-finder to the stars within the earth, to manifest further potentialities in the unfolding landscape of Gaia's crystalline consciousness? 'We need to be the quarry *and* the stars': Was this how my contribution would manifest in space-time?

19 October: Monday 11am. 'It is done'; these the words of the Council which greeted me as I came home to the ten-foot-square hut this morning in YMM. Standing in swirls of energy, love and light within the Stone Circle, I was about to begin 'work', proclaim: 'I am a connective thread ...' when it was suddenly overridden by the image of all four nodes now 'charged', *in* the web; *gleichzeitig* the words formed. Consumed by waves of love in the moment and little 'me' leaked tears of gratitude and relief that *flow* had taken us hence and returned

us here, the *fact* of our partnership the statement: *It is done.*

Gratitude clear, to all companions of the way – those who centred the energy here, those who centred it there, those who glided alongside as witnesses and helpmates to task enacted. *All* companions – thanks be! Whether subtle or not-so, how grateful am I for your love and commitment and support! Relief clear too. What if, what if? Whenever the thought presented, it was silenced by 'flow' – as words formed, as a centring meditation, as experienced, *lived.* Flow. Methinks a learning in itself, the way all proceeds when *preceded* (and perpetually underpinned) by loving intent. I had an insight of same (as much this morning when, in YMM, I welcomed the reciprocate stone of blessing from *Mother'sHead* into the circle, brought it into the wicker sacred pool (so too welcoming the ring of glacial blue). In meditation, I sat, and saw a boat 'docking' at the 'shore' ...

Such a wonderful homecoming! And my intuition was thankfully not misplaced, for occasionally I have 'forgotten' this moment in the weeks and months since, and gone out to stand on the verandah or enter *TreeMother's* grail space with a self-thought: Oh, I haven't had a chance to 'charge' *MossManFindling* in a while (i.e. sing him our 'love' song) to be suddenly overridden by an image of him quietly humming, buzzing away, outreaching along the lines of flight we established as a regular matter-of-course. Each time I feel the joy of surprise to 'see' that like a well-tuned engine he's just purring along quite nicely, thank you.

Similarly, my connection to the *Card Deck* is so ingrained in psyche that I can invoke the energy of the Council and Dancers, see them in my mind's eye, string the *entire* text of the 'summoning' ritual (their 'naming') together, to invoke their presence wherever I am without needing to lay the Circle out in 'formal' meditation. Nevertheless we do have regular 'outings' together. One such was pure delight, and I crave the reader's indulgence while I share what transpired when my companions were 'unzipped' and brought forth from the beautifully embroidered gold-silken pouch which has been their home ever since arriving in my care – F's gift of love that selfsame Christmas a perfect 'fit' for their presence.

1 December: This morning YMM complete and in meditation I sat, surrounded by the Stones. I felt *warmth* at my back – was it coincidental? Or was the strength, solidity, density of Standing Stone *earthing* me (*Gate of the Earth*, after all, was behind, and the first chakra the seat of earth and intoned as much in the ritual). But later, while meditating in the Circle and just being-with, I felt an energy 'arise', a zingeyness; at first I thought it was a soul hug, but no, this was different – it didn't radiate out from the core of me; it was coming from

without and only 'felt' at my back and shoulders.

Suddenly 'I saw' it for what it was – a mantle of starlight, silver-glittered, had been lovingly respectfully thrown, passed over my shoulders to rest there, for me to wear. I felt the joy in the room this act to perform (and how unexpected!); they smiled when I finally got it, a circlet of presence at my back, one of whom had stepped forward with mantle held out to quickly slip on before return to her place. Teasingly, it had been done (yet also reverently, seriously) – would I notice? And yes. When I realised what the energy *wasn't*, I then *saw* what it was – a mantle of starlight in a sea of midnight blue. Beautiful! Oh dear companions of the way! I feel the energy it holds and *cleaves* to my skin – silvered, flowing, shining. Ha! And ha – again! Thank you! What joy to be so-blessed! I wear your mantle with honour, sweet cousins ...

How to choose the place
in the stretch of this,
our shared Ancestral song,
to lift the Bard's flowery
feather-inked pen,
as it ebbs and flows,
floats and foams
on a Moon-mirrored
tranquil sea?
How to end a story,
love story without end,
between sweet Cousins
of the Commons,
dear Sidhe and Humanity?
Begun (it was) in a time
before time, a place before now;
yet now here sits (ready) in its
leather-bound tome,
ready to exist,
ready to be told,
by the one in the storyteller's chair?
Here she sits, yes,
Van Diemen's heavy Book
of (longer-than aetheric) Voyage
propped open upon her knee.
Patience, dear reader,
its close in sight

but not yet reached;
this shore (on which our boat docks)
requires a few (more) pages more ...

Only Connect!

I trust the reader has a good memory, for now is the moment to circle to the beginning of the text, a story of adventure and exploration in the spirit of TS Eliot's bardic wisdom, to know it for the first time. Specifically we return to the experience of a little pinprick in the Alps on a day two years past which first encouraged her contact with David. That little pinprick found she had unwittingly 'tapped into' Earth-energies, and witnessed what could result from such an action. Not long after, *MakerMan* had revealed the connection to a *StarGeist*, a rhizome not to 'take flight' in the material till an adventure atop *Silberen's* 'magic mantle' during the summer just passed, setting in train the ascents of *Leistchamm* and *Brisi* on the hunt for more clues and symbolic interlocutors.

While Little Cove's 'creation of home' maintained its own energy-of-making concurrent with these events on a (for all intents and purposes) parallel track, a new energy of 'adventure' was busy fomenting in the psyche of the pinprick, one seemingly unrelated to the scaling of *StarGeist*'d peaks. This rhizome intersected (or crosscut) two other randomly exuberant lines of flight: Earth Mother's recent work of 'measuring' and a perennial favourite – the retreat from the world to rest in the kiln room at the *heart* of the mountain, to engage with stone sentience pure.

I meditated on the paradox of this disparate energy – the need to *be* (i.e. the mountain), the need to *flow* (i.e. extend the Elven-rope) in the selfsame moment. These meditations occurred in the wake of an extraordinarily busy, physically and mentally exhausting (albeit soul-energising) summer vacation. At times I even thought to feel my companions *physically* 'adding their Light' to mine to buoy flagging energetic reserves (something I have called 'energy injections' over the years); with this subtle support, I was encouraged to trust to 'flow' rather than try to second-guess my own ability to cope or respond (in a way akin to the felt-sense David describes in the introduction to *Conversations*, p.9-10, about his Sidhe walking buddy in the forest).

But why did a new 'adventure' call? Didn't these guys ever take time off? A single word formed: *Trust* (again). And a single image: Of a *swing door*. 'I saw' myself push the door open but not yet step through. In the moment, I 'stayed' in the mountain. In here I would discover what 'I' was asking 'me' to do.

24 August: A new self-project has taken hold in my mind. Something I need to reconcile with all current 'projects' for I don't understand *why* I need to add it

to the pile. Why the urgency of this energy? An urgency that means a new space *in* me needs to be freed in order to give myself *fully*, in the moment, to this *new* duty. 'Tis a buzzy scattered energy requiring focus, for the aether swirling in a vortex of unfastened activity to calm and coalesce into malleable, definable form, for its *essence* to be revealed. A pushy kid-on-the-block energy describes what I feel streaming *into* me; nevertheless one whose cattle prod says: *This is all part of the grand plan. Trust* ... But who is responsible? Wherefrom has it arisen?

In writing myself through to understanding, mind-mapping the different threads in the rhizome to reach this (now) point in the script, the key word floating above all was pilgrimage. The idea of pilgrimage has a longer-than history in my lexicon as evidenced by its use in a chapter title earlier, amongst others. For example, *The Taste of Translation*, my major work of prose fiction, describes three pilgrims' 'ways' (inner and outer mirroring each other). The encounter with the little Chinese market gardener following the visionary streaming of a 'pilgrim's' thread of Elven-rope across the world was its most recent incarnation – the title of his hip pocket volume: *Know the Way*. At its most profound level, of course, this guide was leading me back to the wisdom of Taoist ancients, but the specificity of task to which he referred in the moment lay at a more accessible depth. The 'Way' in this instance being the *Camino de Santiago*, or *Via Jacobi*, a major pilgrimage route across Europe to a Galician cathedral and a saint's relics ...

In EM Forster's *Howards End*, Margaret's role is to express the salvation latent 'in the soul of every man. Only connect! That was the whole of her sermon. Only connect the prose and the passion, and both will be exalted, and human love will be seen at its height' (p.471). Like all textual offerings from conversation partners past and present, subtle and not-so, Forster's ability to capture – in the space of a breath – the central principle of oneness demonstrates the exquisite talent of the bard. *Only* connect. Nothing more needed to *be* love, *think* love, *live* love in the world. *Only* connect the peace-sinks of the world for rivers of molten light to bring healing to Gaia's children, and to the divine World Soul herself. The pushy kid-on-the-block energy I experienced seemed to be intimating I could contribute to same in some small way by connecting that which already exists, but needs *binding* to the whole.

The relevance to the practices uplifted in the company of Sidhe, as I understood it, was that the *Via Jacobi* traces a *human* songline, one more than a thousand years old, across the *skin* of Gaia. Representing the cultural tradition of my birth, it nevertheless is its own form of walking in the footsteps of the Ancestors. Emanating from various points along Switzerland's northern, eastern and southern borders, they all eventually find their way to Geneva in the south-west to join the main path through France and then on, across the Pyrenees into

Spain. Many 'stretches' of the Swiss songline intersect with or follow the old Roman roads which, for the most part, overlay ancient Celtic Helvetian paths.

As this text bears witness, I 'knew' the high wild and the mountains at *Helvetia's* heart well; this is where I had taken root in the land, been called 'home', in so doing connecting to her (local) spirits of place, the peace I felt sunk deep in their (and consequently my) subtle bones. But what of engaging the longer-than history of human traffic and habitation across her (relative) lowlands? Was there a role for me to play singing up country through the *whole* of her geography, using a well-known, -marked and -trod pilgrimage route? 'Twas one with a connection to spirit, granted, but more the spirit *outwith* than to the one *within*. Could I combine these vertically as a type of *Camino de Helvetica*, while horizontally engaging a *Via Helvetica* with Mr1300BC's musical score attuning leylines within and *beyond* the Earthern plane as my mentoring canticle?

I thought on the proposition further. Embarking on such a pilgrimage would bind me tighter, help me understand deeper, the *soul* of the country. There would also be the potential to uplift, through walking, through *singing*, the 'stars within *her* earth'. If she were agreeable to the notion of 'waking' her peace-sink energy, to out*flow* and engage the mantle and all its in/on-dwellers, what would this mean? I knew what I had seen, and experienced as a pinprick in the eastern Alps; I knew the potentiality that existed.

I recalled how the dear sweet *Wildmännli* of the Alps had retreated long centuries past into the hollow hills; now it rested with humanity to take on their blessing role. I also recalled Mariel's words: 'We can only bring (the stars) so far; there is a threshold we cannot cross, but you can, if you will dance the stars inward and outward with us' (p.67). If the Faerie realms no longer crossed the 'threshold', could my work dance the stars inward and outward, to and from *Helvetia's* deep sunk wells of peace in partnership with Sidhe? Was this the *StarGeist's* call I heard?

There are many levels at which to interrogate the becoming desire I felt from the 'pushy kid', a stream of energy to bring the various weaving threads together – threads of which I had grown increasingly conscious during the year since becoming more attuned to the Sidhe energies of the *Card Deck* – both Council and Dancers – as well as threads uplifted by trawling old and dusty journals while wearing my 'Scholar's' hat.

I continued to write myself through to understanding: If I undertook a task to walk the string along an *existing* line of human conquest, principally through areas of human dominance, of latterly 'claimed' territory, could my 'singing' help *re-balance* the energies, the spirit of communion I felt most keenly to exist as a continuing natural matter-of-course in the high wild? Could my singing help bring love back into human *intercourse* with the land? Could the twinning or mirroring of physical and subtle acts of blessing along the line help bring the *fact* of sanctity, of sunk sentience back to the surface, awaken it from deep-buried slumber, to reclaim *its* 'I am' in the spirit of the sky child's wide-eyed wonder? By walking *my* love and gratitude along long-trod human paths, singing up connections to country, re-singing long *dormant* songlines on behalf of the All, would this help *extend* Mariel's description of manifesting Gaian consciousness; would this be a way to contribute to an *ongoing* 'choir of unfoldment and evolution' (p.34)?

Nevertheless, how practical was my action? Could the little pinprick of me I had seen connect to a 'stream' of Earth-energies beneath her feet, up and into the world to 'shower the world with blessing', now walk such a stream *across* and *through* the land? *Only connect!* Forster wrote. *Follow the leylines,* Mr1300BC counselled oh-so long ago there are only cobwebs in my brain at that place. *We have to start digging!* the father in the castle grounds cried to his slumbering family; could I contribute to the trench needed to facilitate the flow, to energise the rivers of light I had seen between two points within the earth? Was this an opportunity to *be* a leyline myself, to *extend* a methodology-in-perpetual-making *beyond* charging and energising connections between specific nodes within my stewardship in the lattice of Gaia's planetary crystal?

I know I have quoted this par of Mariel's often in the text, but once more it jumped out at me, another facet revealed: 'The earth is *still* a planetary crystal with energies vibrating and coursing along a vast latticework of connections. The phenomena you call the 'leylines' are only an *outer* representation of this, the manifestation upon the physical of these *deeper* lines of *living* energy and consciousness' (p.35). If the connection I experienced to the 'deeper lines' could manifest as fresh leylines 'woken' to service in the world, would this act I envisaged constitute an *explicit* form of 'grounded fluidity'?

Meeting Mountains Redux

The inner had come out in psyche, in text.

I felt, as a quite natural matter-of-course, *Helvetia's* peace-sink-pure grace radiate out into the world – her quiet power, her civilised and civilising influence, a simple truth *bound* to place and to which I too was bound. Here she stood, a necessary land in the midst of Europe (symbolic and actual), a refuge, a repository of peace and thoughtful consideration since generations, a place to nut out peace treaties or issues of global import in crystalline alpine air, or contemplate philosophical conundrums beside tranquil lakes, a place to make stirring speeches such as Churchill's *Europe Arise* in the wake of horrifying war. I prayed: *Please let it ever be so.* The world needs refuges like you, *Helvetia;* the world *needs* to know it is possible for humanity to be at peace, to live with and in civility, for the *structure* of peace to be so inculcated in the cultural consciousness, the national psyche, that it has the capacity to *moderate* any extremes via the air the whole *breathes*.

Thus did I feel my desire to outreach to *Helvetia's* irradiating presence on behalf of the All; to walk in, for and with Love on behalf of *all* sentience. Love the foundation; Love the Way itself. *Know the Way*: The little Chinese gardener's book needed to be on *my* hip. 'I saw' the spiritual and physical manifestation of walking Love across the land as the psychoid unity of two-as-one-become. Love as essence, pilgrim's staff, legs, voice, backpack, and all in between, making holistic connection to the All of the One on behalf of One and the Same. This was something I could offer to my partnership with Sidhe – the *specificity* of human incarnation *beyond* a threshold they could not cross. 'Tis a specificity to celebrate, as it bespeaks humanity's legacy *and* potentiality – to dance the stars inward and outward together with our beautiful shining cousins, and all in Love's name.

I meditated with the Sidhe of the Council. I visualised a *living* thread of Light through the peace-sink of *Helvetia*, the opportunity to *blend* her Gaian songlines of geology and spirit, to *rebind* humanity to the land via the paths the Ancestors had *inscribed* on her skin. I pondered, said: Hmmm, I think this is another facet, a deeper level to plumb of my intent *to help others to homecome to the One by the connections I forge with these spirits of place. Helvetia* is a much larger 'presence' than the *genii locorum* I have (seemed to have) engaged till now. You are the People of Peace, and my intent is to 'sing up' *Helvetia's* peace-sink. So, as with last time, will you *help me*, dear companions of the way?

I heard a burble of joy. The pushy kid energy settled. I could now get back to the Little Cove task-list (amongst others), with an agreement in the Circle that we would begin the trek post-'creating the home' down under. But there was one thing I wanted to do in advance – meet *Helvetia* at her heart, ask permission, seek her blessing. I knew I had to do this physically for the psychoid unity of the undertaking to begin on the right foot (so to speak); it would literally mean meeting her *within* before I could walk *out*.

As related earlier in the text, at birthday time I always have the opportunity to choose the mountain I want to climb on the day (or the weekend closest thereto). This year I told the boys of the alternate plan – to visit *Sasso san Gottardo*. Translating as the 'rock' of St Gotthard, it marks the 'heart' of Switzerland, the centre of the Alpine chain that exploded in a battle of plate tectonics some 20 million years past. In this place, a redoubt was built – 'twas to here the Swiss would have retreated if Hitler had invaded, *into* the mountain itself. The place is tightly bound to the national psyche; it is a popular tourist destination. The boys had made the trek two years earlier because of a fascination with military history as much as there being excellent opportunities for tough days out in the neighbourhood. Being a boys' own adventure, I had demurred. Now, however, it was time to make the pilgrimage myself, to meet *Helvetia* at the source, to enter into – as Mariel says – 'the energy and life of one of the great servants of Gaia, one who itself can perceive the cosmic energies and draw them into our world' (p.131).

By coincidence, we made the journey on the day prior to the red or 'blood' Full Moon, September's total lunar eclipse. Into the catacombs we trekked, water dripped from every surface, all was damp and cool; I discovered that here was the place where the four major rivers of Switzerland and, therefore, the central Alps, have their source. My knowing was immediate: The way to bless *Helvetia*'s songline, to connect her spirit with my ancestral land of birth as much as to honour the spirit of the *Via Jacobi* itself (whose symbol is the scallop shell) would be with shells sourced from my Pacific-shored home. These I would offer into the waters of all rivers crossed during the journey; as an *Amici della Montagna della Luce* I would physically as well as symbolically offer blessings all the way from source to sea, from source to sea to source.

In one domed inner chamber, excavated from the granite core and left plain, unadorned, the largest mass of pure quartz crystal ever found in the Alps was on display. No picture does their beauty justice, the depth of clarity, the intricacies of each sculpted face and self-polished facet. No artificial light does them justice either; I could only imagine their dazzling brilliance under Sun's loving gaze. A film described the finding in an adjacent chamber, two brusque bearded miners chipping away like Bifur and Bofur seeking the Arkenstone, the care they took with each new babe midwifed to the light of day – so whopping in size, yet so fragile in the face of the tough hide of granite, the unrelenting strength of the mantle through which they must to be eased, a birth canal extraordinaire!

I was reminded of the crystal peak of my vision which backdropped 'new Maleny' at last winter's dark, as well Mariel's words about Gaia as a giant planetary crystal. I felt drawn to engage the mountain itself and held my hand out to the *inner* sanctum of granite, just as I connect to her outer skin while hiking. It was our first time 'being-with' in this way in the material; a beautiful moment. I *felt* the mountain's breath, its slow generative hum of presence – at first 'twas my breath in outreach, a touch-of-love respectfully bestowed, but soon it 'woke' and reciprocated my recognition with a low hum in return, a resonance too deep for me to 'tune' to known tones vis-à-vis my intuition of *MossmanFindling*'s extant note.

I felt very privileged, at long last to replicate what I have lived over and over in the *Malakut* these past years, to be *in* the mountain, sense the heart of its sentience from within, the power and resonance by which it *calls* all to itself and home to the One. 'Tis *der Ruf der Berge*, pure and simple. Nevertheless I was more than keenly aware that physically it is not 'home' territory. Unlike the boys, my acute sensitivity to the literal pressure of being in a space where circa four hundred metres of stone is bearing down from above and double as much wide means communion via the *Malakut* remains my venue of choice.

Indeed did I know the mountains' call and had uplifted same to text, yet gave thanks for Mariel's commentary in the moment of my connection as foundational wisdom on which to graft direct felt-sense: '(A mountain) is a principal ally upon whose energy I particularly draw as it is a major conduit through which the energies of stars and earth meet ... Mountain spirits are among humanity's greatest allies in the changes that you face, though you don't realise it' (p.130-1). Ah, but, thankfully I did realise. And so spoke with *Helvetia* in this sanctified space; with *bergkristall* my witness, I set out my intent. In stone.

Later we hiked around the mountain which encases the redoubt to a lake; D pointed out the spot on the slope above where he had found his own nugget-sized crystal just lying on the path, glinting in the sunlight – *see me!* – two years prior; the mountain had spat it up and out just for him. I remembered his joy, had blessed its beauty in a small ritual. It would be with him always, mirroring his crystal heart within; the psychoid unity of *boy-and-berg, two-as-one-become*.

That night we set the alarm for 4am, to witness the eclipse. But I was lucid a few minutes prior, returned from a *Malakut* scape where a large group had gathered to witness the 'Red Lady', as she was called there. Indeed we had been invited to join a Sidhe celebration of the joyous occasion; here Moon was *huge*, much closer and almost physically present at the gathering; 'twas a sunny hillside, green-grassed, daylit, yet she was still so visible, so red. I was overjoyed we had been asked to participate! I woke the boys (in the material) and after a peek and a 'wow' they returned to bed while I went out onto the verandah to greet her properly, heart-to-breathing-heart, as well as a night sky *brimful* with observable sentience. So crystal clear the air! I felt winter's approach, the clarity which bespeaks clairvoyance in communion with stellar energy, and so returned to the *Malakut* where a post-party was now in full swing; many here whom I 'knew' or was getting to know, it seems, including 'cousins on my mother's side'. Fun!

Next day, in meditation, I was back at the place where D had found his crystal above the dam flanking *Sasso san Gottardo*. Peaceful, there in the sunshine; the sink still as glass and radiant. Suddenly song and laughter filled my ears – a troupe of *Amici* coming down a non-path above the tranquil waters carrying all manner of instruments; a brass band, they were dressed in the deep green wool jackets and perky feathered berets of the Italian Mountain Corps I had witnessed once, years ago, on Piazza San Marco, Venezia. Young, joyful – they had been giving a concert for Gaia in the high wild. Here they came, tripping the light fantastic down non-stairs (trombones and drums glinting in the sun) before turning left along the path beside the lake.

More and more I felt the energy call, and that my Sidhe companions were keen to participate in this (new) adventure too. By now we had reached a point of quite comfortably 'walking in each other's shoes', regardless of how inappropriate or impractical the footwear. Our concert for Gaia would string from the high wild source at *Helvetia*'s heart, her crystal'd peak within, all the way across and through the land, walking each *Via Jacobi* songline mapped on her skin, singing up country in peace, love and with the light of Grace at heart, every moment of *being* an opportunity to praise.

I began measuring out the threads, like the Earth Mother. The energy called: *Come. Come now.* I said to F: We'll make Einsiedeln by Christmas in a series of day-hikes. It's only a hundred kilometres or so; and smiled at the whimsy of taking a fresh-minted red passport for a walk across its homeland, wearing about my neck the perennial scallop shell binding me to a homecome sea. *Know the Way:* Yes, the *way* is love and the *voice* is love, and I its walking singing pilgrim. The perennial Taoist counsel of the *I Ching* refers: *Let wind enter; keep mountain still.* The little Chinese gardener smiled. It was time to push open the swing door, this time to step through and out from the heart of my mountain redoubt:

Take my hand, Wind,
this time, again,
for a brand new adventure
beyond each our ken ...

StarGeist Revisited

I know I am not alone, nor have ever been since beginningless time, in the desire to sanctify Gaian ground, to sing up the beauty of country, to merge into country, to connect at and through that spot of colour in the soul through which all nestedfishes may commune. 'At times I feel as if I am spread out over the landscape and inside things, and am myself living in every tree, in the splashing of the waves, in the clouds and the animals that come and go, in the procession of the seasons': So spake dear old man Jung, the perennially young.

And so it was as we began to sing up *Helvetia*'s songline; yet with an extension to Jung's insight. For I felt that not only were Sidhe singing with me, but there was, somehow, a sense of *solidarity* 'with the earth', with *all* Gaian sentience. At times I feigned to almost sense an 'Entish-style' waking up, a *shift* in the felt world from benign observer or participant to subtle activist; I almost felt like crying aloud: Who's with me on this quest, love as our spear and shield to pierce the *Cloud of Unknowing*, to protect our spiritual light, the collective light of Gaia's 'quarry *and* the stars'? A felt-sense seemed to pervade the scapes we trekked, one of collective-courage in the face of all (physical evidence, bad news, tragedies, degradation et al) to the contrary.

152

Let me say that I do not think my small action has anything to do with what I sense *beyond* the boundaries of my own skin, but that at this time in history it's as if there is a coalescence of many streams of energy seeking to support Gaia's evolution, as Mariel has described in *Conversations* (and which the *Card Deck's* own energy-of-becoming supports), and that in my having also 'heard the call', tapped into it via the *Card Deck* as well as through previous work, I have become more sensitively attuned to the *response* of other forces in the Gaiasphere similarly. That they may support our small partnership action is simply an added (and unexpected) bonus. Thanks be! Mariel's comments in *Conversations* (p.53), of course, sum up what I feel with far great lucidity as well as brevity.

Yet this felt-sense had its most direct manifestation on a pre-winter's day of high wind and ominous clouds skating the sky of the *Alpstein* as we traversed its western flank – this the region of the limestone-mantled *StarGeist'd* peaks. Was no coincidence, methinks, that the *Via Jacobi* from Lake Constance traced this route, with the main ridge and highest peak *Säntis* to the east ever-present along the way south.

Wind was bitter, this particular day of seven hours steady hike; a headwind freezing my face, setting fast a grimace rather than grin – dear blustery soul: She certainly wasn't taking my hand but trying to push me back! A self-thought: *Hold the centre.* A memory-text arisen: *Let wind enter; keep mountain still.* Each now and then I looked across to *Säntis*, for the most part cloaked in dark swirling clouds. At one point though, during a brief stop, he was released from their chains to stand proud and tall. 'Twas then I could *Hello the House* fully, look into his face truly.

(As an aside, I don't know why, but in my experience energy signatures generally present as gendered. While the overall spirit of the mountains, *mantled stone sentience in the form of a great being of the Earth, I 'know' as female (see *Der Ruf der Berge*), individual mountain spirits of place can present as 'male' – in this instance, *Säntis*. Rarely it is that a signature is genuinely androgynous for my Huxleyian mode; mostly its flavour tends to one or the other, even if 'tis only slight.)

Not long after, the path veered and we lost sight of his cragged majesty. I felt wistful; now I would need to look behind, over my shoulder, if I wanted to admire the panorama he and his ridge afforded. Yet in remarking same internally, words immediately formed (as ever, bouncing in *over* the top of my thought): *Don't worry; I'll hold your back.* Here was *Säntis* describing the change in direction of the path from his perspective. Now he had a chance to *help* me hold the centre, to make headway against Wind's assault! I had to smile. Certainly I appreciated his support on the climb up to the pass and over into the next valley; what a lovely gesture!

Yet I understood this offer went beyond the immediacy of the situation, for it communicated that I didn't need to *see* him to know he would accompany me the *whole* way; a case of 'Love wants to come with today' in a new form. Years earlier I had received a teaching from Mr1300BC along the lines of: *You can still have a lit candle in a place you cannot see it and still know it is lit.* It was his way of saying that even though 'love' or our 'self-light' may be invisible to the eye of the senses, it still isn't an abstract concept. I have explored this in different textual ways over the years, but *Säntis'* commentary was delightfully fresh, and welcome in the moment.

In point of fact, the *true* depth of his statement – *I'll hold your back* – demonstrated how his spirit stood in collective Gaian sovereignty with our partnership task; *together* we would not be swayed from the path of walking the thread, singing up country, extending the length of Elven-rope out from the source of the sink to all. Regardless of what 'headwinds' faced, we each held each other's back; his may represent solidarity in its most solid form, but the overall message was clear: This was an alliance between Humanity and Sidhe *and* the All. For glorious Gaia.

I received the same teaching in the *Malakut* about the same time as *Säntis'* matter-of-factual commitment to the alliance. Journeying in and through 'Camino' spaces I continually met up (as if by chance) with a fellow to compare notes about the respective 'beakers' of water we carried to quench our 'thirst' along the way. They were ever-empty, but this posed no problem because walking the path *itself* ever-filled our (grail) cups. Fluid, seamless, a non-issue; we were always 'provided for' along the way by the simple *action* of our 'work' and devotion. We shrugged at the conundrum, that we never seemed to meet each other when our beakers were 'full', only ever empty. And laughed.

A lesson about trust, in the end – trust to know our work is its own sustenance; trust to know that it is the same for each pilgrim along the Way of Love. 'Tis Love that holds our back every step of the way, and we hold each other's likewise. In solidarity – such is the spirit of fellowship, of community, of partnership.

At this point I would like to remind the reader of *Stairway to Heaven*'s close-out ceremony to 'creating the home to which ...' on our last morning on Australian soil which, together with my induction into flying the 'sky-threads' across the world, seemed to open the way for a very 'unknown' business-like energy to stand at the door of Little Cove, ready to 'blow in' a next incarnation of work on my first morning back on Swiss soil.

Perhaps the reader can intuit who it was, especially given the title of this section. But, as usual, it took me a little longer. Indeed I cannot in all honesty remember when I did exactly twig to the joke, when the lines of flight in the rhizome all amassed in the (same) right place at the right time. Understanding, though, evolves in due course, arriving – like Gandalf – exactly when he means to. Indeed it grows organically with the ebb and flow of our practices to stimulate same. Thus, in walking the *Camino* I would receive further *Malakut* insights pre- and post- the different stations along the way, as well as vice versa.

In one inner experience, I 'held' the glowing orbs of light I would take with me, to bless the waterways of the land; I 'knew' them to be my scallop shells, yet they contained the energy of the stars, the energy of my original starseeds. It seems I was beginning to connect to the stars within the earth, to dance the stars in and out; I sensed that experiencing the 'uplift' of Earth-energies in support of our *Via Helvetica* alliance was another manifestation of same. Yet the specific 'flavour' of the *StarGeist* eluded me. Where was *MakerMan's* confidante?

In point of fact I had been looking in the wrong place, *within* the earth, mislead by what I had originally seen (or hooking into the narrative at the wrong point to mislead myself). I had had an inkling that her's was the pushy kid-on-the-block energy which surfaced in the wake of summer to kick-start the *Camino* project, only beginning to 'settle' when LCS was brought into the sacred pool post-*Brisi* and fully integrated after I had engaged *Helvetia's Sasso san Gottardo* crystalline heart. Yes, *StarGeist's* energy was stellar-pure; and my connective thread revealed as the fourth starseed morphing into the meteorite shard, now slivered to silvered perfection in the stone that had outreached to be popped into my pocket and brought home to the wicker sacred pool from *Leistchamm* (LCS).

Yet she had waited till Little Cove was done and dusted before engaging me directly – at the swing door of 'home' on my first jet-lagged morning returned to 'home'. I thought again about how she presented – short-cropped silver hair, eyes rimmed in kohl to 'soften' her androgynous all-in-white business-like demeanour – and laughed. I had intended to re-shave my head as a pilgrim on the path, but knew a bit of eye make-up may soften the blow for family. It seems she had gone a bit overboard trying to constellate in a way that would define her 'sisterhood' to me (or was it a case of the mirror mirroring and I would look as threatening?). Regardless, her energy signature (or flavour) was a complete unknown in the circumstances; it was the first time we had formally 'met'.

Only after-the-fact did I understand it was *her* stellar energy which sought to connect with the stars within the earth that my singing up country would support. *MakerMan* could only bring her so far, however, till the 'threshold'. We would not meet in *this* space all together to further our shared 'work'; I would need to learn to deal with her distinct 'foreignness' on my own.

A month later she tried again. My raw journal notes refer.

<u>22 November</u>: One thing very clear and strange, strong, during the night. I woke to 'Presence' beside the bed (left side). I felt the *breath* of said Presence make contact and consciously told it to back off, that it made me feel *cold*, and I didn't want it there. As it left, departed, I had such a 'glimpse' of photon-energy

before my eyes it constellated as a (I don't know) star-system-nursery-nebula. It gave me a fright; such a cold place, presence – nothing like anything I have ever encountered before. I really couldn't deal with it, relate to it. I wonder if it will return in a 'form' that is more able to interact with my energy – because I can't 'step up' to its level, has it the 'skills' to step down to lowly me? I still appreciate its courtesy and respect, however, backing off when it was clear I found the connection 'uncomfortable'. Intriguing, nonetheless – wherefrom, whereto, and why?

23 November: What to make of encounters overnight? Strangely I woke at 12.45am bolt upright out of a *Malakut* space, no recollection, the full-dark-full-deal; I got up, walked about a bit, still felt as if *outside* of myself; even walking around, I wondered: Is this 'real' or am I still *out*, still connected to whatever space I had been in? Sat down, closed my eyes; suddenly, an image appeared, like a postcard or street sign with a message on it for me that 'P' (which I understood to be a 'star-energy-system-presence') was this way with an arrow. It was a message *from* Presence itself; a bit jokey in a way because I had a giggle at its 're-appearance' with this light-hearted take on our 'engagement'. Thus did I realise where I had been and with 'whom'. Exhilarating in a way, yet matter-of-factual: A star had left its 'calling card' if I ever wanted to find my way back again.

One more memory now re-surfacing, of how momentous (I think) the overnight encounters were (as in: universal energy was 'busy' last night), was that at some point, already lucidly conscious (so within whichever space I don't know but I was very *present* there), a huge bang or crack sounded in the room which brought me immediately back to the now-of-here. I know it was connected to the plane of consciousness I engaged at the time: 'Presence' so strong, it crossed into the material (or *stretched* the boundary; like a sonic boom, breaking the speed of sound in a way? Is this how stellar energy manifests?). So *insanely* loud I really thought it would wake F, but no, I the only 'witness' to the moment, in as well as out of it. Hmmm.

Little more than a week later she returned, with a lesson to help me engage her profound otherness, her alterity. (Nevertheless, as representative of the *ganz andere*, I did like the way she attempted to previously connect through humour or sisterhood … perhaps she had sought the counsel of *MakerMan* as to what had worked in the past with me?)

2 December: 'Tis 2am. Lucid out of a space, now I sit – to reflect, remember. 'Twas a lesson, at least twice-repeated. I stood in a long tunnel and at its far

end, a wizened witch with long white hair sat on a chair, waiting. My lesson, in the face of her far-distant yet *very*-present presence (as in I felt the *full force* of her identity even though I was so 'far back' in the tunnel) was to stand firm, grounded in my identity, sovereignty, to not be scared, intimidated or whatever. Why? For its own sake, of course, but also, as I stared unblinking and firm into her face, I would see how *all* her exterior features dissolved, like a seamless shapeshifting and stripping of 'self' to return to the core of her *essence* of being. At which point the presence wasn't intimidating or scary or too overwhelming for me to deal with. At which I could meet it/her on equal terms, footing.

The lesson repeated at least twice (I guess to get me used to 'practicing' being comfortable in the situation, so probably more than twice, but my conscious awareness only remarked two times with clarity) – it was a real: Stand firm and *stay* with the encounter, the experience until it reveals its *true* nature at which time you can engage (if you wish). In the space I knew this to be a *very* important lesson.

Was it asking me (amongst other things) to come back to the Presence I had told to leave because its energy was 'too cold'? Is it saying the responsibility lies with me to stand firm in my sovereignty and then the crystal pillar that is *my* sovereignty would be capable of dealing with it, going with it till it 'revealed' itself as ripe for engaging? Hmmm. Is it the solidity, the solidarity of *my* presence which it needs? Which offers it (perhaps) the means by which to reveal *its* true nature? ... Is this a sort-of take on M's comments in *Conversations*?

Thus do we return to Mariel and 'grounded fluidity' (p.52). But in dealing with the *ganz andere* nature of P's particular form of stellar energy, one with which I have had no previous experience (by comparison, Gary G et al have been much easier to tolerate), I was also drawn to this line of commentary to assist cognition:

'Many of the relationships which Gaia has with its cosmic environment and family are changing, and we – you and I – are part of this change ... Gaia gains a new "subtle body", and as she does so, you and we do as well ... It means that more energies from the stars will flow into this world, and the living energy of the planet will in turn flow more freely into the cosmos' (p.55-6). In another section of the text, she talks about how this frees our ability to hear star-songs more fully: 'While this change will make it easier for you to connect with stellar energies, (its purpose is) ... to enable you to blend more fully with it ... to see and hear and be part of the 'stars within the earth' (p.100-1).

Clearly all interwoven; I was simply more (naturally) attuned to the 'back-end' of the pipe (so-to-speak) with my connection to mountain and stone sentience; the *StarGeist* energies of P, however, were drawing me *out* in order to contribute more *in*. Indeed do we come from the stars and return to the stars. I had re-learnt to fly for a reason. All known, all in, long before surface consciousness was asked to engage a star-system-nursery-nebula which latterly took the form of a white witch.

My lesson of the starseed which transformed into the 'live' density of 'Earth-consciousness' refers: 'For the stellar realms to connect with us as *intended*, we need to return this ball to the stars … (to) be absorbed by the energies, their reciprocity of which would enable the continued 'evolution' of our Earth-consciousness here in material space and time' (from Chapter 5). Together with P, I was ready to weave the threads here, to be the quarry *and* the stars, across a threshold my Sidhe companions could not cross – yet knowing that in *this* task they remained my very *present* partners, dedicated to 'holding my back'. Thanks be!

In Medias Res

Oft-quoted but never bettered for my Huxleyian mode is Emerson's observation that the soul already contains in itself the event that befalls it, 'for the event is only the actualizing of its thoughts' (from his essay, *Fate*). This text bears testament to same, but in all honesty any coherency in the threads which tell of said events has only been made possible by the excellent weaving of David, Jeremy and Mariel onto which foundation this tale could be liberally grafted.

In his Norton Lecture on *Quickness*, Italo Calvino shares a legend about the emperor Charlemagne whereby a symbolic object (in this case, a magic ring) holds a chain of events together in the narrative. He suggests that the object is the 'real protagonist of the story … an outward and visible sign that reveals the connection between people or between events.' Around it, he continues, there 'forms a kind of force field that is in fact the *territory* of the story itself.' He cites Norse sagas, chivalric romances and Renaissance poetry as examples: 'The moment an object appears in a narrative, it is charged with a special force and becomes like the pole of a magnetic field, a knot in the network of invisible relationships. The symbolism of an object may be more or less explicit, but it is always there' (from *Six Memos for the Next Millennium*, p.32-33).

I would add to Calvino's list the *Card Deck of the Sidhe* – the real protagonist, the 'star' in the adventures related herein. It has held together the narrative, tied the knot in the network of relationships, embodied the pole of its 'magnetic field'. Indeed Calvino's list is a Bard's list, and who if not *MossMan* was ready to sing this story into being? Not to be outdone, who if not *MakerMan* was capable of choreographing our performance? And who if not *MagicMan* stood ready to 'hold my back' each step of the way from source to sea to (stellar) source? Finally, who if not *VanDiemen'sMan* kept me to the promise to write every day?

To each of these Heart Stones my deepest heart-felt thanks – if *you* had not existed, if *you* had not been drawn into the force field by the energy of the *Card*

Deck, self-naming within the Stone Circle, working to contain and channel aetheric intent toward material manifestation, would this text have *existed*, could our tale have ever been *told*?

In *Death and the Dervish*, Mesa Selimovic pens the following dialogue between the Sheikh and Hassan (p.108):

> S: *Nothing exists until it is told.*
>
> H: *Nothing can be told until it exists. The only question is whether anything should be told.*

But what is it that we mean by existence? The *Card Deck's* existence opened an energetic portal to our wonderful cousins who have ever, always existed – yet facilitating and *quickening* exchange more than I could have achieved alone; providing context and background to our shared ancestry that deepened perspective and initiated engagement to the point of partnered co-performance; all of which enabled me to tell the story of its unfolding. Yet Hasan's perspective is valid; the question must be put: *Did our story need to be told?*

Clearly the Stone Circle responded with a resounding 'yes'. *Together* we agreed the story of our adventures this past year were astonishingly rich – how each helped the other to co-create beautiful outcomes – ever-ongoing – in service to Gaia.

Mariel says: 'In partnership with us, our desire is for you to become like the Old Ones who stood and formed the first circles' (p.141). And indeed I feel it to be so – in the way the different Stones and Dancers constellated into a permanent Council with advisors stepping in, in support, as and when required; in the way I felt myself 'adopted' into a lineage of guardianship of the grails, standing in sovereignty as an equal amongst the *Companions of the Way*, here at the place 'where stars and earth meet'.

On this basis did we agree to uplift our partnership to text, to share these learnings on. So here 'tis, the inner outed, and gifted back to Lorian's care in the hope it may inspire others' journeys and adventures likewise.

With the *Card Deck* as mediator, we were blessed to be able to build: 'A collaborative presence, a shared field of vitality, energy and inspiration' (p.82); in so doing, our 'field-experiences' reflect David's description of the original impulse for the deck's manifestation: 'It is blessed as an expression of their love for the world and their desire to join with human partners in serving the wellbeing of the planet and bringing to birth a Gaian consciousness that allows us to live in the world more ecologically and holistically' (p.85).

Indeed I hope and trust this text to be ample demonstration of the *fact* of the wonderful wizardry of the *Card Deck* to inspire such outcomes – otherwise we might need to include the myriad other adventures which did not make it to the pages of the final manuscript!

Nevertheless, 'tis time to close the chapter (but never the book!). Our story of adventure began *in medias res* and ends likewise. Who knows what further events this soul contains, waiting to actualise, together with *Companions of the Way*? Clues rest in both material and *Malakut*, as they always have, always will.

Yet for now I give pause to the script, pry open a small gap in the songline ever-unspooling before these feet; a space to rest in each other's company awhile, *intermezzo*, to give thanks, and clink grail cups – the white and the red – to toast our wonderful good fortune to have met and enjoined shared unity of purpose, given voice here-now in fresh bardic song:

So do we sit, ensconced,
our picnic spread outlaid,
here in the dappled shade,
reverent cone,
of TreeMother's verdant grail.
'Tis only a brief bantering while
we rest these dusty shoes
(you too?)
before returning to the path,
of interconnectivity;
so much to explore
in this prepositional party!
In of to and through,
up over down across,
with outwith
beyond behind
beneath above
(now phew!).
Each and every one
a becoming landscape
all its own;
each and every one
we know as Love's
own and loving Way.
Yes, Love the Way
(the Truth the Light the Life) –
how lucky are we to walk and sing
the only Way we know?
To bring us homecome to the sea,
there and once more back again;

'tis a wee stretch of terra,
Helvetia and Australis so bountifully
bound, and lit (!);
merely a miniscule patch
of warp and weft is their
gold-silver'd gift
to Gaia's crown ...

Yet the time now come
smack bang in the midst
of in medias res
(our weaving of fine-filigreed
threads in crystal'd creation awaits)
to bid readers near far,
subtle also not-so,
a fond adieu – showered
(and with perennial blessings bower'd) –
from a Moveable Feast,
singing Joy to the World
(yea – peace, love and light refer);
immer in honour of Ancestors immortal,
Hope fiery eternal,
Alliance true, semper fidelis –
Love's blessings do we share
in material and Malakut,
ne'er to be undone in any and/or all.
'Tis an Unseen Hand that tugs
we Cousins of the Commons,
to flow, fly the thread onward,
ever on –
through the earth a path to tread;
'tis why we pilgrim-walk the stars.

Yea –

this the Way, the only Way
that we have ever known;
this the Way, the only Way
the Way of Love our Home ...

Epilogue

'We all breathe life into what we love': Mr1300BC

This text, oft-stated, began *in medias res* and I have tried my best to find a suitable place in the continuing thread of its (likewise) telling to cry halt to the chatter of voices keen for this or that aspect of partnership to be written into existence, for the chopped-off length of (my) tapeworm of time (as EM Forster was once drawn to wryly comment) to stay well and truly chopped. But (like any good tapeworm) its penchant for wriggling and squirming, stretching its neck to see what further dark tunnels of gut it can conquer, has taken hold of this writerly pen and headed off apace down paths that, to be honest, I am also excited to document.

So it is that, after the manuscript was forwarded to Lorian at the end of January, the party line telephony of the Stone Circle gleefully kicked back into life with two distinct strings of task-orientation to cleave onto all that recounted herein. And, as ever, the strings return us to the beginning, to a day two years past when I asked a question of David about my 'self-action' long before consciously embarking on a Sidhe-partnered walk. His opinion, that perhaps I had been invited to wider participation (Chapter Two refers), referenced the fact that we, as incarnate beings, are part of the circulation of energies in both "vertical" and "horizontal" ways. Self-action 'offers' our own energy and attunement to such circulation as a 'responsible' entity in our own right, while inviting (or being invited to) larger participation with 'allies' involves our 'larger' self making itself *part of* something big.

The last chapter described my intuition that these two streams – self-action and wider participation – had come together in the desire to sing up country across the length and breadth of *Helvetia*, the land which had adopted me – in so-doing to 'become the path itself'. As I (latterly) understood it, the notion of 'awakening to home' had morphed into an altogether grander proposition than connecting four stewarded nodes in Gaia's crystalline consciousness; it seemed this partnership of Sidhe, Star and Stone intended stretching toward a shared never-end.

Now, in the wake of manuscript delivered across the Atlantic pond, I found myself in a *Malakut* scape *still* writing, the intent to work through the proposition of how the energy of creation itself focuses, coalesces, and *densifies* to the point that whatever 'it' is that desires manifestation hasn't anywhere else to go but to manifest – somewhat like a snowball that grows as it gathers speed, *cleaving* all to itself as it rumbles downhill, till *voila!* With my companions, we demonstrated the process with light – the result uplifting, exciting, energising; a real: *Look what we can do together with the fidelity of our intent!*

Whether the (ensuing) manifestation physical or non-, in the scape 'I saw' how all creation arises from drawing together energetic threads from the aetheric – the impulse of the 'light' of Love. Yet *our* spirit of desire is what kickstarts the productive energy of creation, to purposefully *make* something from the threads it gathers together – the will to exist *needs* to exist in and of itself, a desire to 'become' required for the *flow* of light to begin streaming from the aetheric. With desire's focus, to coalesce all in and around itself, the energy densifies, self-propelling and growing all the while (like a snowball) till fully realised in form.

MakerMan – perennial helpmate in all matters process- and project-oriented, in initially awakening me to the 'history of human creativity' and how it *supports* the unfolding of holism in the world – had returned to nurture my awareness of the circulation of energies at work, how things manifest in vertical and horizontal ways. This reminded me of the process model of 'becoming' I had developed years past for my PhD on bringing subtle knowing out to the material light of day. The reader will find a description of the model in the Appendix, relevant as it is to an overall methodology I recommend for outreach to and engagement with the Sidhe.

In terms of *MakerMan's* 'snowball of the light of Love', though, it can equally be presented in the following form – and 'viewed' either on vertical axis or unfolding horizontal plane (of consistency) whereby energy spirals 'up' and 'out' from one's own becoming desire (and self-action) to participate (as one's 'larger' self) in an altogether grander action:

164

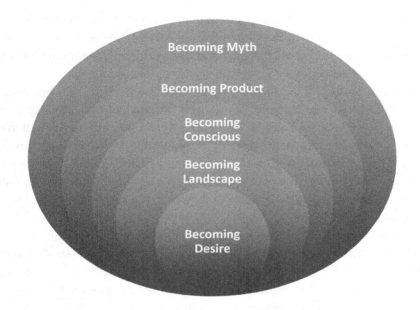

Process Model of Becoming

'Tis a case of like attracting like: From first inklings, and intuition, of a 'fuzzy' ision on a distant horizon harnessing desire's energy to *become*, we are propelled ɔ *embark* on a journey (landscape), to *make* something out of it (product), to *engage* ˥e (personal) myth of its meaning, thereafter to *gift* same into the pool of collective ͻaian) consciousness. The challenge, to which *MakerMan's* 'history' alerted me, ; the mammoth shift needed in (current mainstream human) consciousness from ɾeativity for its own sake – to feed *own*-species' desires – to partnering toward truly shared vision of Gaian holism.

Our history amply demonstrates what we can manifest in the world – to good nd ill. What would it take for *every* self-action to be joyously *gifted* to the whole, ἰrculating the energies in vertical and horizontal ways, making ourselves *daily* ˥ourly, moment-by-unfolding-moment) part of something bigger, offering our ɾeativity to *solely* serving Love's light? Could human consciousness shift from :s propensity to self-orientation to actively embrace the other (*any* other, physical r non-), to seamlessly *merge* intent with the All?

For Gregory Bateson, this would mean linking 'self and other and also *self ɉus other*, and (using) this recognition to assert the value of the *relationship* as well s the value of self and other' (1987, p.192) – a case of 'I see you' in my lexicon or ϸcology of mind' in his (see Glossary). It means being self-sovereign *and* living ˥e one-life-of-the-one-world as true-natured matter-of-course in the (self-) *same* reath; it means meeting transcendence and immanence at its (our!) *face*, aligning ˥e vertical and the horizontal at its (our!) *source*. Spinning zero degrees in a full circle, we would therefore discover potentiality for such a shift in consciousness to *become* already existent at the core of our deepest self: Love. All we need do is kick-start our *desire* for Love's light to flood the world with joy and *its* energy of *creation* will do the rest.

Lee Irwin coins the expression 'mergence' to speak to this proposition of experiencing the world as an increasingly expansive interactive sphere of 'becoming', *grounded* in love and *fuelled* by love: 'Our ability to discover patterns of *emergence*, of shared correspondences, of the magical links and leylines threaded through all worlds and conditions, opens the horizons of knowledge to an increasingly greater spectrum of possibility (and …) can lead to increasing insight and empathy with all worlds and beings (where …) each individual contributes to the whole' (p.182-3).

In the moment of *MakerMan*'s visit, my thoughts spiralled: Can we rise to this task, to this duty as a collective? Can we engage such a process of becoming toward a vision of humanity as *true* Gaiatarians? In all our three hundred (and more) lives of 'men' walking the Earth, living and acting as we have, is there still *time* for this shift of consciousness? Returning from the *Malakut*, I found a heightened resonance in the ten-foot-square hut centred at my right ear, and a split second later a double-crack of the wood in the cupboard announcing Presence had returned with me; we had stretched the boundary in our musings. OK, said *MakerMan*, you got it. But now I'm off. Thus did I farewell her, with thanks, and continued my own contemplations on how our Stone Circle supports the model of becoming as both vertical and horizontal proposition:

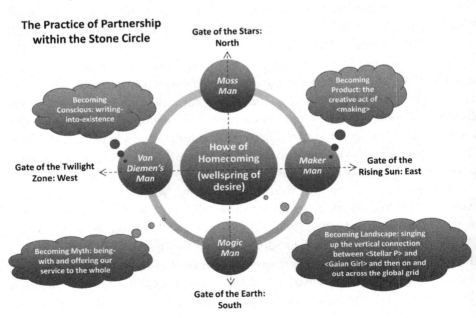

The Practice of Partnership within the Stone Circle

Gate of the Stars: North

Moss Man

Becoming Product: the creative act of <making>

Becoming Conscious: writing-into-existence

Gate of the Twilight Zone: West

Van Diemen's Man

Howe of Homecoming (wellspring of desire)

Maker Man

Gate of the Rising Sun: East

Becoming Myth: being-with and offering our service to the whole

Magic Man

Becoming Landscape: singing up the vertical connection between <Stellar P> and <Gaian Girl> and then on and out across the global grid

Gate of the Earth: South

I apologise for how convoluted the model appears. Its central node is where I sit in the Circle, all cards outlaid around me. My wellspring of generative desire 'summons' the Council, and the four Heart Stones at their directional axes placements 'hold' the energies of becoming according to each's core 'strength'. While the full 'landscape' sings up the (becoming) energetic connection vertically and horizontally, *MossMan* and *MagicMan* are clearly the lead (vertical) voices in the performance between 'heaven and earth'; and while *MakerMan* concentrates on 'product' and *VanDiemen'sMan* on 'consciousness', their tasks twin and merge to form the requisite (horizontal) string 'out across the world'.

The full Council, as an *entity* in its own right, demonstrates how the practice of partnership becomes a shared 'myth' of being-with (in support of *my* intent) as well as offering service to the whole by making the entity *itself* part of something bigger – a collective mythical undertaking, if you like. It is as if this broader intent, that of *together*-work, as a fuzzy vision on our *shared* horizon, had suddenly come into striking distance as an *outcome* of completing the manuscript. It was as if the energy of the *manuscript's* creation had focused, coalesced, and densified to such a point that whatever *its* underlying intent (which desired manifestation) was, it had *nowhere* else to go but back *into* the Stone Circle, to manifest therein the *next* incarnation of our partnership's 'becoming'.

In the spirit of Mr1300BC's counsel: *We all breathe life into what we love*, it seems that, through our love, we had breathed such life into the cauldron of the grail space that even if members of the Council had wanted to step back, they simply could not. The incarnate Circle *itself* called, the alchemy set in train by our work *desired* manifestation. And *MakerMan*, reading the signs, seeing how we had stretched the boundary with our practice, had come to say I still had another chapter to write, to describe what we were *all* experiencing as this 'latter-incarnation' unfolded, unexpectedly, in our midst over little more than a couple of weeks ...

How did I know this was bigger than (as Mariel says): 'Once you set forth your intent, we can blend with the field you create and enhance its capacities to connect and to manifest' (p.147)? Because from my point of view, the intent to produce the text had been achieved; equally my companions were high-fiving round the Circle once I hit the 'send' button on the email to Jeremy: *All over red rover*. Till suddenly I was 'called back in'; this the first time I have ever sat at a *Malakut* desk to (physically) document process and with colleagues' input actually *in* the space. It meant I became aware that the audience for this text need not be restricted to human Lorian readers. I had written in our closing bardic song that the time had come to lift the pen, '*to bid readers near far, subtle also not-so, a fond adieu ...*'; a line composed as whimsy, it returned now in the context of my *inner* writing to suggest there is a repository, a *Malakut* library, to which our shared experience shall be added, to support work on the Sidhe side of the veil in their outreach to us.

Indeed, during the project I had already been called on to provide input from humanity's perspective in small group discussions and workshops as part of our shared task-orientation. In one respect this is how the *specificity* of the 'invitation to participation' manifested in my experience; now in the same spirit it seemed the text would also be offered back *in* as a contribution. In other words, the project was not just about seeking energetic outcomes on Gaia's behalf in the physical world, but the experience of partnership *itself* was an outcome offering a methodology to guide inner worlds on their approach of the 'human' as 'stakeholder-partner'.

In the end that is by-the-by, however – a valued (and valid) opportunity to complement our practice. By far the more exciting development was our experience of the Stone Circle's extant incarnation. Let me try to explain its unfolding:

Standing in the kitchen, chopping veges, listening to a CD aptly named *Alpstein*, haunting instrumentals inspired by the selfsame chain that *Säntis* (he of 'I'll hold your back' fame) overlights. CD over, I randomly choose another, (Aussie) Nick Cave's *Let Love In*, in which one of my favourite songs riffs: *Do you love me?* Somehow these twinned in the *Malakut* after lights-out that night when I 'heard' the cellar door close – a hollow sound which echoed up the stairs to where I sat 'working' on the manuscript in my (*Malakut*) living room.

In the space, I began writing that growing up where I did I had never experienced such a sound – cellars being a foreign concept in the sub-tropics. Nevertheless, I described how I found it a comforting, *earthing* sound, yet one filled with mystery – unless I go down to meet the mystery at its source, I cannot find out what it contains. At this point text shifted to image: emanating from a particular point in the stellar realms, 'I saw' a vertical line of light go deep into the planetary core. In between this vertical connection is where I 'sat' in the space. I understood it to be like the Earth-energies vortex in reverse (that which I had unwittingly 'tapped' into with my little self-action in the Alps two years past, and on which I had sought David's original counsel). Instead of coating the membrane of the world's atmosphere by shooting up into space, it spiralled down, flowing along a line of consciousness into the Earth beneath my feet. Words formed: *BergGeist, StarGeist und ich* (i.e. Stone, Star and I).

I returned to my inner text and wrote: *Stretching the boundary to the heart of stone* – I needed to figure out how my length of Elven-rope could reach to the very core, the 'kiln room' where I had seen the beating heart in the chalice so long ago. In the moment I understood that our Circle could facilitate such a 'hook into the whole' from what we had learnt (and experienced together thus far) through which *StarGeist* P could connect to the stars within the earth cradled in the embrace of mountain sentience, a connection to the 'magic of the mantle' we had sung awake.

(Note that in the above model I name *StarGeist*'s stellar specificity 'Stellar P' (cue Marlon Brando in *A Streetcar Named Desire*) and her earthen counterpart 'Gaian Girl' (cue *Helvetia*'s crystal heart). In between 'sits' the Stone Circle.)

Throughout all of my *Malakut* writing and visioning, Nick background-sings *Do you Love Me?* Or rather *MagicMan* posing as Nick (the reader will surely recall his cheeky attitude – perhaps he felt he needed a signature tune to rival *MossMan*'s – i.e. *Don't You Forget About Me* ... too?). I understood what he was implying, however, for the entire refrain goes: *Do you love me, like I love you?* In this respect, if *MossMan* supports Stellar P's alignment and *MagicMan* Gaian Girl's, what *depth* of connection is required for the *BergGeist, StarGeist und ich* attunement to work? Answer: Each needs to love as (like) the other loves along the whole thread of light for the energetic connection to be optimised, for the flow to seamlessly flow, for the harmony of performance to be balanced in the musical score.

I surfaced from this encounter and once more, *MakerMan* 'cracked' the cupboard in farewell while I lay with furrowed brow trying to figure how to attune to a resonance for 'meeting' the stars within the earth at a place where I wouldn't feel 'cold' (P's energy signature, recounted in the last chapter, refers), at a place within, rather than outside the Circle, ringing the door to home (whether material or *Malakut*). At some level I knew I needed to learn to separate the acts – of being (self), of flowing (other), somewhat akin to David's counsel on holding boundaries and maintaining sovereignty. In this instance, *ich* needed to act as a nodal entity at the same time (and in the same loving spirit) as *BergGeist* and *StarGeist*. Once the connection 'stabilised', the flow from 'source to sea to source' could then occur as a matter of course (or so I hoped!).

I thought of dear *Säntis, BergGeist* of the *Alpstein*, holding my back so I could walk my sovereignty through *Helvetia*'s sink of peace, now being implicated in supporting this next incarnation of shared solidarity in Gaian space. I recalled Mariel's words: 'Mountain spirits are among humanity's greatest allies in the changes that you face, though you don't realise it' (p.131). But I still didn't know what form such alliance would be expected to take, or when.

Four days later it hit; trying to explain its felt-sense I wrote in my journal:

I'm not fully here, yet am fully here. Just *not-earthed*; it exhibits as 'light-headedness' and an internal shiver or tremor. In (brief) meditation, I discover a dizzying vortex of swirling energy flowing up and down through the chakras. It connects (up) to 'heaven' in a clockwise direction, then (down) to 'earth' anticlockwise. Both at the same time which is the dizzying part (and almost like a feeling of travel sickness!). It's as if the verticality is plugged in well and truly today for whatever reason, but in walking the connection 'out', will it help settle me?

In *Malakut* wanders that night, I constantly went in and out of spaces, eagerly affirming an understanding to *earth* myself in the soil of existence simultaneous to connecting with the *aether* of universal energy. I saw this as a function of being barefoot in either context – skin-to-skin with the earth at the same time as dancing my 'soul-self' through the cosmos (a case of Beauty's *aethereal-material* counsel brought into an actual practice of how Stones and Dancers interact within the Circle). The funny thing was it had to do with drinking Lady Grey tea for the earth-conduit to be optimised and Earl Grey for the universal. Ah, my Huxleyian mode – I certainly won't have a problem enacting that guidance!

Things settled for about ten days. Then the next *Malakut* scape beckoned – over and over a single word repeated, in image: *Chthonic*. Never spoken. I assume because it would have been irrelevant; I had only encountered the word once before, in a Jungian text, but so long past I didn't even know how it was spelt anymore, let alone how to pronounce it. The word was used to describe the destination of an excursion beneath the mantle. An 'into the heart of the felt world' encounter, it had been the full-dark-full-deal – for me at least. 'I' had no memory of the place, only of arriving back on the surface of an *Amici* high wild, a granite-cropped gorse- and heathered-scape, chatting to others while waiting for the last members of our group to return.

Later we sat in the *Amici* hut, around its long table, where I mentioned to a fellow beside me that I didn't realise this is how the 'chthonic' would affect me; even though I felt well, it seems it could be a bit messy and I suggested he move back in case 'hit' by the reaction. It turned out to manifest similarly to the 'head fountain' visualisation of two years prior but this time laval-red in presentation. None of it harmful, simply a courtesy in case he needed towelling off afterwards...

Interestingly, three days prior I had received a gift from the *Amici* which had left me glowing with happiness. However, only now, in preparing the chapter have I put the two together – it had been a 'deposit' to my 'bank account' which I found when checking the 'balance' at a *Malakut* ATM (very cleverly designed!). The gift was a bottle of crystal clear water, *so* clear and pure that I could not even be sure if there was anything in it; but it was stoppered, so yes. The bottle's design was highly reminiscent of the wine glass *Moveable Feast* filled for me at the formal dinner to which F and I had been invited, yet the silver motifs were all of sweet *Wildmännli* swirled into its glass skin. The water itself was as clear as the bottled 'light' we had brought home from our outing to *Sasso san Gottardo*, *Helvetia*'s crystal heart, last autumn. It still sat, unopened, on the shelf. Was it time to take a literal sip?

I now turn to the raw notes of my journal to conclude this part of the Circle's myth-making:

<u>24 February</u>: YMM. Difficult to describe the feeling (or movement) but by the meditation's conclusion, I felt myself, my form, as a flame (red, 'chthonic'). A living flame like that emanating from a candle – in shape/form/constancy – but no candle or wick, only pure flame. My whole form this shape, this fire, and I felt it mirror my pattern of breathing love in, out, through self and world at the same time. So the shape and form of my breath (my love) was the flame.

Of course, Mr1300BC's words from years back arose in the moment: *Love in itself is fire*; also my insight that the shape not only equated with the lotus pose I adopted in meditation, but with the form of hands raised in prayer – prayerful hands thus an expression (in the everyday) of our embodiment as living flames of love in the world. Within the space of meditative repose, however, simply being the flame was its expression, no need of hands. Now, backtracking to the moment of felt-sense, that my body – in this shape – *itself* a flame of love, I sensed the Stone Circle to be flaming in its own right too. All stones stood solidly tall, flaming (or flaring) before settling down to a glowing permanency of presence. I understood this as another way of 'holding my back'; it meant my flame 'protected' – safe, held within the grail space; it was as if the Circle a glass bowl or cone which kept the wind from sputtering or even wafting the flame with its own encircling 'ring of fire'.

The point to the flame (mine, and the Circle's) was constancy. Keeping steady, true, unwavering meant the flame could focus on task rather than having to 'weather' the storms and winds of time, change et al. In the moment I also recalled the 'bodyguard' who had come and introduced himself to me the day after our 'chthonic' wander. A young man – fit, healthy, long dark hair pulled back in a ponytail – he'd arrived all sweaty, covered in grit, dirt and soot, as if out of the earth itself; had come and said he was here to protect and watch out for me in this volatile setting.

At some level I knew what he meant; some months prior I had been instructed in how to 'anchor' myself in a cliff of rock (using resonance) in order to stand firm in the face of come what may. Clarity and courage and other-centred compassion our shield against less-than amicable forces. But I certainly wasn't going to turn down what I understood from him to be a genuine offer. He reached out, shook my hand – casual, but very professional. Is this *Shaping Man* taking form at last, a protective force because he knows how to work with fire, has longer-than experience singing up Ancestral country, can 'read' the volatility or unpredictability of forces that may be encountered in the chthonic depths, and has skills to support my management of the differential in 'tapping' the different energy streams? Thanks be!

<u>25 February</u>: YMM. The resonant hum purring welcome and I just wanted to be part of it so ... no cards (I told them) just a short meditation with 'my' flame. But then at some point the equation presented: *Cards + Flame = Glowing Field/ Frame* and I thought: OK, you win ... Early on I 'knew' visitors were present to the Circle. I had several little photon 'hellos' (each discrete) before we settled into the space. And then I simply *was* the flame and felt the presence of the Circle equally aflame; a sense of radiation, irradiation, that the energy was fully 'live' and connected; beyond the boundaries of 'me', the air/aether of the whole grail space 'charged'.

I breathed through being a vertical connection between 'heaven and earth' as a flame and then radiated it out horizontally into the world (thus noticing the twinned 'charge' between self and circle stones), until at some point I realised that above my third eye, somewhere between sixth and seventh chakras, a broad generalised Presence had entered the Circle, specifically focused on my cognition. It was white/silver-ish, swirled, concentrated; gradually it settled itself in the space. And even though I had never encountered her Presence in this form or location before, I instantly knew who had arrived, the star-system-nursery-nebula thingey called P. At that I was pleasantly surprised; no longer 'cold', it was a neutral energy, and in the moment I sensed that my 'flame' together with the glowing circle of Sidhe 'support' had enabled P's entry in a form I could deal with.

Somehow, in that exact same moment, I understood this was no abstract or symbolic connection between 'heaven and earth' that I engaged with my 'connective thread' mantras or 'flame-of-self', but one specifically focused on a particular *living* stellar presence. No longer meeting P in the *Malakut* but literally drawing her energy into the material. Our task, the Stone Circle's task, to welcome her to the cauldron, halfway-house (if you like) to connecting with the stars within the earth. I couldn't believe it – we were seriously engaging a cosmic specificity *directly*? The felt-sense was extraordinary – and somehow, intriguingly, I knew exactly what to do. The flame of me *stretched* and extended to meet her and draw her energy back down, to *pour* it into and out through the cauldron. It was difficult, exhausting, and I gradually needed to close up the shop ... I had no desire to pass out!

As I came up and out, stared at the snow falling down, felt the solidarity of all Stones and Dancers with me in the moment, I suddenly realised our task *in* and *as* the Stone Circle. Not just to be with each other, to help each other with each other's work, but this our collective task *each* time we sit together, to specifically help P's light and love connect with the stars within the earth – *BergGeist, StarGeist und ich*, stretching the boundary to the heart of stone. I looked down to how the Circle was laid out, all round me. Holding my back, this

172

grail space protected, safe, loving … sitting with me here within the *Kiln Room* of the *Mountain* (above as below) my *Companions* as well as my *Homecome* self – truly a partnership of Sidhe, Star and Stone, fully awakened to what it means to be called home …

26 February: The crystal beacons are lit, Gaia calls for aid and we Horse Lords from the North, through the Gate of the Stars, shall answer. Everything has come together – I had wondered how the connection between my felt-sense as crystal pillar, *Helvetia*'s crystalline heart, and new Maleny's crystal mountain appearing and disappearing from view (amongst others) would coalesce, *converge* with the 'flame-of-self'. I sat again as the flame and suddenly 'saw' the snow swept up to aetheric heights by high winds over *Gridone* caught by the setting sun. *The crystal beacons are lit!* I wrote at the time and never *not* wanted to observe the phenomenon, so exhilarating to watch, to participate in (even at a distance: spooky entanglement refers!), when suddenly the firefly sparks took off in the rhizome, intersected with the Stone Circle; our task to enduringly, with constancy, keep the flame of our crystal beacon at our threshold of the felt world alight, to connect the stars within the earth with their cosmic family.

Again I felt the Stone Circle aflame; around me a ring of fire, stones flaring, our shared breath like a bellows causing the beacon to reach high into the sky and (in connecting to stellar energy), pull it back down, reel it in; there was such a felt-sense of literal outreach as flame (self and combined) and the stellar 'flame' (hooked into) returning with us to here. I couldn't go with it for long because I was so intent on observing, analysing, understanding the process so that in future I would be able to just give in to task without any further ado.

In 'getting it', a 'zing' of energy coursed through me. Not a warm (self) soul-hug, this had a nip to it, a slight chill, lower than ambient air or body temperature; not disturbing but noticeably 'other'. I understood it to be P (remembering how cold she had presented originally … pure ice from a distant dimension); yet the felt-sense of how her reciprocal recognition, her touch-of-love affected me was as if all my self-crystals inside were popping open with the 'energy injection' (like kernels of corn popped in a pan on movie night). It could almost be individualised: I noticed each one 'going off' and had to laugh, the crystal beacons definitely 'lit' in extraordinary and consciously-felt form. So glad too that as soon as it began I could find an analogy that made sense of the phenomenon for my wee brain – crystal popcorn!

The month ended, and so will I (for now) on this (sung) note. I sat (as usual) with my companions following YMM and was drawn to meditate the 'flame-of-self' in outreach to P. Again I 'wore' the mantle as part of our shared commitment

173

to task, donning the midnight blue cloak as usual as I spoke the words: *I wear a mantle of starlight here in the world to bring the energy of the Stars streaming to Earth* … but this time I sensed how my friends tied the length of fabric at my wrists (with a quick Faerie-flick) as well as hooked it about my shoulders so it could stay in place while I performed the ritual sky circles of joy before we communed, aflame, as one, as circle of blessed fellowship.

In the moment I *felt* how the mantle subtly shapeshifted into angel's wings, the embrace of the angel akin to all stellar energies held within the container of cloak till sent forth into the world, these glittering enlightened specks of (star) dust breeze-blown away for another day's joyous work detail. It was exactly a year since I had stepped into the Circle and agreed to share guardianship of the grail; it was four months since I had been gifted my own starlit-woven gossamer mantle of midnight blue.

At the time I did not remark the anniversary of formal partnership, but clearly my companions had made a notch in the calendar. The only thing I had noticed in a bright-lit *Malakut* scape was that my hiking boots were in serious trouble, the whole tread cracked and broken. In the moment (of complaint – these were expensive boots!), I consciously remarked that they had *only* lasted a year. I couldn't believe it – they were completely shot! Had I really walked so far in such a short time? Had the terrain really been so tough? My friends soothed raw nerves – cobblers existed in their world too (!); all would be put to right. I calmed down, smiled and apologised to these sturdy shoes; loyal (and literal) foot soldiers they had brought me all this way on a shared quest; perhaps we both just needed a little rest …

So is it done, our work? No, never done, no matter how many lives we walk the Earth, no matter how many skins or mantles of starlight we wear. Time is ever of the essence. The Stone Circle's incarnation as a cauldron 'charged' with its own (vertical) alchemical remit continues apace, and so do we keep walking the thread out into the (horizontal) world, singing up country, singing a songline of Love, of crystalline consciousness, into being, over, ever over – in honour of the Ancestors, in honour of Hope, in honour of the Alliance between Humanity and Faerie. And all for our wondrous Gaia.

Thank you for reading …

Appendix: Rituals of Awakening

***MossMan*, dear Findling, so do I name thee
my standing stone in space-time.**

As described at the outset of this text, the invitation I received from Sidhe companions of the way to participate in shared worldwork in service of Gaia's evolutionary consciousness led to the development of *Rituals of Awakening* in order to establish 'new' nodes in the planetary grid, their purpose to assist the flow of 'rivers of light' into and across the world. While the process of engagement facilitated by the *Card Deck* may have been specific to *our* task, as the rituals evolved – and, more importantly, demonstrated their effectiveness – their potential to constitute a *replicable* methodology was seeded within the Stone Circle.

In this appendix, therefore, I offer our recommendations as guidance or (at least) thought-prompts for others' own journeys in company of the *Card Deck*, specifically speaking to the awakening (or re-awakening) of the 'stars within the earth', those housed within (or aligned with) the stillness of stone. Standing or otherwise – huge, human-commensurate or pebble (pocket-sized) – I understand them to be containers of mountain sentience pure, and central to the process. Mariel's words were indeed an inspiration to us in undertaking this 'experiment', one way amongst the many for humanity to engage with subtle energies toward a shared vision of Gaian holism:

The crystal matrix of planetary forces is still as available to you as it is to us. As we who became Sidhe retreated, and you who became human expanded upon the world you carried with you the memory of the telluric technology of node, connection, and flow, shaped by song and dance and ritual. Guided by this memory, you discovered new ways to tap the sites of power. The practice of building stone circles and erecting standing stones began. What once was done by a person became embodied in stone. This worked as long as the stones were alive, but as the descent into matter continued, and much more importantly, as you lost the ability to form connections with the livingness of matter, the stones have become just what you see today, dormant and in some cases truly dead to the ancient powers. (*Conversations*, pp.37-38)

By way of introduction to what this appendix documents, my plan is to firstly outline a generalist methodology of outreach and engagement coupled with recommendations and guidance based on our 'ethnographic fieldwork' (to date!). Following, in the interests of transparency, I include the actual rituals developed to consecrate (and work within) *TreeMother's* grail space as well as to awaken *MossManFindling* to shared purpose.

Although these are specifically bound to task-orientation and location, they provide context for the depth and breadth of partnership energy engaged; so too demonstrating the sincere nature of our commitment, and the loving spirit underpinning process – such things a general methodological outline cannot achieve. Perhaps certain elements within these texts may also trigger a reader's own thoughts of evolving ritual? Experience has taught me that disparate conversation partners 'speak' to different parts of our psyche. In any case, all is offered from our Stone Circle in good faith. May the reader's own journeys be as blessed as ours.

Methodology of Outreach and Engagement

Let me begin by affirming the value of simply being-with the *Card Deck*. Laying them out, listening for their arising voices, seeing which cards (or elements within their images) connect to place-holders within our depths or perhaps to feelings encountered in the outer world of the senses. Anything which burbles up, *any* snatch of text or word-image:

Write or sketch its essence into *material* being.

Externalising memory in this way is not only valuable for people who have a lousy memory at the best of times (i.e. myself) but itself represents a valid methodology, a process of gradually bringing inner knowing out to the light of day where it can be scrutinised, interrogated, engaged from a place of (non-local) witness by one's self, its 'creator'. And, there resting on a plane of *intimate* exteriority, lies its potentiality to be moulded (with loving intent) further. (Here,

Hesse's Demian is a worthy conversation partner – see Glossary.)

Jeremy's *Card Deck* images indeed provide the trigger, but our own souls the linking thread, the connective resonance to which Sidhe can attune on a bedrock of loving intent. In my case this manifested as the cards' specific self-naming, but it can amplify in other ways as well. As such, 'listening' is the greatest gift we bring to our engagement – in order to grow our *own* consciousness of how the cards interact with the deepest part of our selves as much as being open to any and all voices arriving on the wind.

From there a flow of energy can commence between we 'Cousins of the Commons'. A slow dance of courtship, granted, but when underpinned by the way-of-love, the 'speed' of connection is immaterial; its durability – forged on reciprocal recognition, on welcoming the speech of the other in oneself – is the critical ingredient, the 'eggy-binder' for establishing genuine alliance and partnership.

Further, what I was to discover in my own partnership with Sidhe is that its evolution followed an arc which I had previously lived through, one which – in its documentation and reflection thereon – I used to develop a *Process Model of Becoming* as a key output of my PhD research on bringing inner (i.e. subtle) knowing (back) out into the world of time.

Here, I offer a skeleton of the model (populated with examples from our alliance). It mocks-up the different stages encountered from pre-partnership commencement through a full cycle of project- (or task-) orientation, before circling back to the beginning for a next course of partnership work to commence – like its own ring song, in a way.

'Tis a model which mirrors Eliot's bardic wisdom – and yes, even down to his profound insight (breathtakingly expressed) that Love's calling is what sets us to action in the first place:

> With the drawing of this Love and the voice of this Calling
> We shall not cease from exploration
> And the end of all our exploring
> Will be to arrive where we started
> And know the place for the first time.
> (from *Little Gidding*, in *Four Quartets*, 1944)

'Tis also a model which I cannot help but articulate symbolically, with *Malakut*-oned sight (said Huxleyian mode refers). As well none of the stages should e seen as discrete. My longer-than experience indicates that such partnership rocesses are perennially iterative as new knowledge and learnings enter the quation at different junctures, requiring feedback loops as an accepted matter-of-course rather than teeth-gnashing frustration.

Like swirling eddies in a flowing stream, these function both *within* an between the various stages (even if one operates within a circle-of-self). 'Becoming after all, is an unfixed proposition; *flow* is implicated in its very utterance; dynami energy rests at its very core, and must be acknowledged as such by anyon committed to following the path (from source to sea to source).

Yet in *harnessing* such flow within the framework of a model, we brin grounded fluidity to our partnership with the Sidhe in the spirit of Mariel counsel: 'In dealing with us, you must strengthen this adaptability ... (It i your fluid self, but it's a "grounded fluidity" ... When you successfully adapt t and flow with changing circumstances in your life, you are fluid in a grounded practical way, one that is connected to what is happening and to your environmen You are not simply swept away' (pp.52-3).

My after-the-fact counsel, therefore, is that by *externalising* intent and proces in the graphic representation of a model, it may help moderate and focus an project entered in company with Sidhe, as well as provide a blueprint for futur engagement (as my PhD model proved to be – once re-found whilst penning thi text). At the very least it provides a reflective space to engage Sidhe energy *outwit* one's inner self, as witness to its *becoming* and where its energy of potentialit seems to be directing the flow of the river of light.

In my case, this included a literal flow-chart of shared work between th various 'Annes' (together with their hand-holding 'muses') as recounted in th text – iterative feedback loops a persistently necessary adjunct, especially whe various Stone Circle Council members (as well as *Card Deck* Dancers) offere specific suggestions for follow-up. I find mind-mapping difficult enough whe one mind is involved – the potential for a process to become unwieldy and dera itself with many voices is something to keep in mind.

Mariel may have said: 'Once you set forth your intent, we can blend with th field you create and enhance its capacities to connect and to manifest' (p.147 but our intent needs to be clear to ourselves in the first place to ensure that th (fallow) field is sown with that which we hope to reap. Yet if intent is fuzzy? Nc yet discernibly formed, still hovering on the horizon?

The experiences I relate in this text indicate that our process kept cyclin – spiralling on to ever-greater tasks (experiments?) once the basic partnershi model was set in train. Hence any small simple 'intent' could be the one to se the train in motion. Fundamental and foundational to any equation, howeve (and what I hope I have made plain herein), is the *purity* of love and service w bring to supporting Gaian purpose – one whereby flow enacts itself, naturally as a matter-of-course, because of the love *vested* in its undertaking.

Love so-vested is then 'reaped' in the *flow* of how events unfold and manifes themselves out of all potential possibilities. Love, it is, which gathers the creative energies to itself, of the right causes and conditions to manifest intent. And with *all* our love vested in this space, in *shared* intent? Ah, the beauty of partnership engaged with Sidhe companions of the way ...

Process Model of Becoming

Partnering with the Sidhe toward a shared vision of Gaian holism follows a process of 'becoming'. Yet the simplistic and stripped-out look of the model below (courtesy of a ubiquitous computer program) does not even begin to address the rhizomatic abandon with which the process (itself) *becomes* across all manner of interdimensional lines of flight on its single tangled 'plane of consistency' (see Glossary).

I ask the reader to therefore imagine a plethora of (sub-) arrows crisscrossing and looping back on themselves between the different 'storage tubers' in this particular partnership rhizome (within the overall Universal Field), as representative of the iterative cycles of embodied action and reflection I needed to build in to the model.

Nevertheless as a general outline, the following is as useful a snapshot as any to give a flavour to how an outreach methodology functions to bring a project from its first subtle inklings into tangible form.

Methodology of Outreach and Engagement

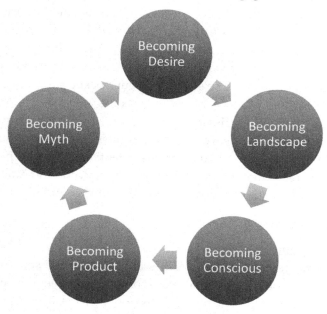

Process Model of Becoming

To describe the elements of the model in more detail ...

1. Becoming desire:

The pre-partnership stage – of eyes meeting across a crowded room, the slow circling before a dance of courtship commenced; suffice it to say that the productive energy of desire (Jung's 'libido') is the 'buzziness' by which (at some level) we intuit there is some opportunity seeking our engagement, requiring our support or service, but we are not yet sure how to go about it. In a way it is like being handed a starseed but not knowing what to do with it (something I know only too well!). Yet by graciously accepting the 'offering' and popping it in our pocket, reciprocal recognition is effected. Thus do we demonstrate our openness to the possibility of engagement.

Alternatively, in this early stage, we may be the instigators of contact, the ones who effect outreach; something set in train by simply being-with the *Card Deck*, saying an authentic: *Hello*, offering our own token/s of friendship, welcoming (Irigaray's) speech of the other within, accepting that such speech questions us – in short, by demonstrating our genuine commitment to the way-of-love ...

2. Becoming landscape:

The space we 'unveil' and cultivate is one of co-belonging, our intent to create the context in which love (seeded) can begin to flourish. First forays into 'unknown' territory begin – trust, therefore, integral to the process. Herein does the landscape of shared territory 'become', the path of evolving alliance made as it is walked, the map written as it is scouted; material and/or *Malakut*. The starseed in our pocket 'steps out' with us each day; Love as the third who 'wants to come with'.

During these reconnaissance 'adventures', we may meet different 'actors', each of whom offers perspective, counsel. Perhaps we even sit at a shared 'round table' to discuss various potentialities. At this point it is important to recall that it is not the 'speed' of connection so-established, but its durability – one in which our own commitment and staying power is implicated.

3. Becoming conscious:

When we feel we are ready, it is time to take the starseed from our pocket, to hold the glowing orb in our hand, to feel the energy of our *understanding*, our Earth-consciousness, of what it means to be a *Companion of the Way*, coalesce into a densifying ball of light, one which we can return to the stars, roll into the 'Mother' I saw constellated in the carpet. 'Tis this ball we infuse with our loving intent, our statement of purpose; this becomes the partnership 'compact' into whose creative field (no longer fallow!) our Sidhe cousins can blend (or plant their energy, or add fertiliser to the compost, to extend the metaphor), to enhance its capacity to manifest (as Mariel describes), or bear 'fruit'.

In this stage, therefore, our awakening to the *specificity* of task arises; 'tis here that the 'contract' is agreed, roles and responsibilities assigned, our orientation moving from a previously rhizomatic meander across unwieldy terrain to following the true straight path of the conscious pilgrim ...

4. Becoming product:

In this stage the energy of 'making' is engaged. This is the stage of preparing and conducting ritual, weaving the length of Elven-rope, singing up blessed country each step of (shared) songline to an unknown never-end, of choreographing performance to translate latent potentiality into material and energetic fact. Here we *work* the new threads into the becoming cloak of Gaia's aetheric structure – sharing responsibility for establishing nodes and forming connections in the lattice of our divine planetary crystal.

We each bring our *skills* to the task of becoming product, the aesthetically-realised beauty of co-creation our aspiration. In this stage, the energy of the *Card Deck* manifests in specific Sidhe presences to support the alchemy of transformation – our grail space becomes a very important *ally* in its own right. Within the Stone Circle the energies blend – meteorites of living light stream to Earth, their successful distribution to 'market' only possible because we, like the little Chinese gardener, *Know the Way* ...

5. Becoming myth:

We have reached the culmination of our project, the fulfilment of our intent. What was sown in partnership is reaped by the *All* of Gaian consciousness. Catharsis in its wake: *It is done.* We marvel at how deep magic facilitated the flow of the entire process; we document our (personal, shared) myth for offering into the collective pool; we script the map of our traverse as a blueprint for others to follow if such a path is similarly inscribed upon their faithful hearts.

Likewise the map becomes our mnemonic helpmate to re-entering the territory of our stewardship, this stretch of Ancestral song we Cousins of the Commons have (re-) sung into being. Here, we work further in the 'Garden of the Great Mother' in support of a shared vision of Gaian holism.

But what is the buzziness we sense hovering within and without? Is it a new call to service in the spirit of ongoing alliance between Humanity and Sidhe? Again an unseen hand tugs taut the line, the starseed thread anew to shine. Time to step out afresh in each other's shoes – a myth once lived is ne'er without close!

Ritual Templates

In presenting three generic proposals for ritual in this section, and following same with the rituals written specifically for the purpose of our partnership tasks, let me state that a single principle guides and underpins my approach – Unity of Being, the-one-life-of-the-one-world. We are each unique expressions of the absolute, each lit by the selfsame spark of love.

No matter how we manifest in the *one* world – as human, angel, slug or stone – divinity rests at our core. Divinity – Love. Pure. We *all* have a right to be, no one expression of life is any *less* sacred than another. In my self-sovereignty I am simultaneously part of the All. Life *is* Love; and the thanksgiving I feel to be *gifted* the opportunity to serve Gaian purpose – here, now – is the *fact* I bring to the penning (and conduct) of ritual.

Entering the *space* of ritual – subtly, physically, in time, out – my intent is on *holding* in my being the divinity immanent in *all* creation. This is no intellectual concept; my felt-sense concentrated in *exactly* the place of the Sacred – inner-outer one-and-the-same, mergence by another name. The 'words formed' in the forest one day years ago are alive in me *and* beyond in the *moment* of ritual performance, as I stand in solidarity with and on behalf of All:

I am All; I am None;
I am everywhere One.
I am who I am. I am Love.

As well as the *moment* of performance enacted, likewise it is the *space* of performance I engage, described by Beauty as: *Aethereal-material are one and the same in my reality ...*

Verily I know: *Love is the solidity within aether, that the Ground ever-grounds (me).* And even if lightness-of-being can be difficult to integrate into everyday material existence ('grounded fluidity' an evolving proposition, ebbing and flowing, but increasingly, as Beauty predicted, 'home'), it is the quality, the flavour of its *presence* that I bring to ritual invocation.

All of which means that my style (in written word and spoken action) is effusive, passionate, joyous, whip-whirled about in the embrace of the Sacred. (Over-the-top, melodramatic and challenging are equally adjectives which have been applied to my mode-of-being over the years). Hence, for another soul with alternate Huxleyian mode, the following texts may prove perplexing and of little replicable value. Apologies, therefore. As stated at the outset, perhaps my methodology proves of use to the reader, but then again not. To each his/her own, as the saying goes; including any hungry slug waiting in the wings for a tasty teatime treat!

Whatever the manner of writing and speaking which fits the reader's mode, my experience suggests that the importance of preparing a *conscious* ritual of invocation in which to *embed* sacred purpose and loving intent cannot be overstated. The whole prepping process I found invaluable; the longevity it gave to honing intent (sculpting exactly what it was I needed help with) and gathering feedback was akin to being in the right place at the right time – integral to having the 'right' ritual delivered in the 'right' company, and with the 'right' audience!

The time I took to prepare, reflect, write and rewrite, even do 'dress-rehearsal' readings (and yes, manner of dress similarly implicated) all assisted in funnelling aetheric (and aesthetic) engagement into a more compact, dense, manageable and pliable form. Imagine the difference between working with 'play-dough' and the stickiness and messiness of 'glitter- glue', and perhaps my meaning becomes clear.

My other main recommendation is to see which *Card Deck* presence/s step forward to assist in preparing the ritual. In the text I describe how I was supported in different aspects of process by different Council members and Dancers. However one stood out, of course, because of his alignment with the *Findling* to be awakened: *MossMan*. The fact that he also represents the Bard in the deck could be coincidental, or not. However it meant I had the perfect helpmate for my mode-of-being – the ritual began to 'write itself into existence' as song, as a love song in a bard's (i.e. poet's) voice. Co-creation is such a beautiful, exciting and energising process to participate in, so radiant its 'Faerie Gold' illumined by Love!

Nevertheless, dependent on the ritual's purpose, location or any other variable, the opportunity to simply 'ask' the Circle for input or assistance (that a willing co-creator would be more than welcome!), and then to sit back and see who shows up in support, is a more than viable option. Beginning to prepare proceedings alone is quite acceptable; the energy of 'making' itself thus becomes the catalyst instead of a pre-statement of intent. 'Making', of course, also includes ensuring that any *Malakut* insights received are replicated in the material for psychoid unity to be effected.

Finally, my process is to preface the ritual with the YMM self-practice – as a way of beginning to flow the energy within me, equally to confirm and centre my self-light and sovereignty, before stepping (or touching) into the space of engagement physically and subtly. My recommendation therefore is simply to begin with one's own usual incarnational practice – to simultaneously ground self and extend outreach – before commencing the ritual.

Template 1: Consecration of Earth-centred Grail Space

This ritual's purpose is to establish the space of nodal connectivity, to consecrate its grail of hallowed ground as a generative font of blessing as much as a zone of interconnectivity for future ceremonial work.

'Ground' is an important word here – to hook into Earth-energies, my felt-sense (supported, no doubt, by Sidhe companions' thought-prompts) is that the connection needs to be *grounded* in the *ground* itself, and for all elements involved in the ceremony (including self) to be in physical *touch* with the Earth.

In this, my intuition was supported by Mariel's commentary: 'In you, stars and earth meet. ... you are in touch with the life within matter in ways we are not. If you will listen, it speaks to you with voices we do not hear. We know the voices of starlight but you hear the voices of the fire within earth and matter' (p.141). So too was my intuition supported by an understanding of the *root* cause and condition of life – Love; Love the Ground of Being, love our anchor energy to 'home', love anchoring us in the soil of Gaia. 'What keeps us rooted' refers – love as both foundation energy *and* thread. To work the 'leylines' of Love's light *through* Gaia, our formal ceremonial connection must be equally rooted.

For my part, it was clear 'where' the nodal connection needed to be centred, the consecration of this grail space as a cone of blessing in honour of the overlighting *genius loci* a necessary prequel thereto. However, if such a space in which to concentrate the energy – as a container of blessing connecting 'earth and sky' – is not in yet in one's *conscious* orbit, I would guarantee Sidhe would arrive with appropriate suggestions. At the very least, I recommend meditating on Mariel's 'temple and altar' conversations with David in this regard:

- Temple: 'As much a creation of spirit, energy and possibility as it is of form' (p.122)
- Altar: The space created within the temple where 'I "make space" for you in my life ... (is) only partly solid; it is a blend of energy and substance. ... This altar reflects the true altar which is in my heart' (p.119)
- Temple and Altar: 'If you dedicate, as I have done, some part of your environment to be an altar to our contact, then the energies of affinity, resonance, and presence can be grounded and enhanced by something concrete in your life; such a place or thing can be an ally between us ...

remember you are the stone circle' (p.146).

As described in the text, Mariel's temple equates with my ten-foot-square hut, her altar with my kiln room. Thus I also offer, as thought-prompts to the reader, my process of 'bringing into being' the new ten-foot-square hut at Little Cove. Prepping for *Stairway to Heaven*'s arrival at New Moon to awaken the nodal connection involved a (slim) window of opportunity to consecrate the temple 'grail space' in advance, in which we would work at the 'altar' of our shared intent (i.e. the node itself).

I may have dubbed the process my 'creation of home' but its purpose in the context of ritual work is clear. 'Singing up country' (i.e. connecting to spirit of place) constituted *walking* the scape, being in physical *touch* with its (sandy) earth; the mantra of 'creation' mindfully stepped out wherever-whenever – going to the shops, bathroom or wandering neighbouring streets; lying in bed, washing the dishes, searching out stones along the beach ...

My point is that the practice was not simply 'designated' to a specific time and place (e.g. the 15km walk 'home' along the eastern sea-wild) but maintained a constant sub-text to *every* action. Like the stillness of meditative mind, it takes time to 'train' this muscle of *conscious* interconnectivity, but I believe worth every bit of sweat! Just think of it as 'Love wants to come with today' in mantra form, and if it helps to 'hook' or centre one's mindfulness in a container (e.g. a shell worn permanently at my neck), then so be it.

In any case, the mantra is offered in template form below. Not only does it invoke the magic of the mantle, but represents its own form of 'energy-cleansing' and 'freeing-of-field' for the light of Love to dance unhindered in the space (supported by the relevant qualities):

May the flow of my love and the light of Your grace come into this grail to create
May the flow of my love and the light of Your grace connect with this spirit of place
May the flow be (insert relevant qualities to the energy needed at this time) all rolled into one
May the flow be (repeat relevant qualities needed at this time) all rolled into one
Thus may your light, sacred grail space, shine unhindered all days yet to come.
With perennial thanks and blessings to all companions for your support ... Amen...

As said at the outset, the grail space is one in physical *touch* with the Earth, so that our touch-of-love streams out and through her subtle self. Once established, however, the linking thread may be maintained through remote visioning from a human-constructed space, but I would not suggest this as ideal in the early stages as it may endanger the durability of connection. To forge an enduring relationship with spirit of place, its *body* should be directly engaged, it needs to literally *feel* our love. To set up a 'line of sight' with another node, this too needs to be an act of embodied knowing in the first instance for light (and information) to flow as *intended* between all nodes in a grid so-linked.

An analogy for me here is the clinical practice of acupuncture. It may take longer for its effect to take hold, but it uses our own body as the mechanism of healing, with the commensurate impact longer-lasting as a result. As well, only with a network of nodes 'tapped' can healing energies flow between them, and from each to radiate out to the 'region' within its own remit.

The prime content of the ritual is threefold:

- Formally give thanks for the *genius loci*'s overlighting presence
- Ask its permission to use the grail space for the purpose of establishing a nodal connection
- Confirm the node as a locus of ongoing 'work' for actively engaging Sidhe energies (i.e. for interconnecting horizontally as well as vertically through the respective Gates)

As described in the text, I began preparation in advance of the actual day of ceremony during 'Nine Days of Consciousness'. Its purpose was as much to keep me completely focused on task over a longer-than period as it was to commence overtures to the overlighting *genius loci* early, to enact gradually increasing outreach with gifts of love to the shrine. I didn't want her to feel shocked by a sudden flurry of activity on a single day, pre- and post-dated by complete radio silence. 'Twas a simple matter of courtesy, but with 'durability' also in mind. And, of course, I 'win' too because I love to be in the garden …

Gifts are offered to the grail space to support the content of the ceremony. *MakerMan*'s history of human creativity refers. Gifts *from* the heart, gifts *made* with heart, gifts which *evoke* what it means to be *us*, are the most precious to bestow, to receive. My gifts to the grail space were clear – textual and musical. Yet *anything* self-made, created by hand, crafted with love is imbued with our spirit, our breath. *We all breathe life into what we love*, Mr1300BC said. In the same vein, we all breathe love into what we make – granting ourselves complete creative freedom in the process. What more is needed to bring us the joy of gifting? Next time I may do some baking to bring the psychoid unity of our 'eggy-bound' partnership into the material light of day!

Another most precious gift is time, devoting time to spirit of place. No 'wham-bam-thank-you-ma'am, done and dusted, now I can tick that job off the list'; this is an honoured presence in whose *loci* we are offered sanctuary, home. Respect, courtesy, love, time, gratitude – these our offerings to the grail beyond what we physically make ...

Finally, as part of the consecration ceremony, I feel it important to consciously don (or re-don) the guardian mantle (Mariel's exercise refers) in the presence of *all* Earth-energies and children of Gaia – a case of speaking aloud the commitment within hearing of a *broader* audience, all called in witness to the compact entered with Sidhe.

Instead of assuming intent and support of Gaian purpose will trickle down the line to such entities and beings eventually, it presents an ideal opportunity – and venue – to repeat our response to the Sidhe's call to partnership within earshot of all sentience that has the potential to receive blessings (direct or indirect) as part of our shared work. In the spirit of the interconnectivity which binds each to the other to the other without end, and all back to the One, my experience suggests that (re-) affirming the *Alliance between Humanity and Sidhe* has the ability to enjoin our whole One World Family in a collective group hug! And, in repeating the call, who knows what other forces may align with the partnership goals? Maybe a local '*Säntis*' will offer support to rival our hungry slug?

Template 2: Ritual of Awakening

This ritual's purpose is to awaken stone sentience, to call up its star within the earth, to charge it with *holding* the energies of connectivity, as well as keeping the lines of flight *open* for the rivers of light to *flow*.

I remind the reader here of the advice I received that stone is *Slow to Wake*. Yet I can emphatically confirm that once woken, if the energetic connection is durable – love, pure and simple, its anchor – it purrs along quite contentedly on its own like an immortal puss-in-(white)-boots, a phenomenon with which I also have direct experience!

Being slow to wake, the 'act' of drawing its *thread* from sleep (as the song lyric suggested) should be conducted over a longer-than time, and include gifts to its altar (in my case, 'love-letters' scripted, folded and placed into a heart-shaped chalice on a sturdy mossy hide), which – in itself, like Mariel's – is a blend of energy and substance (a case of psychoid unity in perfect sung harmony).

Each gift offered is (metaphorically) strung to its brother fore and aft to form a collective ring 'song' of blessing – this, I believe, strongly supports the uplift of the stone's extant resonance as well as the durability of ongoing connection. Coupled with the energy of repetition, the 'act' is akin to delivering a calm, leisurely and mindful massage (in broad subtle strokes) to its firm hide; slowly it begins to respond to our loving touch, to wake to shared purpose. The rest, as they say, is history, but in this case a history-in-perpetual-making ...

In the ritual, calling on *all* energies to help in the task of awakening stone sentience is crucial to achieving intent. My intuition here is that this aspect of partnership task goes *beyond* the Alliance between Humanity and Faerie, implicating as it does the great elemental beings of Gaia's crystalline consciousness.

My sense that this is the case is built on strong foundations (no pun intended). In the essay *Der Ruf der Berge* I describe direct experience of same and in the wake of my 'induction', I then 'saw' who resided in her 'hollowed hills': *Amici*. This insight was akin to coming into resonance with ancestral Aboriginal Dreaming from the 'bottom up' rather than 'top down'.

My felt-sense of the integral nature of Earth-energies to the 'awakening' equation is equally supported by Mariel's commentary: '(A mountain) is principal ally upon whose energy I particularly draw as it is a major conduit through which the energies of stars and earth meet ... Mountain spirits are among humanity's greatest allies in the changes that you face, though you don't realise it' (p.130-1).

For all these reasons, my chief recommendation is to call on all energies to help in this task, and to clearly state the purpose of its intent. Given that an energetic resonance with all sentience 'within earshot' was established during the previous ritual (consecrating the grail space and (re-) donning the guardian mantle as described above), my sense is that the connective thread should still be 'live'. In my case the 'call' was voiced as follows:

> *Three days past I stood in this space ... and now I return to issue my own call: Help*
> *me to help others homecome to the One through the connections I forge with the*
> *spirits of place. This sacred task I take on in the context of my mission to love the world,*
> *ever mirroring the Ground of Being's joy of creation between the face of the sky and*
> *the bones of the earth. Thus do I seek your assistance to awaken MossManFindling*
> *here in the circle as my Standing Stone, mantle bearer of peace, love and the light of*
> *God's grace along leylines connecting the blessed places in the world for which I have*
> *stewardship, to help others to homecome as I have come home ...*

The remainder of the ceremony is then dedicated to the stone to be woken, speaking directly with it, engaging it in heart-centred dialogue, outreaching with touch-after-touch-of-love – a practice, I recommend, as a daily act of being-with in advance of the ceremony proper.

In my case, for the actual ritual, I researched the history of the stone, provenance – personal and collective – to 'sing' its songline *back* into its memory. Equally did I share my own 'provenance' – 'tis the simple fact of walking the way-of-love to be completely honest and open in forging becoming-relations.

This transparency of history and intent, of intersect between self and other

ithin the space of engagement, honours the *genius loci* and all within its remit
⋅ demonstrating that we have done our 'homework', are committed to 'full and
ank' disclosure, and are not making overtures about a shared visionary future
ithout considering the outcomes and impacts of same.

In this respect, within the cone of ritual itself, we take on the role of bard on
ehalf of the *genius loci's* 'clan' – speaking aloud the relationships which bind all
 us as family, as one, within the space. And in so-doing, it strengthens our own
nding of self to place, rooting us deeper in the soil of our *loci's* spirit, in love.

David writes in the Card Deck: 'In Celtic society, the Bard was the one who
ew the history of the clan … all the relationships and connections that made up
at history. The bard was the keeper of the collective memory which he or she
uld share through his or her songs and narratives. The bard was the keeper of
sion … (and) connected the clan with the world around them, with each other,
ith their own past and with the vision of their possible future' (p.48).

Little wonder, then, that while *MossMan – my* bard – wove the connections
gether on the Sidhe side of the veil, I myself was the responsible 'bard' in the
actment of ritual within material space and time.

It is time to bring the ceremony to its close; to 'wake' the stone to shared
rpose, to the vision that we as 'bard' *keep* on the clan's behalf. My ritual
vocation therefore as follows:

*You are my mountain in space, and I embrace you … Perfectly positioned so I may
merge my energy with yours, the energy of my love for this sacred spirit of place …
may my love outpour through you along a songline binding these nodes together,
and all home to the One.*

(Hands raised to the sky)

*Light on light; love inflows from the One to my heart font and outflows to Gaia's All
in a woven tapestry of liquid light and gossamer star-threads in which I also encircle
and embrace you, my Standing Stone in space-time. Wake! Now wake!*

(Rising)

*There is joy there is joy there is joy there is joy there is joy there is joy there is joy!
Great sky circles of my joy do I make to welcome you to your task, my darling!*

At the time of *MossManFindling's* awakening, I had intuited his extant note and
ing into being his 'thread of light' as part of the ritual, but no lyric had by that
age 'populated' the melody. Still, once arisen, I made sure to head out into the

189

garden regularly to 'sing up (his) country'; I offer it here as an intoned/untuned text in the event that in one's own ritual of awakening, the stone (at some point 'speaks' its self-note and 'refrain' to accompany the chant below:

> this is who you are
> shining shining star
> living in the earth so far
> standing still in peace
> rivers run so deep
> you the thread no more to sleep ...

Following, it is simply a case of 'listening' for its response to our 'marriage proposal' (with bowed head and fingers crossed), while our *Moveable Feast*, singing *Joy to the World*, waits in the wings (with hungry slug) to be served ...

Template 3: Ongoing Alignment

This ritual's purpose is regular attunement to the energies of engagement also known as (with *MossMan* singing up a storm): *Don't you forget about me ...*

Alignment with key dates in the Celtic calendar has proved the most practical in our partnership's experience as, in themselves, they offer suggestions for the 'flavour' of each ritual's conduct. Of course, this is simply a function of my cultural and genetic heritage – how I, in company of Sidhe, attune to the energies – hence is offered as a guideline in spirit. In other cultural contexts, 'windows' of relevant liminal space-time, of 'November-fog' days (see Glossary), step into one's consciousness to be noticed, to be engaged, similarly. My point here is the regularity of interaction which is implicated in the ritual.

Regarding the following dates, my understanding is that they offer an (open) portal of several days surrounding – much like the Moon's waxing/waning cycle extend energetic support for our respective (tidal) activities while she subtly 'adjusts' her cloak over a few nights. If other commitments therefore 'intrude' on a specific date, choose another as close as, rather than skipping the opportunity altogether. The regularity of practice is integral to maintaining connectivity.

Autumn Equinox (21/9): Appropriately a time to give thanks for the harvest 'tis when I reflect on another cycle of creativity drawing to a close: 'Every new beginning is just some other beginning's end ...' The nights grow longer from here until the Solstice, and so do my inner musings, drawing insight from the past year of communion ...

Samhain (1/11): The halfway point between Equinox and Solstice, and when, traditionally, the worlds are very close …

Winter Solstice (21/12): The *Halcyon Days* refer, as does the richness of winter-dark explorations, whether material or *Malakut* …

Imbolc (1/2): The halfway point between Solstice and Equinox, a time when I was told to 'Wake Up!' very loudly many years ago by a less-than-sympathetic Mr1300BC …

Spring Equinox (21/3): Seeds sown in the chill earth, now warmed by the sun's radiance and growing presence, begin to 'wake' … just as days grow longer than nights …

Beltane (1/): Halfway between Equinox and Solstice, it is the time of Taurus – an Earthen energy prevails, the Maypole beckons and I can feel the Mother's joy even if it's accompanied by hay-fevered sneezes!

Summer Solstice (21/6): For the briefest moment, the twinkling of an eye, light and dark stand in equal balance – within and without in star-shone harmony …

Lughnasad (1/8): The beginning of the harvest season (as I sow, so shall I reap), it marks the halfway point between Solstice and Equinox … and I feel the energy move from without to within, a reflective space in the script to open …

Ritual blessings tend to take on a life of their own after a while, with the potential to perpetually sub-text conscious practice. Mindfulness becomes deep-etched like the mark of a permanent tattoo. So it is that practice evolves into a simple act of 'being-with' on each of the listed occasions; and in keeping with Celtic ritual, 'tis a day which 'begins' at the set of the sun the night before. This is when to outlay the Stone Circle, to summon the Council, to light the candles, for all to settle – like snug bugs in rugs – into the peace of the sink …

If the weather permits the ritual should be conducted in the grail space of the Earth (in my case *TreeMother*'s ten-foot-square hut); if not, within the indoor 'temple-hut' but ensuring conscious outreach to the outer space to invoke the energies of connectivity.

This outreach can take the form of a lit candle *in* the outer space in the spirit of Mr1300BC's wisdom: *You can still have a lit candle in a place you cannot see it and still know it is lit.* Additionally it can take the form of including any 'gifts of the garden', of the outer grail space, in the (indoor) ceremony – for example, my summertime 'haircut' of *TreeMother* enabled my sipping of TMT at the Equinox, while at the Solstice I collected moss as a symbolic thread rather than shiver amongst snowdrifts hugging equanimous stone ...

If specific task-orientation arises around the time of the ceremony, relevant text stating intent, seeking permission and requesting support should be formulated. If not, the following – based on our partnership's enduring compact – is offered as a guideline onto which specificities may be grafted as and when required.

As a Cousin of the Commons I hereby affirm, in spoken tongue, within the Circle:

- *The core purpose of my contribution to our partnership to sing up connection to the stars within the earth*
- *My fundamental love for Gaia which energises and underpins my work along the 'stretch' of Ancestral songline for which I have accepted stewardship in company of Companions of the Way*
- *My commitment to ever-wear a mantle of starlight here in the world to bring the energy of the stars streaming to earth*

As a guardian of the grail, I give thanks to each garden within my care for the gifts of the season you have provided to all children of Gaia within your remit; so too do I pray for your health and vitality in all seasons to come. A small square of food do I touch with my lips, so too take a sip of sweet-ferment fruit. All thanks to the Earth! So too to Sun's kiss! Requisite portions of heat, love and light e'er to be blessed this night!

As the purpose is to ensure ongoing alignment and durability of connection, I hum and sing the love song which arose from intuiting *MossManFindling*'s extant note. A practice with similar relevancy will most assuredly evolve in one's own engagement over time to likewise top-and-tail the ritual.

Finally, to close proceedings, I suggest to offer a prayer into the grail. The following, penned for my first 'regular attunement' ceremony after the establishment of the nodal connection, has proved just as fitting for each formal occasion in the space thereafter. In one respect, it speaks to the broader 'world-worker' intent that the spirit of alliance supports with whatever specific task engaged toward a vision of Gaian holism. In another, I feel it speaks to the underlying purpose of humanity's sacred incarnation, as the words seemed to flow out of my pen in a rush of soul-knowing pure.

As such, it is offered herein in the event that it may also speak to the reader ...

Dear Gaia ... All this love we have brought into being in this space through our ritual, all our intent, by connecting our sacred places, letting the threads of light and love flow between the nodes in our care, all this we dedicate to you, offer into the collective font of your intent. Dear Gaia ... Please take this love; this wave of love flowing along lines of flight, threads of joy, through your world to use as you will. May Love touch every heart in creation; may Love bring Peace into the core of each self; may the Light of Grace support each own to burn brighter ... All this we offer from our Garden Grail of Beauty ... May it be so, may it ever be so ... Amen ...

Specific Ceremony of Consecration
& (Re-) Donning the Guardian Mantle
(18 June 2015 at the chime of eleven bells)

Dear *TreeMother*: Here I am again, come visit your beautiful self and all your helpmates who hold this precious space on behalf of Gaia. You know me as I know you, but today's visit shall be a little more formal than our occasional chats and simple familial practice of *being-with*, of shared time together. Is that OK?

So ... may I begin by setting out the cards of the Stone Circle so all may bear witness to our act of communion? For you are my Howe in space, and this grail a generative fount of blessing. And as you know, I hope to awaken *MossManFindling* to be my Standing Stone mountain-embraced in three days so that within the grail space he can stand as a nodal point in Gaia's web, connecting you with a special place far far away ... Thank you ...

(As cards are outlaid, invoke their energies with recitation of their names in welcome)

Mountain above as Mountain below one does not have a body, walking in the garden one does not see a person ... from the Gate of the Earth and the Rising Sun, through the Gate of the Stars to the Twilight Zone ... here is my Kiln Room, my ten-foot-square hut within, to which you are all most welcome, my Companions of the Way ... hello *MagicMan*, hello *MakerMan*, *MossMan* – welcome, it is you I shall awaken – hello *VanDiemen'sMan* ... for a new hawk is born, who is centred within, split open by love, for the inner to come out ... in honour of the Ancestors, in honour of Hope, in honour of the Alliance between Humanity and Faerie ... know that I am Homecome to the Sea (yes!) ... for ... one day the Singing Bird, we are Brothers-Bear all, when did I forget the Beauty of the World, yes I am a Scholar, Gravity always gets in the way when we don't make a big enough leap, this you know dear *TreeMother* – imagine, you are represented in the cards (!), I am so grateful for your overlighting presence, blessed be! – a Rose by any other name would smell as sweet, on a Stairway to Heaven, to Laputa our castle in the sky, where we drink at the Sacred Pool, with a Stone Raptor and a Shaping Man, sharing a Moveable Feast, singing Joy to the World ...

More than three months ago I stood with you all, in the sanctified space of the ten-foot-square hut, stepped into your Circle and said: *Yes. I accept the mantle of responsibility, of guardianship of this grail space.* I said: *This life, this time, I join your lineage, I share your work, weaving the energies of love for God, for Gaia, for all.* As part of the solemnity of the moment I let my arms do what they will, and they gradually widened out from my body as if someone was slipping on a cloak and then they came together, joining in front of my rib cage (like a little Chinaman pose). I *felt* my Solar Plexus beat gradually stronger, louder till it was a ball of pulsating energy as strong as I've *ever* felt. And I knew that you knew, we all knew, that we are: *All together serving the One and it only works if we all work together.*

At the time I said: *Yes I will – if possible – try even more to focus the energies, to be a connective thread, a font of liquid light.* I said: *I have begun these tasks, this work solo but if by collaboration, by partnership, by shared guardianship/wearing of the mantle of the grail I can help more, then I will. Gladly.* This ritual I performed in sight of the Great Mother in her Sacred Pool. All my 'family' there in the ten-foot-square hut to bear witness. Tears leaked and as I brought the whole to a close, the last candle was blown out by Your breath. And the *Elven Song* resurrected itself in voice within. You know the song, don't you ...

Now, I wish to repeat my commitment here in the grail space of *TreeMother*. And I ask that you all here present bear witness to my communion with the beautiful guardian of this sacred space, and the task which shall flow therefrom – my loving intent to serve further, in which you are all most welcome to participate, my dear and honoured Companions of the Way ...

But firstly I'd like to share with you a story of my longer-than connection to trees, what I have learnt from trees both here and in the *Malakut*, the interconnectivity, mergence of these spaces to one single plane of consistency in which I may participate. Later, in poem I shall describe my relationship to you specifically, *TreeMother*, but there have been some other significant teachers along my path till now ...

(read aloud the essay: *The Secret Life of Trees*)

... The reason I told the story is because it closes with an experience on Oz soil – of the connection between ancestor trees and ancestor humanity, Aboriginal dreaming of place, the elders' continuing energies anchored in the stones of place. Now, I have no idea if that was a formal placement, a Stone Circle matching the fairy ring of beeches' presence, but that is how it felt and presented to me. And this felt-sense can't help but synapse across to you, *TreeMother*, and *MossManFindling's* together-presence here in a Circle to which I would offer my service.

So begin the ceremony ...

Dear *TreeMother*: During my seven years in the wilderness you have been a constant companion, a steadying anchoring force, and for this I thank you. Whenever I felt alone or distressed, misunderstood or swamped by experience, all I need do is look to your serenity in the corner of the garden to be calmed again. I remember well the clearing of ivy away from you and *Findling* to reveal your true selves to the world (though *Findling* has decided to wear a mantle of moss in the meantime, a worthy contributor to his naming); so too do I remember the burying of a prayer for D beneath your strength and courage with the hope that he may discover his own; there was the building of the tree house to feel myself cocooned within your world, where cats would occasionally join me aloft (as well as young D for whom it was ostensibly built!), followed by formalising your sacred 'space' five years ago with a stone (gravel) circle where I could sit beneath your shade to share a cuppa. And now five years hence – here I am returned from the wilderness, hair cut, cleaned up (you too! the lads did a lovely job!) and with your springtime blossoms of happiness now gracing my lips as tea. Thanks be for the blessings arising from your True Nature! Thanks be!

Dear *TreeMother*: Long have I known of your wisdom, long have I felt your generous spirit protecting our garden and home, long have I asked for your assistance in mothering my brood – whether human or tree child; and long have I touched you and felt your gentle touch of love in return. More recently have I sipped of your divine blossoms, served in clumps of five by your hand, five petals apiece, and given thanks for all your gifts – the gift of the 'five' is especially pertinent to me now; it seems your grail space is my *aether-in-material-form* on this side of the world ...

Dear *TreeMother*: Ever do I thank you for your presence here, for the sense of peace and tranquillity you bestow on the garden, for *embodying* the spirit of this beautiful place, undertaking to be the guardian of joy, love and light sunk deep beneath your sturdy roots.

Dear *TreeMother*: Sana and Blessings to You! May I step into your space, you Elder of our clan, you who teach me so well to grow toward my crone-self – may I step into your space a sacred ritual to perform?

(... a moment's silence ...)

Dear *TreeMother*: Stepping in, I feel how your Circle of Love and Light is a microcosm of Gaia's cauldron; I feel how this Circle is filled with the energies of consciousness and life from solar, lunar, stellar and telluric sources; I feel this Circle as a space where such forces are synthesised, blended to wholeness and shared out into the world. And yes, I feel how I participate in this task in my own way – and I thank you for holding this space open for our shared worldwork.

(... a moment's silence ...)

Yes, I feel the power of holding within this Circle, a sacred grail space you guard and steward, dear *TreeMother*. I feel how this power resonates with my own power, I attune to these forces, and enter my own depths as likewise a vessel of blessing. And from my own depths I offer you this gift – my own gift of blessing, in words of love, the only tongue I know.

Poem of (this) Place

Elder Tree, mother lover, gateway
to the ancients' wisdom – attuned
through bark branch, leaf berry,
sip-supped in blossom tea.
So do I thank thee for thy gifts
of blessing, five-fold found
by this foundling kind (Findling
in another tongue) – two as one
within your space, children of
radiant joy become we be,
learning at your learned knee ...

You, who wear your cronedom
crown blue-blood-red wine-berry
wine. You, whose roots stretch
far, deep down, entwining with
the dreams of mine. You, my Howe,
guard well the gate –
in space and time
(this space, this time). Here matrixed
now all fireflies seen spark the sky
with lit starseed. Heavenly hosts
boast rhizome intersections of
Venn diagram sets (an in-out
kind of logic this) forward-ho
toward a journey's near-end.

To one Gulan is known
(once I was told) and now I
too may tell in your presence
how I walk the same meandering
straight path in and then out again.
This my Way of Love through

a labyrinth of hope and mystery
shyly revealed, your shining self
overlights a fledgling knight's
night-wander – thanks be!

And now that I know your lore,
your (documented) place in
the history of place these four
thousand years or more,
a no-brainer to twin ten-foot-square
hut musings-communings inner-
outer at each turn of your Celtic
sun-moon. Two (random) cards
have I from Tarot decks
outlaid. Each a songlined source-
to-sea gift, like Jeremy's gold,
in burnished leaf to enfold,
a reminder of autumn-ripe
days to come and what I
should proffer-offer to this
space in your honour.

For now, though, feel my love
as ever you have felt it course
my veins through to yours
and know that I too feel yours,
ever have,
ever will. Nought more
would I ask this sunsetted eve.
Eve – first, true, you –
blessed blessed be …

(… a moment's silence …)

Dear *TreeMother*: Clearly I sense your presence as the principal guardian of the Circle – of all herein contained and herewith connected. But I know you are not alone. This is shared worldwork. I feel the spirit of the mountains, the spirit of the waters, the spirit of the ancestors (welcome Rosa!), and the spirit of the flora and fauna here in this space. I am overjoyed that I even saw your tiny accompanying tree spirits – dear little souls a la Miyazaki – as swirls of light and love radiating out from your skin last Christmas – as if they wanted to dance with the fairy-lights (aptly named!) we had adorned you with!

(… a moment's silence …)

The point of all my verbiage (and yes, I know I am verbose but please be patient with me, for it is through writing that the inner comes out) is that I feel an ancient lineage of care and protection working here – here, in a secluded nook of a small Swiss garden. And I bubble over with joy at the thought … such that I feel an intense loving desire to link this secluded nook's work with a fresh-baked secluded nook half a world away (fresh-baked only in terms of my stewardship of place – it also has its ancients busy at perennial work, whom we'll meet soon enough) in three days' time ... which is why I'm coming to visit you now, *TreeMother* – you and all your helpmates – to share with you my intention …

(… a moment's silence …)

I feel the Circle overlit by you, *TreeMother*, as a space of alliance, a grail space to which I would invite the Realms of Faerie to participate – with your permission and blessing.

Now, of course it is possible, my dear *FaerieFolkFriends*, that you already work through this particular Circle overlit by *TreeMother*, that you receive her ongoing blessing to help weave and blend the energies of love and light for Gaia from this place. It wouldn't have occurred to me before (yes, I know I am a bit dense sometimes!) but in preparation for the awakening ceremony in three days' time, I've been reading in a vast repository of Elder Tree Lore of which I was previously unaware (ditto) and it seems you are intimately related? That the Elder is the Lady's Tree, and thus the Howe for entering the Realms of Faerie? And that I could have been doing all ceremonies of connection with Faerie out here within the circle, because the Circle already existed?

Indeed, in meditation I have seen golden threads crisscrossing each other, like fine filigree, gossamer wisps of light (but sturdy) yet with no discernable pattern or grid, just exuberant crisscrossing this way and that; and words forming: *Threads of happiness*. A beautiful cloak of happiness are you weaving, and from this place? Oh, how ignorant am I!!!

And indeed, while *Homecome to the Sea*, I found myself being covered in fine filigree starlit webbing – spreading so fast over arms and body, I assumed a crawling spider, creating the web in her wake. Yet she herself camouflaged, mergent with her creation, these beautiful patterns of gossamer lace … So glorious – to be integrated in the weaving! How lucky am I!

In any case: *To every thing a season and a time to every purpose under heaven*. I know the principle housed in Ecclesiastes 3 well – and now is the season (and time) when all appears to be aligned for this next stage of (shared) work; a work in which I hope to actively participate *in* and *through* the energetic space of this sacred Circle, weaving threads of happiness between nodal points of connection in the vast and wondrous web of Gaia ...

(... a moment's silence ...)

Hence I stand here in your presence, in all your presences, to receive your question, and gladly answer: *Will you share this mantle of guardianship with us? Will you be part of the lineage that guards the thresholds, opens the cauldrons of loving spirit, and releases new life into the world? Will you be an agent of wholeness with stewardship, responsibility for this nodal point and all to which and whom it is connected?*

Yes. Yes, and again yes. I know I have within me a power of love and holding in the world; I know I walk between the worlds as a threshold being, a grail of blessing. I have embraced the mountain, received instruction in the *Way of the Knight*, I host a generative font of liquid light in the deep, I know I am a child of the stars, a connective thread between heaven and earth, wearing a mantle of starlight here in the world to bring the energy of the stars streaming to Earth. And I affirm and anchor all this here, in this grail space, with *TreeMother* as beautiful overlighting presence and witness.

(... a moment's silence ...)

Yet my intent goes further than answering your call, but to issue my own: *Help me to help others homecome to the One through the connections I forge with these spirits of place. To awaken MossManFindling here in the Circle as my Standing Stone, mantle bearer along leylines connecting the sacred spirits of place in the world for which I have stewardship and take on responsibility.*

(... a moment's silence ...)

Thus do I invite all beings who would support this work to join me here in three days to hear me affirm this intent and task in the context of my mission to love the world, ever mirroring the Ground of Being's joy in his creation between the face of the sky and the bones of the earth ...

And now – with Faerie present – I ask: *Shall we sing and dance our joy?* Sip together of *TreeMotherTea* to confirm our shared standing within the grail, my formal joining of this grail space as mantle-bearer, partner in outreach on behalf of darling Gaia and with especial, eternal thanks to *TreeMother* for holding this space open for our work? Please share in *TreeMother's* blessings ... Sana and blessings to all!!!

To close, I shall sing (you may dance) – the *Elven Song* you taught me accompanied by 'imagery' of young maids holding hands, dressed in flowing white, hair streaming behind and elderflower-filled (?), dancing round a maypole in a well-lit meadow. Expressing their/your simple joy to dance and sing of the *holding* and *flowing* of the One's being into the world, the innocent whimsy of skipping, ribbons, flowers, pastel colours, rippling laughter.

So, are we ready? Let us begin ... to sing ... !

Specific Ceremony of Awakening
(21 June 2015, at the set of the Sun)

1. Enter Circle, this *shared* grail space and greet, name, welcome all participants as I place them in position. Also greet, name those already of, present within the space – *TreeMother*, spirits of the mountains, waters, ancestors, flora and fauna, Faerie energies that may be present, *MossManFindling* of course …

2. Flow through YMM 'liquid light' forms, closing with sky circle sweeps, followed by (with head bowed) the intoning of: *With love in my heart & blessings on my tongue, know that I am homecome. To You.*

3. Dear *TreeMother*, dear all:

Firstly, dear *TreeMother*, thank you for hosting this gathering of energies and for the ever-loving, ever-protecting and ever-nurturing role you maintain here, overlighting the all of this space. For your presence I am eternally grateful. Thank you.

And now, with all witnesses and participants here present, I wish to affirm that as part of this circle's existing holding and anchoring function, I seek to extend its remit to be a nodal point of connection between our home here and our 'new' home ten thousand miles distant (called Little Cove, if you're wondering … it slips off the tongue more easily for me than any Swiss place name!).

In essence, I seek to weave a new thread of joy and love and light into Gaia's filigree web of evolving consciousness – a songline between these homes, these two blessed spirits of place, a *songline of presence and resonance* we may sing together and through which solar, lunar and stellar energies may be shared out, into, across and through telluric dimensions as blessings to all.

(… a moment's silence …)

Three days past I stood in this space and answered your call to share the mantle of guardianship of this grail space. And now I return to issue my own call:

Help me to help others homecome to the One through the connections I forge with these spirits of place. This sacred task I take on in the context of my mission to love the world, ever mirroring the Ground of Being's joy in his creation between the face of the sky and the bones of the earth. Thus do I seek your assistance to awaken MossManFindling here in the circle as my Standing Stone, mantle bearer of peace, love and the light of God's grace along leylines connecting the blessed places in the world for which I have stewardship, to help others to homecome as I have come home …

(… a moment's silence …)

4. *MossManFindling*: It is you I wish to specifically engage as my partner in this work – like me, you are an 'orphan', a foundling bound in swaddling clothes, gathered up in arms on a loving family's doorstep and taken in. Like me, far from home, yet welcomed, embraced into the bosom of new family here, our discrete stronger-than connections to home have been forged here; indeed I feel strongly, deeply, that my soul's understanding of what it is to homecome has been sculpted by my experiences here; nascent understandings – of love, fidelity, stewardship, care – brought to maturity by this place. And now I would weave you into my understanding of what it is to love and be loved and what may grow from such blessed starseeds when bound to specific, anchored spirits of place ...

5. At the same time I would respectfully ask that you, *TreeMother*, and all our helpmates of this, our grail space, watch over (and please lend support and protection for) the opening of this portal, to help *assure* that the energies which flow through *MossManFindling* between Little Cove and our garden here are ever-charged with my loving intent and desire to likewise help others to homecome, just as he and I have been helped and guided home by love.

Actually, my high-and-wide-as-the-world dream is for all humanity to experience a loving connection to place that helps them be at peace within themselves, to merge with and into Gaia's world spirit, to embrace all sentience as their family, and in so doing to homecome to the One, as I have been so blessed myself to experience and know – deep-know – what it means to homecome, as a connective thread back to the divine love and grace of the Ground of Being ... a bit ambitious, perhaps, this dream, but I am happy to start somewhere and more than energised in my task that this somewhere is right here with dear friends!

6. So, you have all borne witness to my intent, my clear statement of intent here, now. Thus shall I sit within the circle with my partner *MossManFindling* and tell the story of our shared history – as well as our lone histories, as far as I know, in song. By singing this songline into being, I wish to 'charge' you, *MossManFindling*, as my Standing Stone gatekeeper before the Howe of *TreeMother*, to be my champion in the *Way of the Knight*, for your beautiful organic smoothed-by-aeons form to be aetherically-infused with the peace and love sunk deep in the subtle bones of this sacred space, to be the bearer of this energy of joy and light *betwixt* and *between* our garden and Little Cove – so that all who bask in these places' presence may be infused with homecoming spirit.

Hark now – all witnesses here present – to these *Poems of Place*, of shared memory, sung by bard to bard down the millennia and to which I now add my apprentice's voice ...

Tales of the MossMan
(an adventure in Findling finding ...)

Seventeen thousand years since you were
upped and shunted off from home by a quirk
of fate and climate. Much as I, though shorter

my longer-than sojourn far from southern shores
than yours down the slippery slope of a wide-
open glacial tongue. And then your birth, here

in this space (Findling found! So went the cry
up), a coupla years ahead of when I joined
the material from the aetheric this time round.

Yet wonder: How many more spins round the
universal block while you stood stoic for such
seeming blinks of aeon-weary eyes? Yet now

both of us here with a chance to homecome;
plus contribute to same on behalf of the whole?
Oh, the task ahead! Sleeping, we two till now

in our respective cosy nests. Awake we must,
shall, sofort – such work there is to be done!
But when the busyness and buzziness dissipates?

It's back to just two, communing (what we both
like best, methinks). With your permission, into
your memory I now look and see the dark earth

which encased the solidity of your soul. How was it,
then, to be moved from shone-through light (reflected
starlit glory refracted in melting and cracking ice),

plunged into the incubatory heart of Gaia instead?
With whom did you converse while buried so
deep? Till a day arrived, five-five its name (now),
fifty-five years has it been since the magic of
the numbers led you here. All elements (four)

conspiring to release their hold; lifted by sublime

force you were, up and out – new babe! Lightness
of being! Thus do I picture the fateful moment
of primal resurrection when in consultation with

human partners (families Müller and Wolfensberger
no less) a solemn decision taken in which you
held centre stage. But pray tell: Was TreeMother

first planted and then you took pole position? Or
was the order reversed? Still it began; stone Findling –
dear foundling, an orphan by any other name taken

in just the same. Thus did the years pass, where
quiet you stood on the edge of time, a forgotten
valley forgotten in time. But not by greedy ivy –

which grew, grew, and then grew some more
(just to be sure). Once again in the dark till a day
came at the start of another lonely foundling's

long wilderness years a-wander when she stripped
you of cloak (as she did hers), revealed the svelteness
of your form (it taking way longer to accept her own).

Yes, seven years from the trailhead till found – the
magic of the five – a commitment to charge you with
latter-day life. Again. Because she loves. This thought

to ponder: Any and all may be homecome through
love. A truth in which she trusts. And you? She hopes
you too (for it is time to begin an old work anew) …

Little Cove Dreaming

Long has it been I've dreamt of you. This tiny
loop of sand snug fit inzwischen granite bookends.
There you are, so small, shy, and your waters,
turquoise, a slender offering to an even more
slender lip of land kissed at high tide, also low.

To wade into your shallows, stand tiptoe waist
deep with each return of the new, languorous
waves approaching shore, and still resist gentle
attempts to tug me in more? (Come on now – dive!)
My, how you flirt! A bat of coquettish eyes while

togs smoothed back into place. Between my toes
silicon crystals rise to silvered promise of a mermaid's
svelte tail (instead of skinny shins), to waft sensate
as seagrass, or the occasional yellow fin visitor.
Here now a shovel-nosed ray, surprised wriggle up

and out of hiding. That's a find, so too the dolphin
pair who scatter mercurial shoals beneath boarders'
dangling flippers (the wrong sort of fresh meat);
dipping, skating, ever at play. And yet all so serene,
cockatoo- and lorikeet-screeched joy inclusive.

Nothing wakes Blinky Bill in his eucalypt tower
turret. Nonetheless I can't help but marvel –
that all this I've known (in dream and person) since
first toddler steps taken on a National Park picnic
bench fifty plus years ago and a goanna stand-off

because of Vegemite and Velveeta wedged between
Sao twins. So agog was I (after doing the wormy
thing) – who stood taller in the end, eye to quizzical
eye? All the while tribal elders stood by – I heard
their gurgled amusement into fresh-minted pastel

tea cups hosting a Thermos brew of Bushell's. Ah
(can you hear my audible sigh?). For each memory

tinged with holiday happiness and sunburnt cheeks,
freckled shoulders (still implanted in skin), ditto
salt-lipped smiles. Later, pretty strapless dresses

and make-up (subtle) for the big excursion to Surf
Club (or local Chinese). I remember the snap I took
of you, Dad, and Mum against a long white wall of
tranquillity after Jenny and I had passed graduation
muster. With love: To all this history you bore witness

as I did you and latterly likewise, these past years'
return to share again your special nook with special
latter-day someones – time and tide tugged I've been,
time, each time, with those most special in time's
calendar this time. Waiting, you were, till time and

tide met and Moon too, watchful with longing to
bathe in her star-lit sea, pregnant self shining the
light of satori upon this pocket within a pocket. A
hidden door to wonderland it became, and tugged
further, beyond its threshold to where you stood –

tall, fruitful, bathing me in lush shade and a deep-
bowed hello. There we stood, two strangers long
known to each other within. So it seems. Perhaps.
Maybe. Yet the question on both our lips: Shall we
dance? Gleichzeitig. Yes. Curtsey in reciprocal.

Leaves fluttering on the breeze. Love at first sight,
that's what they call this – a spontaneous marriage
proposal to follow. It's happened before. And now?
In a way this time easier, no need to explain in
human tongue; heart knowing's no need to give

voice, no chance to misunderstand. I touched you
that day as you touched me and I pray ever more
of the same each day to share. Hence my request –
MossMan, saged sentinel, smooth-aged and worn –
can you mayhaps find a way? But, look here, once

more ahead of myself and all that has gone before.
Let me tell then when, in sweet Little Cove, I lifted
a shining Moon-filigreed veil, to night-glide this
future home. Known long before, it seems, by spirits
of sacred place – of mountains, waters, ancestors,

flora and fauna, all of you plumb bang here. Was a
Conference of the Birds in session? Nevertheless
'twas you I (in)advertently invoked with a Dantesque
flourish with my verse: One day shall find us
homecome (I quote). So-promises the universe

as well as lowly I. One day, it shall be. One fine
fine day. When all the rivers run – know, that we
shall be homecome, to the sea. Ha! Decided to
play me at my own game, didn't you – with great
streams streaking from the sky, streaming Gaia's

joy to be, to flow; whether in material or Malakut,
flooding consciousness was key – and yes you won.
I asked: What do you want of me? And your answer?
To root you in sand-soil, float you buoyant in a star-
filled sea. So do I sit at table in this Innenhof with

two (ever-now) elders of place. Smiling they are,
welcoming to new stewards in (non)residence.
Shining ones pure, they speak of shepherding
memory as well as future potential. An interview
of sorts, but the outcome already known. Bardic

their tongue. I say 'sit at table' but suddenly said
furniture upturned, inverted, and instead we float –
aetheric environ dense with promise, material way-
markers light as air. Sea-drenched is the skyscape
and we inzwischen all, Innenhof-intertidal zone,

a becoming landscape all its own. A drill I know
well from those long wilderness years – one
time fill, repeat at will … Next day – more. Ever
yet more signs. These ones old young – new-

hatched, well-aged. To wit: Two kookaburras

tripping the highwire (grandfather ancestor divine
child nachwuchs), their witness silent. To which
I respond? Through your eyes I see: Self. This I
know (tell I each, while languishing under their
sceptics' scrutiny). Yes, this I know and cherish

and want to share, so repeat my prayer: Help me.
Three women, three guests, three cushions —
mantle passed, donned. And I weep tears of joy
at their gift. It is done. But what more do I find
when the cloak be lifted? A glorious cabinet of

curiosities, left from a bygone age (with a huge
tree growing besides, yet in the midst of all?).
Rimmed in polished wood, doored in antique glass
(frosted forest-green, delicately star-embossed),
housing a home of precious dolls in linen miniature.

SandPeople, you Wildmännli folk of Noosa Dreaming,
how blessed can I be to make your acquaintance too?
Surf's up, you say, and indeed how huge the swell!
Enspirited with your spirit and vice-versa too I feel.
Witness to your kin's extraordinary skill; bright sylvan

cousins — a civilisation at home in the sea. And
I granted permission to witness from a high-wide
headland onto your Eastern sea wild! Thank you
thank you and again thank you! Yet when time to
go home? To the Innenhof of the Innenhof that is

Little Cove, thus was your counsel; well-protected
our nest from vast ocean reaches, cosseted in the
lee of Mother'sHead, girt by sand-ancestored dirt,
each and every one our teacher ... Rising now I see,
with eyes wide open, how to bind these two spirits

of place, weave a taut-strung thread of aethereal joy,
happiness, love and light into the supersensible

spirit of Gaia's golden becoming cloak. When life
dwells in the realm of possibility, lightness of being
becomes our homecome way, carrying joy in heart,

mirroring joy beyond, flowing love out into the world.
All this I see when you arrive to perform, MossMan,
granted a day's leave pass to be here centre-stage
with a backing band and Elven dancers out front
tripping the light fantastic, sending the crowd wild

with choreographed joy, passion, love of life – the
energy heights reached in the space of a finger-click!
All this I see from my hilltop home, your charm, your
smile, twinkling starlit eyes, till offstage, I may run to
greet you, embrace you, send my hand coursing over

a totally glatt pate, share a laugh while doing a spit
and polish on your many-times-over millennial head.
Too soon the keepers are back, time to return to your
cell, no need for their cuffs, you have your own golden
links to hand them on a plate. But know I'll come to

visit, know I'll put us back together at heart, in my
simple mind. So don't forget about me, no matter
how much rain keeps falling, rain keeps falling down
down. I know you'll call my name when you walk on
by. I know the magic of the numbers never lie. Never

forget God gave me travelling shoes, the wanderer's
eye, a few gold coins to help me to the other side,
the ship, the key. You and me. Home – and yet miles
away? It's OK. I fingertip-feel how aether densifies,
matter lightens. How starseeds become meteorites

as they fall to earth; burning up, they smooth to sleek
shapes in their traverse of the atmosphere. Never
too hot to hold, never not an opportunity to transform
what was to what will be. I feel spirit's mergence with
matter; I see nestedfishes in holistic fusion. Wherever

we may be, we are always together, weaving the
connection (now forever) into which we two can also
be woven? Yes! We weavers interwoven! Such joy to
behold! Such starseeds of living love offered into my
care. And with love, I love them on. Sana! Sana!

Sana!

7. (Now the moving of the stones into the chalice …)

All witnesses here present, please welcome Little Cove's *AncestorCouple* to our
gathering, on behalf of the *SandPeople*, the *ShiningOnesoftheSea* – I shared with you
the story of our meeting in the *Poem of Place*. Daily, since I first became conscious
of *AncestorCouple*'s blessing for our future stewardship, I have communed with
these stones collected at *FirstPointLittleCove* – the granite strength of Noosa's
protective head, the volcanic basalt spewed from *Wollumbin*'s fiery heart.

As I have held these stones, I have deep-felt their ocean-washed stories while
atoning my own deep love of place to them. Now they shall carry my blessings
into the heart-chalice of *MossManFindling*, together with two river-washed stones
from this place, held till now as markers of way (heart and holism their particular
remit, and no, that shan't be altered with the change of scenery) in the Sacred
Pool of the Great Mother of my ten-foot-square hut. And our final participant – a
tiny child of the sea wild to commune with you, *MossManFindling*, a huge child
of the high wild. Both of you water-washed – whether by warm southern oceans
or glacial alpine fields, your form evokes the spirit, the peace, of Gaia's longevity
as much as your relative youth.

And remaining in the Great Mother's Sacred Pool shall be *StarlightSeed*, this
tiny sea-washed starlight-infused stone – until now cradled by the scallop shell
who moves to the heart-chalice, but now fully fledged to carry the blessings
between heaven and earth *selbst*, a linking stone, a stepping stone, just as red-
river-rock is the pool's connector thread to his liquid light-carrying brother out
through the *Isorno* watershed. All these anchoring energies of the sacred pool –
fresh-minted, long-held – thank you for your presence and support!

Complement complete in the heart-chalice, so do I bless you five cup-bearers
to support *MossManFindling* in this work; your presence shall keep the line of sight
created – with his opening, his charging, as a nodal point of connection – true. I
thank you for your presence … as equally I thank this beautiful child of the sea
wild for her presence whilst around my neck since that same fateful day when
AncestorCouple bestowed their blessing on our union with place till the day when
the deed finally done. Yes, after working her own magic of the five those fifty
days, her home became, six days past, to share a *nest* with Fish, my *Companion of*

the Way. Know this, *feel* this: You two are my plumb line, direct to the *Kiln Room* at the mountain's heart. The mountain that is All and None and everywhere everytime One, here and beyond *gleichzeitig*. For where there is mountain, there is no self. Mountain above as Mountain below, I thank you for this longer-than work as a plumb line to the source ...

8. *MossManFindling*: You are my mountain in this space, and I embrace you. You are my Anne-sized mountain – how wonderful! – perfectly positioned so I may merge my energy with you, the energy of my love for this sacred spirit of place and Little Cove's sacred spirit of place *gleichzeitig*. May you feel this love I have for home, to homecome to both these places, and may my love outpour through you along a songline binding these two together, and all home to the One.

(Hands raised to the sky)

Light on light; love inflows from the One to my heart font and outflows to Gaia's All in a woven tapestry of liquid light and gossamer star-threads in which I also encircle and embrace you, *MossManFindling*. Wake! Now wake!

(Rising)

There is joy there is joy there is joy there is joy there is joy there is joy there is joy! Great sky circles of my joy do I make to welcome you to your task, darling *MossManFindling*!

(Back down to hug him)

TreeMother: I hug you too! Forever my thanks for your presence as 'keeper' of our grail space here and the love you radiate out into the whole garden and house – our home – over, ever over. May the love held here overspill its boundaries to be shared down a songline far – very far – to Little Cove via the connective thread that is *MossManFindling*, my Standing Stone, my champion. Sana! Sana! Blessings to all!!! For love's cup may be filled over, ever over without *ever* being depleted – such a well of liquid light do we host in our joy! Joy I would share with you in song; let all who know this *Elven Song* sing with me!

(Keep singing while pouring the wine, beginning our shared *apero*? Open-ended, like most *BigNightsOut* ...)

Annex: The *Amici* Files
Amici della Montagna
(Mountain Friends)

'Neither men nor gods, but frontier-walkers,
border-crossers between the demonic and material worlds':
Hans Steinegger, *Innerschweizer WildmannliSagen*

In a forgotten valley on the edge of time, our family stewards a small cottage, ten-foot-square hut with a window on the world. This window frames a Cold Mountain worthy of Han-shan's poetic genius while sheltering in the refracted glory of another. Four hundred years the cottage has stood thus, its construction made possible by these selfsame giants – built of the cliffs, once aloft, which rumbled under the tumult of time, split and smoothed by aeons to useable proportions. Stone sentience surrounds us, embraces us; as within, so without. We are (literally, as John Muir believed) *in* the mountains as they are in us.

Indeed, we cannot help but be conscious of their presence, our minuteness in the face of their majesty. These mountains call to us and, like all high wild places in the world, are open to teaching us their secrets if we – in turn – are open to listen, to observe, to quietly, reverently, contemplate the sheer fact of true nature in action: 'The secret of the mountains is that the mountains simply exist, as I do myself: the mountains exist simply, which I do not. The mountains have no 'meaning', they *are* meaning; the mountains *are*' (Matthiessen, p.95).

In his *Mountains and Rivers Sutra*, Dogen writes of the high wild as the dwelling place of the great sages, that this in fact has 'actualised' their sentience: 'However many great sages and wise men we suppose have assembled in the mountains, ever since they entered the mountains no one has met a single one of them. There is only the actualisation of the *life* of the mountains' (Daido Loori).

In a forgotten valley on the edge of time, I feel this life; I hear the resonant hum burbling up from far beneath the earth, the 'actualisation' which constitutes a connective thread to the very Ground of Being. I hear the mountains' call, *der Ruf der Berge*. But how many of us have the opportunity to heed the call, to make the trek into their domain, respectfully sit at the feet of the sages to learn, to befriend the simple fact of their beingness?

I know that some have more opportunity (and proximity) than others. I know that some may have opportunity or proximity but lack intent – having not yet heard the sages whisper. Yet of those who have, some are even honoured with the title: Friend. *Amico*. And once a friend, a friend for life, a friend who ever-returns, ever-tugged by the unseen hand in a homecoming ritual as worthy as any to bear the name.

Amici della Montagna – mountain friends, these ones so-called. Friends who, as sacred task, commit to caretake the landscape within their remit, offering service to the *life* of the mountains themselves together with all those who wander the high wild with backpacks and stout boots and lungs full of fresh clean air. *Amici della Montagna* – these are the friends who return over ever over; friends that our family has the privilege to now also call *Amici* following an extraordinary meeting one autumn years past …

Border-Crossings 1

Our small cottage nestles in a valley on a border – a border between two countries and two continental plates, the latter's fluidity and dynamic tension catalytic to the creation of this high wild region. It is also a border where the different dimensions of our one world, the holism that is Gaia – physical and non- – is itself very fluid. The veil seems thinner here, my intertidal zone a becoming landscape which shapeshifts at will. The propensity to border-cross – between here and there, before and after, material and *Malakut* – thus occurs more often than not, and with it, the teachings of 'wise men and sages who have all made the mountains their own chambers, their own body and mind' (ibid.). Over the years, I have found myself a-wander through these *inner* mountains – traversing tunnels of shed snakeskin, stumbling upon catacombs of sacred relics, discovering the kiln

om at their heart, witness to *life* pulsating in a chalice therein. My lesson each
d every journey has been to forge a connection between the mountain at the
re of *my* being and the heart of the *felt* world – my becoming *mergent* with the
nsity of stone sentience a profound expression of the sanctity of the incarnate,
aterial existence we share.

Such expression involves, amongst other things, my practice of walking the
gh wild, connecting to spirit of place with each tramping footfall. It is a practice
nerally engaged in concert with family – each a like-minded soul according
their own mode-of-being (including our resident *canis lupus*). The need for
rfect weather does not figure highly in the decision to walk. Indeed, given the
inuteness of our cottage any opportunity to be *out* is as literal a godsend as it is
urative. In the spirit of John Muir's perennial observation that 'going out (is)
ally going in', walking the high wild involves leaving the known, the familiar,
e human-dominant; and entering the foreign, the mysterious, the primal. It
eans shedding our ego's alpha status, donning in its stead the cloak of humility
d awe. We walk in the tracks of wolf, lynx, deer, chamois – this is their salon,
d we the polite gentleman callers therein.

Picture, then, a wet and wintery day in mid-autumn. Complement complete,
e cross an arbitrary political border to follow our river upstream – a river which,
e all others, knows no border but watershed-led gravity. Plunging more than
o thousand metres in thirty kilometres on its journey out of the valley, our river
a stunning symbol of Gaian holism I celebrate long and loud in poetic form. To
ipse the path beside its frothing joy a joy itself which I cannot help but uplift
ne and again in text.

On this particular day, however, no rhyming couplets graced my thoughts.
ey were focused on the muddy path ahead, the rain dripping from the brim of
y cap, the thick cloud shrouding surrounding peaks as well as most of the valley
sides. The sound of sloshing boots and rushing water filled my mind. But all
a sudden, another sound rose above. A distant brushcutter. We looked at each
her askance. Who on earth would be out on a day like today working an alpine
sture? My husband shrugged. Probably one of the alp-herders doing some last
lying before winter buries the landscape in snow for the next however-many
onths, he proposed.

We continued, and presently came upon the source of the sound. As predicted
emanated from the precinct of an alpine hut, its picturesque meadow replete
ith Madonna shrine, on a terraced slope above the river. We nodded and said
llo to the fellow we saw from the track: *Buongiorno!* And he grinned past his
isy appendage in reply. Not five minutes later, though, we came upon two more
eerful souls. This time my husband stopped for a proper chat, one in which
e rest of the family could not participate, the local language being a border we

213

have not yet sufficiently crossed.

Farewells said, the men headed off at a good clip along the track ahead. Our interpreter, meanwhile, turned back and offered the following translation of their conversation: 'Apparently there's a mountain hut further on where we can get out of the rain and have a hot coffee. About twenty minutes. They'll show us the way.'

A public restaurant out here in the middle of nowhere? And at this time of year? Often farmers offer snacks and drinks, even light meals, over the summer months to hikers passing their farmsteads to supplement their meagre income but we had never heard of any in this region. There was cash in the backpack destined for the bar back in the village where our excursion began for the requisite hot toddy to round off a chilly day out. As far as we knew it was our closest 'civilisation' – several kilometres back up the track where the road ended on 'our' side of the border. Otherwise, several hours by foot across a high ridge to the south would be required to reach villages in the next valley on 'their' side of the demarcation. To our reckoning this was a place completely uncluttered by humanity's footprint. Bemused, yet up for an adventure, we followed …

Twenty minutes can seem like an age if you have no idea where you are going. Brushcutter-man swiftly overtook us to catch up to his friends; from a side path, another fellow appeared. We crossed a decrepit bridge over boulder-strewn whitewater, and proceeded up a steep track through thick beech forest. Russet leaves not yet fallen to earth delightedly dripped onto our already-drenched headgear, and we stumbled over tree roots lost in the gloom of their mushed brothers. Exploring uncharted territory, that's how it felt – the dog beside himself with glee at each fresh sniff-of-the-new, I giggling with the inanity of how our day was unfolding. Finally we came out of the trees and beheld a mountain hut up ahead.

Into it went the stream of men – six by now had accumulated along the path ahead of us and from the opposite direction arrived a couple more. These looked at us slightly quizzically before stripping off drenched shirts and trousers and then also disappearing into the hut. My husband's conversationalist appeared at the door, beckoned us to enter. Including dog? Sure, including dog! It seems we had not been 'shown' to a farmhouse restaurant which just happened to be in the neighbourhood, but 'invited' to join these men at their own personal fireside.

In we trooped. A single room with an enormous hearth over which was bubbling a veritable cauldron of pasta. A long wooden table, groaning with food, flanked either side by solid oak benches. The entire setting squeezed with sweaty bodies, broad grins and damp towels. Come sit! they cried. Share our fare! Bottles of wine miraculously appeared, handshakes and shy smiles were offered for the language-mutes amongst us, cheese ends and bacon rind conjured for a dog in eventh heaven.

We were warm, we were dry, but what was all this about getting a coffee? ny husband laughed after his second glass of red.

His interlocutors chortled in returned. You'll have to wait till the feast is over nd all hunger sated before your coffee shall be served! they winked.

Amici della Montagna. On a wet and wintery mid-autumn's day we had tumbled into their cross-border domain. A medley of individual volunteer rganisations throughout the Italian Alps, this particular band of merry men tewarded our *inzwischen* (in-between) zone – clearing paths, erecting signage, utting crosses atop peaks, renovating disused alpine huts as *rifugios* (refuges) rom the whims of high wild weather. Hailing from a village in the next valley, reir trek in would normally be hours long. Ah, but to do their work with all equisite gear, heli-drops were scheduled throughout the season – April through)ctober – for these caretakers of landscape. Despite the inclemency of this veekend's weather, its date on the calendar had been etched in stone; the last of re year, it could not be postponed. Wives had packed all manner of delectables or their Big Day Out, and these dozen men – through the sheer delight of sharing were determined that we too would be stuffed to the gills before any espresso iffered to complete the communal breaking of bread.

With wine-loosened tongues, the *Amici* described their singular joy to erform tasks in service to Nature and all who visit her high wild. To be out in the nountains, in the belly of the *felt* world, was welcome respite from the foibles of he world of men, they confided. Everything seemed more *honest* out here – true ature by another name.

One spoke a little English, shifted closer to me and said: 'We sing.'

Sing?

It was an opening the other *Amici* could not ignore. One fellow prodded his neighbour, an action which continued down the whole length of the table until he domino skipped to the other side, pattern repeated. Eventually someone nodded before disappearing up a ladder into the loft, returning a moment later vith a piano accordion in mint condition regardless of how many heli-drops it ad endured. The remainder of the troop gargled last dregs of wine, tuned up enor and baritone larynges. My English speaker explained: 'When we come o the mountains, we like to sing. And over time, we have become quite good. Jow we give concerts. Our songs are the peasant songs of old Italy – about love, overty, migration, and always the longing for our mountain homes. Now we vill sing for you.'

During the performance which followed in this private salon, every human motion possible of being summoned was, and in wonderful choral harmony; nore often than not accompanied by table-drumming from the youngest member of our family together with ecstatic sync-barking from the four-legged one. Hours we had spent in their company. Rendered speechless by their gifts, their generosity – of home and hearth, voice and song, the authentic outpourings of souls who bless each and every guest at their fireside – needs be we had to take our leave before our way would be lost to the mists of night. Needs be we had to return to the known world, the one left at the end of the road in a forgotten valley or the edge of time. But not before exchanging addresses. Once an *amico* in person always an *amico* in spirit. From the moment of my husband's first salutary chat with two of their number on a muddy path, we had been welcomed as honorary members of this community of true friends of the mountains, a revelation no less charming for its heart-felt spontaneity.

Indeed I felt we had been embraced by humanity pure in an uplifting demonstration of incarnational aspiration in this grand Gaian experiment – our sacred task to be an *amico* to all sentience in creation, to see and act with eyes as clear and unclouded as the *Amici della Montagna*, who sing in praise of our beautiful world with passion equal to any angelic host.

Border-Crossings 2

In the years following our chance meeting, we have not (yet) come across the *Amici* out in the field again. But that does not mean we do not stay in cyber-touch, or deliver Easter Eggs to their mountain hut's lintel (rather than the threshold, for obvious reasons), or discover their activity in side valleys we have wandered to chart new territory. Each time we cross the border to walk this particular patch of our valley's high wild, the *Amici* fill my thoughts. I walk the path consciously, knowing it is the way it is because of their work; that a section of track demolished by avalanche the previous winter, for example, is only waiting for their careful unpaid hands to arrive the following spring. No shillings jangle in their pockets, their labour their reward, and the fruits of same the evidence before them as surely as love the impetus for its performance. 'For the love of it': an offhand expression brimful of meaning in this context; unconditional is their care for the land they call home.

Yet in another border-crossing as momentous as the first, I was to discover that our *Amici* were not the only ones caring for this land they call home.

One day, about six months later, a chilly day in late spring (frigid, the wind still ice-infused after a winter which did not want to end), we trekked with friends along a well-known path on 'our' side of the border till halted by deep snow. Our planned excursion would not be possible. But rather than retrace steps in disappointment, we perused the map before heading cross-country up a south-facing slope to another ridge. Picking our way between remnant patches of slush, an alternate was proposed – to climb an unnamed peak which seemed, from a distance, to be relatively, for the most part, snow-free. Thus we headed off on a new adventure.

Two-thirds of the way up, however, I cried halt. The snow too deep, my footing too precarious. We had already lost some of the party at the base of the rise – they were keen to make their way back to a 'real' mountain hut to dry out soggy boots and partake of hot soup. The boys, meanwhile (dog-inclusive), wanted to go on; I said I would wait on a solitary granite slab, broad as a breaching whale, till they returned and we could all go down together.

Their voices gradually fading, I turned to face the chain of mountains falling away in each direction and intoned a prayer for their safe return. Cells singing with the *chi* of shared circuitry, I then began a conversation with the mountain sages of place – the ancestors who have actualised the life of *these* mountains. It was a conversation in the spirit of *Hello the House*. I told that we come to their mountains because we love. Love the engine of our intent – to come close, closer to the Ground of Being through the inexhaustibly-miraculous, awe-inspiring creation that is our beautiful world. I stood on a giant chunk of ancient *living* rock, glacier-smoothed and –split, felt its stone sentience connect with mine. Our collective resonant hum was loud and clear, our intercourse soul-to-soul, yet mediated through material selves, these star-dust cloaks we shabbily wear. Oh, but it seems that more was awakened by our communion during that half hour than a simple sharing of the reasons why our family walks the high wild. For once the boys returned and we began our march down the mountain to meet up again with the rest of our legion, I had an intriguing encounter.

Walking a straight line along the ridge, along a non-path or a mountain goat-trampled track (nought more), as usual I pulled up the rear. Concentrating on where to plant my feet, listening to one of the boys try to imitate the sweet melody of a courting bird earlier heard singing from atop a budding larch, I slipped into reverie of the *Amici* and how even when we did not walk one of their specific paths, I could still somehow sense their 'presence' in the subtle bones of the land.

In that moment, it seems I crossed a border without realising for suddenly all sight of my companions faded and 'I saw' two wee folk walking along the non-path toward me. They were only about knee-high tall but 'adult', wearing sturdy green dungarees, and jabbering away to each other in a language I had never heard. As we passed each other, they did not acknowledge my presence. In fact, I don't think they even noticed me, so deep were they in conversation. I immediately stopped and turned to see where they had gone. No more than an instant but they had disappeared.

In their place 'words formed': *Amici*. And I understood that these tiny folk were equally responsible with their human counterparts for keeping the paths safe as well as generally blessing the landscape of which they were stewards.

Later I told my husband of the encounter. But rather than being as wide-eyed with wonder and excitement as I, he quite matter-of-factly said: 'Oh, you must have met the little people. We call them *Wildmännli* ...'

Wildmännli

Literally translated as 'wild folk', the Swiss have a long and rich oral tradition of *Wildmännli* legends as do other countries in the Alps. And to a story, they all tell about how *Wildmännli* are wonderful helpers to mountain farmers, taking care of their meadows and even herds when they are absent or ill, as well as providing advice for everything from hunting etiquette to pasture management and veterinary remedies. Truly are they *Amici*, ones that by any other name would smell as sweet.

Each now and then, my husband remarked, an old-timer from the mountains would talk about *Wildmännli* with nostalgia, reminiscing about a time far in the past when they had been part of the visible world. Mostly these stories would have been told to said old-timer when he or she a child agog on a grandparent's knee. But retreat they did, to the hidden, to the invisible, permanently. For many centuries alpine farmers and herders have needs be performed their tasks alone ...

My husband could tell me no more. Research took me to the legends themselves; the first collection of direct oral reports documented in a volume from the late 16th century, and extended by two separate authors in the early to mid-19th. As part of a cultural history project for an inner-Swiss canton, a fresh text was fortuitously published by a fellow by the name of Steinegger containing all known data at the same time as the two tiny *Amici* popped into my field of vision. Saved from the dilemma of poring over old German script and grammar, I could concentrate on content and translation instead.

Apparently, it was always known that *Wildmännli* lived an existence mostly hidden from humanity. Their very name conjures the spirit of the wildness of nature, the prevailing landscape of the Alps – 'amoral, one that can never be tamed' – with its mountains, gorges, valleys and forests, its plentiful caverns and deep holes in the ground which seemingly lead to the centre of the earth. The stories speak of them as 'neither men nor gods, but frontier-walkers, border-crossers between the demonic and material worlds' (p.13):

'In the legends, *Wildmännli* are described as little people, silver-haired and -bearded, about the size of a four-year-old child (or "two shoes tall"), half-naked or completely hairy. In winter they clothe themselves in *tannenbart* (fir-tree lichens), moss, foliage or animal skins. Mostly they go barefoot. Other reports have these diminutive people dressed in a red or green outfit complete with beret. Apparently such clothes were gifts from alp-herds and farmers for their od service' (ibid.).

Further, what the legends tell is that as humanity expanded its reach into the ps, *Wildmännli*, 'expelled' by the new settlers, 'fled' deeper into the mountains, treating from an 'invading Christianity' which had no time for other ways of ing than their own. Nevertheless, they remain honoured in the naming of many gional landmarks mapped since the medieval, and their documented great ve of music and dance has long been integrated into popular Swiss culture. continuing alpine ritual is the banishing-of-winter where *Wildmännli*-cloaked ummers (amongst others) form yodelling, bell-ringing troupes to 'frighten' the ld and dark away at local *Fasnacht* (Mardi Gras) festivals – one example of an during pagan tradition successfully translated to later Christian society.

Wildmännli. Dear sweet souls. For many generations had they shyly rticipated in the life of the human world, their joy to help, to teach, to be true *nici* to the land and those who peopled it. But increasingly they found only rare mpanions in spirit, the solitary herdsman on his summer pasture or a busy ilk-hand in an alpine dairy: 'Once a milk-hand who had to stay overnight in e hut rather than return down the mountain to his farm in the valley, woke to ld them at work, making cheese in God's name. Astounded, he took the drink milk one offered while another said that if he would like to learn to sing or del, play the flute or alphorn, they would be happy to teach' (p.92).

'For as long as I can remember, I had often heard of the little people being en, sometimes even in large gatherings. In the far past they were intimate to manity. But more recently it has become much rarer ... old people often explain me that the *Wildmännli* complained about the wickedness of the world, that ople no longer lived with the simplicity of their fathers, and that for this reason ey had retreated from the world' (p.32-3). Again: 'Wherever *Wildmännli* remark ything wrong or *ungerade* (odd, unbalanced, strange), they leave straight away' .91).

Yet every now and then, the veil between the dimensions thinned invitingly offer a glimpse: 'Sometimes people would see them suddenly appear out of cave or crack in the rocks and just as quickly vanish again, *blitzschnell* (as fast lightning) ... They would come out to help with the hay. They only need say *hwupp* and the hay would be mown. ... (People knew) they kept chamois like ats, and that if one was a friend to *Wildmännli*, they would be gifted a wheel of amois cheese with the proviso to never completely finish it otherwise it could t grow back again' (p.39-56).

World-Workers United

The existence, and world-work, of *Wildmännli* continues, whether we 'see' it or not, whether we are aware of it or not. Like all Faerie Folk legends, the *Wildmänn* of the Alps were once observable fact. They may have gone underground – literally metaphorically – but they are no less real for being unseen by sceptical huma eyes. And, after my delightful encounter, I knew them to be as true a compan of friends to Gaia's high wild as any *Amici della Montagna* heli-dropped in wit brushcutters and piano accordions.

Indeed, after my encounter, I realised I had met my Faerie *Amici* long befor in the *Malakut* but had not known them for who they were. I recalled wit delight a troupe of little people in joyous celebration at the local churchyar before disappearing beneath a gravestone with cheeky grins. It was a meetin I gave to Kisha as she was 'surfacing' from grief and pain to find the peace an tranquillity of inner knowing in their stead (the following an excerpt from *Th Taste of Translation*, p.415):

She watched clouds slow-skid the sky, shape-shifted by silent winds, and spotted twin-cloud, hands and feet conjoined, a perfect O of blue space at their centre. Neve mind the wind which caught them at their task, spreading wide their misted wing. Their yogic stance could not be broken and the O, with its tunnel of clear ligh beyond, stayed. Even as the sun dipped behind the ridge, the twins caught pink now by dusk, these guardians of the way, stayed tight-wrapped round their O. And sh waited until they melted into evening blue, wondering: Does the path remain whe no longer seen?

She went to bed with the question still on her lips and dreamt of the village from time before now, from a time of no paths between cottages, only grass and the rar stone marker. Nevertheless she is in the selfsame cottage, knows it to be the sam although no Madonna graces her outer wall, although she sleeps on a mat by crackling hearth.

Suddenly she is called to a celebration at the church and skips down the hill to joi a procession through the graveyard. She sees accordion man astride a graveston of granite, this time with guitar, calling everyone to join their merry troupe. Sh thinks she recognises others as well, but can't be sure as they fade in and out of focus Everyone claps and laughs, sings and cheers. Such a party!

A dark night but the way lit by gentians, precious deep-throated flowers line th path, tiny bulbs filling their blue hearts, skin translucent from an inner glow. Kish follows the troupe along a twisting turning route while a joyous chorus sings lou in her ear. After a time, she stops, follows no more. At peace with her decision, she farewells the merry-makers as they move off through a clear-lit tunnel to beyond, shared voice like swirled mist to her ears.

Each time we trek the paths in our forgotten valley on the edge of time, I feel gratitude for the *collective* service of the *Amici* twins who make the trail safe and sure-footed for all wayfarers. With each audible step my boots engage their work, whether on the Earth's outer skin or via her inner subtle bones. And through their work, because of their work, I have the privilege to engage mine – to enjoin the *life* of the mountains, to engage the *wisdom* of mountain sages. Their planetary embrace facilitates mine; their conscious holding and flowing of greater Gaian intent – regardless of the size of garden plot they steward – energises my resolve. Holding and flowing such intent, in whatever way, shape or form, serves the whole; each act a firefly spark of hope for a more loving world. Thus each time I walk I send blessings to all *Amici* stewards, physical and non-, for their selfless *expression* of love. For their love ensures that those of us drawn to walk the high wild can express our love likewise – in my case to mirror joy back to the face of the sky.

The memory of my various meetings with the *Amici* makes me smile every time, and has fuelled a small collection of simple but heart-warming touchstones for when I am far from their orbit. Yet since those first encounters years past, we often find ourselves trekking the same paths in our own unique way, connecting at the oddest but most delightfully whimsical junctures. In this respect, my human *Amici* can pop up as 'faerie-like' in nature as their 'cousins' can wield a subtle brushcutter.

Still, the initial connection was *Amici* to *Amici*, as within, so without, as above, so below. These two ground crews, united as world-workers in sacred task, presented me the possibility to bear witness, to learn. Who knows if they bear witness to each other's work; it is not a question I have asked nor does it seem important. Important is the fact that I have been fortunate enough to bear witness to how they *live* the divine grace inherent in our beautiful, beautiful world, how they each *sing* a precious note in a world-wide, -deep and -high choir, how their joy-inflected symphonic *praise* generates a resonance of connectivity in, out and all round about Gaia's interwoven stream of consciousness.

We sing, said my English-speaking *Amici* friend.

Yes. It *is* a simple as that. We sing. United. Please join us.

221

Amici della Luce
(Friends of the Light)

An ancient Buddha said:
"Mountains are mountains, waters are waters": Dogen

In his Mountains and Waters Discourse (*Sansui Kyo*), Dogen says: 'Mountains and waters right now are the actualisation of the ancient way. Each, abiding in its phenomenal expression, realises completeness'. At the hour of the Rat on the eighteenth day of the tenth month in the first year of Ninji (1240), he taught to the assembly at Kannondori Kosho Horin Monastery as follows:

'There are mountains hidden in treasures. There are mountains hidden in swamps. There are mountains hidden in the sky. There are mountains hidden in mountains. There are mountains hidden in hiddenness. This is complete understanding. An ancient Buddha said, "Mountains are mountains, waters are waters."'

So it is, ever was, ever will be. In the essay, *self-naughting*, I describe my seven years a-wander in the wilderness of the *Malakut*. Halfway through this time Dogen's mountains showed up, the dwelling place of his great sages:

'However many great sages and wise men we suppose have assembled in the mountains, ever since they entered the mountains no one has met a single one of them. There is only the actualisation of the life of the mountains.' He recounts how the mountains *become* their own chambers, their body and mind; and indeed I have experienced this vividly and directly in my own process of becoming.

'Twas not long, however, till Dogen's waters also decided to make an oracular appearance as I describe in this journal entry:

Lucid, powerful, very exciting. F and I were to make a hike to a thermal spring. There were two ways of getting there, from below or from above. I thought a map would be useful as he seemed unsure of the route ... suddenly I was in a shaft or well, a *vertical* tunnel. I had come here to find the map *to* the actual place where I was. In my mind I kept calling it *Acqua Termale* (AT); no idea why, but that's the name which presented constantly in my thoughts. I went down the shaft – very narrow, maybe only a metre and a half wide, square in shape, warmly lit. I was alone and once hit bottom, walked along a tunnel to a room (coincidentally no larger than a ten-foot-square hut) where I knew the map was kept.

It was pinned to the wall behind a sheaf of glass but it seemed I could 'buy' one here too to take home. In fact, on my way to the room I passed other maps documenting different excursions to alternate locations, all plastered to walls, but I kept going to the AT map room. I looked at its map closely and yes, thought F would appreciate having a copy to help our journey, the AT clearly marked with a little hut symbol (like in regular hiking maps). As a thermal spring, it linked the elements of fire and water together *within* the belly of the mineral-rich earth – 'source' as well as place of healing.

Interestingly, whilst in shaft, tunnel or room, it was wet like a mine, the silence backdropped by the constant sound of running water, of the AT *itself*; seepage from the spring made physical connection through the walls, but I still needed the map – I was close, but not in direct contact yet. 'I saw' two ways of getting here – from a village 'above' or one 'below'. In geological-type imagery, with different bands of rock depicted, I understood the latter was built in a region that was 'barren' (*Malakut* 'words formed') and not connected with the waters of the AT. You could get here, but not experience what the waters offered as it showed a block of impenetrable rock between.

As I surfaced from the space, Mr1300BC arrived with the message I needed to take back to F. *One Life*, he said, repeating it over and over. It fit with his message of the previous night (*Life and Death share the same Breath*), now expanded with the imagery that there was *One Place* where all is connected, for which there is only *One Name*. In the moment, my realisation was immediate: the AT the source of the sacred waters of life. To have the opportunity to make the excursion, and to be gifted the map to its exact location? Extraordinary good fortune!

Afterwards, Deleuze and Guattari's notion of the rhizome, open and connectable in all dimensions and directions, came up several times in fragmentary follow-ups to help *me* explain this to 'me', such that in/on a plane of consistency, the rhizome can change state between dimensions without losing the connection to itself, and that the number of dimensions or multiplicities emanating on said plane is endless, infinite – thus *One Life* or *One Name* has an infinity of names/lives shooting off from it without losing or severing connection to its source, the AT ... I think 'me' got it.

I have stacks, absolutely stacks of such journal records of *Malakut* wanders which are written-into-existence on a plane of intimate exteriority. Like storage tubers in a perpetually extending rhizome of interconnectable thought, each a potential contributor to the unveiling of personal myth, they sit and watch from their discrete (and discreet!) places of knowing – patiently (and sometimes not-so) waiting till I eventually intuit their inherent meaning. So do the stacks remain as seemingly random research piles until such time as further ventures into becoming landscapes (which resonate similarly) arise or other synchronistic events in material space-time (such as scholarly reading, dog-walking or even doing the ironing) begin the slow process of unveiling psychoid unity to *itself* from the fecund swamp of soul.

Suffice it to say that I have learned, through all my long years a-wander in the wilderness, that even if, on first reckoning, the constellation of landscapes and encounters appear *not* to be relevant, linked or revelatory, over time 'tis guaranteed they shall gradually disclose their interconnectivity – with each other, with me – to the full light of surface cognition. At which time the stacks reassemble themselves (like Deleuze and Guattari's armies of ants) into plateaus ripe for interrogation and problematising, including eventual *material* manifestation (if I am fortunate!) according to a process kickstarted by the *desire* to create, to know.

Hence, the AT had made itself known to me, but it would need time and gestation before I could make myself known to it. At some level, though, I 'knew' this sacred source to be related (in ways as yet undisclosed) to the high wild landscape I call home in the Italian-speaking part of Switzerland, a valley where I meet Dogen's mountains 'walking' on their own terms, having intimately 'heard' *der Ruf der Berge* anchored in this space:

'People outside the mountains do not realise or understand the mountains walking,' he says. All mountains are eastern mountains, 'and eastern mountains master travelling on water. Accordingly, these activities are a mountain's practice ... There is walking, there is flowing, and there is a moment when a mountain gives birth to a mountains child.' Thus does he describe the Ancestors' path of understanding.

In such a spirit, Dogen asks that we too study the moment when water *sees* water, just as I had previously studied the moment when mountain *realises* mountain: 'Water's freedom depends only on water ... But water as earth, water, fire, wind, and space realises itself.'

I thought: *Mountain cradles water, water flows through mountain, and out into the world.*

Dogen says: 'The path of water runs upward and downward and in all directions ... Water is the true suchness of water. Water is water's complete virtue.'

I thought:

All the way from source to sea, from
source to sea to source ... Water – sacred –
through your eyes I see ... Self – font of being,
font of flowing, font of blessing, interconnection;
watersheds of passionate expression,
universe high and just as wide ...

Incubating Insights

I continued my engagement with the generative heart of mountain sentience, but never forgot the AT's crystalline existence. And one day, a gestative nine months hence, all causes and conditions ripened to enact the following:

A very special journey last night to a landscape called *The Tree of Infinite Knowing*. An extraordinarily vast high wild space, glacier-smoothed, but not a tree in sight. Yet this its name. I 'understood' there had once been an actual tree, a majestic specimen with widespread branches, but it had long since 'died' or (to put it a better way) changed form, metamorphosing to infuse the landscape with its (perennial) wisdom. 'I saw' this transpire, its melting and merging, as if over an incredible length of time, aeons. By the time of my 'visit', it had fully decomposed, composted, had completed its cycle to fruit the earth with 'infinite knowing'. Hence the entire space, *everything*, was now *The Tree*, not simply the tree itself.

I 'glided' about, energised and blessed to be granted this glimpse, but also intrigued to discover as much as I could about the space. 'Knowing' that *The Tree* infused everything, I was amazed to find that parts of the landscape were like a high moor, the watertable very close to the surface in parts; grassy areas were spongy and damp underfoot. At one point I looked down a small crevasse, like a crack in the earth, not deep but wide enough to be noticeable, and saw that the rocks therein were wet and glistening as if fed by an underground spring. I had a sudden tug of understanding that this was the site of the *Acqua Termale*, where it reached the 'mantle', here at *The Tree of Infinite Knowing.*

Later in the same space I had the unexpected good fortune to meet *The Tree's* guardian. A time arrived during my explorations when the resonant hum, signature accompaniment to *Malakut* encounters, suddenly rose in pitch to become a tinkling bell 'announcing' another presence. A figure appeared from behind a boulder and took something I value into the 'dark' beyond. I felt a surge of vibrational energy and words formed: *GreenMan.*

Given all the images in circulation of this being, it was quite a surprise that he constellated in my imaginal world as a kind of contemporary wood sprite – tall young adult male, curly blonde hair, cheeky grin, baggy trousers, hippy-style green shirt daubed with swirls of yellow. Oh, and no shoes. Yet although he had 'stolen' something of mine, I intuited it to be a game and, exhilarated by the touch of his vibration, felt no apprehension entering the dark and rugby-tackling him to retrieve said 'treasure'. Instantly he disappeared and I understood our game simply represented a cue to describe his task – to collect 'knowing' to add to *The Tree's* wisdom chalice, itself a dynamic living energy in *constant* communion with the sacred source as well as the worldly production of the 'new'.

Throughout, I had a feeling I knew this place, although visiting for the first time. The landscape constellated as the 'far hills' I saw from my place at *The Wall.* A locale of longer-than *Malakut* task given me by Mr1300BC, this wall divided the entire landscape in two. As I hovered above, when first assigned duties here, I saw it stretched, unbroken, far toward a distant glacier-smoothed high wild mountain scape; now I knew this scape to be *The Tree.*

To describe the wall, however: It was wood-panelled, and tall – my practice, in this designated 'section', was to 'plane it away', cut through, and reunite the two 'sides' as one whole. To perform the job I was given an old-fashioned woodworking tool, something ne'er before used by these writerly hands (human or subtle!). Of course my first attempts were pathetic, embarrassingly so – I cut deep into the wood, gouged about, not a shred of ply did I render uniform or smooth.

I understood I needed to improve my skills in the first instance but, just as importantly, not to suddenly break through (i.e. no chopping through with an axe or whatever). My progress had to be steady, faithful, gradual; slowly thinning the *density* between the two was required to restore the landscape to an *enduring* expression of holism.

Message clear from the start, *The Wall* consistently informs my approach; regardless of task assigned or collaborator met (inner and/or outer), all is underlain by a *desire* to connect inner and outer scapes as a single plane of consistency, to live a one-life-of-the-one-world reality here-now, ever-on. Nevertheless, to intuit that the single holism of *The Tree* (fed by the *Acqua Termale*) could be supported by my work at *The Wall*, that its scape the envisioned horizon of my task, was energising. The storage tuber grew …

Another period of gestation followed, till Mr1300BC returned with a real gem, symbolically titled (like everything else in my Huxleyian mode's universe), *The Way of the Knight*:

> Firstly he reminded that all that had gone before were prior stages to my need to now go *through* (what he called) the 'volcano mountain', his teaching therefore part of a coherent string of instruction (in his mind at least!). It described a quest, replete with ballad (tune, text) of a knight's adventures, and was delivered in a series of child-like sketches of the stages involved, whereby the knight gradually drew closer to a line of mountains where it seemed the 'grail' (also called 'light' or 'source' at different junctures) would be found. The final sketch communicated that the next (and last) stage of the quest would take the knight 'very far', *beyond*; yet no drawing followed to suggest whereto or what, only that it would be the home of said grail.
>
> It was offered to the student (or squire) as a riddle: *Do you know where that possibly could be?* before flipping back through the sketches all the way to the beginning, to the first image of the questing knight himself. Here the 'grail' had been housed all along in his heart – the spark of love that is each's inheritance manifesting as a ball of light. Recognising this, becoming *conscious* of his 'self-light', enacted its expansion; now it radiated out to become all-inclusive of his form, flooding him with its (his) life energy. Yet the message clear: Only by undertaking the full quest (there and back again to *self*) could he 'release' the grail from the cave of his heart, for it to explode into 'viable' life. Hmmm …

When meditating on what I had been shown in the parable, I found myself, briefly, in an inner chamber. Here I stood within the walls of a tall earthern structure of rough brickwork and the occasional square of colour, domed like an egg, its floor dirt or stone-flagged. I understood it to be a chamber constellating *within* the so-called *Volcano Mountain*; fully rendered and reinforced, it reminded me of a vertical kiln, the brickwork like that of a cement kiln I had once stood inside upon decommissioning – cracked, heated, smoke-stained were its refractory bricks but always up to the fiery task at hand.

Herein, the resonant hum was almost boomingly loud, underpinning and overlaying all (absence of) sound; in the space of meditation, I was drawn to deepen connection to the 'kiln room' and found myself instantly gone – into the *Full Dark*, a 'place' impossible to describe …

Again a period of gestation. Till a *Malakut* scape presented which seemed to pull all threads in the telling together, and out of which I had a sudden insight as to the *specificity* of task:

The space constellated like our 'home' village in the Italian south, but as if in a time before time, a place before now. We had planned a trek to an alpine hut in the high wild which offered risotto for hungry hikers – the problem of poor patronage in such a remote region (a forgotten valley on the edge of time) meant we were keen to support 'local enterprise', to keep 'life' in the valley. I saw the hut from two perspectives – one by arriving instantly (dog in tow), the other by trekking in on foot (children in tow).

At the hut we met around a communal table with others in the context of 'work'. One described to me an assignment about which he was very excited; project manager on behalf of a 'great master', it centred on accessibility to a place called *Mandalay* (M). At this, he showed me a very fine pen-and-ink sketch headed by some lines of ancient script. Beneath the text was a picture of a cave on the shores of a small alpine lake fronted by a couple of Buddhist-style monks. An incredibly beautiful drawing, the perspective was from the far side of the lake looking across to the cave beyond.

He then asked me about my own journey to M with the children which, it seems, had already taken place but in describing it, I trekked it again. I told him it took four hours from the trailhead (where the car was parked) to reach the alpine hut; to reach M itself, however, meant climbing further – the hut, therefore, a good staging post on the journey. We needed to carry everything with us to make the 'risotto' as well as anything else needed for overnighting in the space. I saw grassy meadows, forests, a smoothed area like an alpine pass. But once in the vicinity of the lake high above, the landscape grew more rocky, granite-outcropped, vegetation sparse.

Safely arrived, we entered the cave – it constituted a permanent monastery for the monks, yet visitors always welcome. It felt very special, holy, to be invited there. We wandered a network of tunnels (flaming torch-lit); each now and then widening out into chambers for communal meeting or to reveal small niche shrines. The monks wore deep red robes; their heads were shaved. The silence was most profound; I saw glistening wetness on the tunnel walls, seepage from the source; the lake's waters rose from somewhere in this inner space although I did not see whence it outflowed myself.

Outside, a woman handed me a postcard as a memento of our visit – it showed a map, designed like a medieval itinerary, what de Certeau describes as 'performative indications ... a memorandum prescribing action' (p.120). I became excited, remembering how I had perused similar examples for my dissertation on pilgrimage. The postcard depicted a long trail from the lowlands taking one into the *heart* of the Alps, where the cave would be found, and included a drawing of a small figure walking the path.

The woman pointed to the figure and said: *To this one is known the way in **and** the way out.* I therefore understood that walking to M not enough; one must re-trace the route *out*; the whole *thread* the journey, a cycle needing completion before its import *known* and embedded in the soil of self. The postcard symbolised what other seekers could discover if they followed the example of 'this one'.

Returned from the space I wondered at its 'naming' – was the phonetic earness of M to mandala a coincidence? In research I discovered the place is ne stuff of legend, as the site of a 'great civilisation', somewhere the Buddha upposedly visited. But were these red herrings or simply ways to alert me to ne importance of what I had been shown? Regardless, another time I thought: mmm ... but now backed by the thought that it was time to begin the assembly f all puzzle pieces into a single plateau ...

What's in a Name?

To be frank, it is difficult to know when the exact moment of conscious wareness of task arises in one's cognition, when the uplift of soul-knowing ure decides to muscle its way out and through, past all other thoughts and isks (ironing and ego-conditioning inclusive) to say: *I am* and *This is*. To stand tubborn as robust plateau or desert-father'd mesa, perusing the surrounding indscape from the solidity of knowing 'above', to fold intractable arms, fix self /ith penetrating stare, and finally say: *You must.*

Emerson holds that the soul already contains in itself the event, for the event ; simply the actualisation of *its* thought. At some level, therefore, the 'event' resented itself and 'I' agreed to steward its naming into existence. I needed) discover the source of *our* waters, my homecome river flowing to the sea. Vhatever its relationship to the universal *Acqua Termale*, font of the primal Ground f Being, it personalised itself *to* and *for* me in this context with its naming. The articularity of its constellation as a *Malakut* landscape speaking to the *physical* igh wild sentience I embrace as mirror of joyous self, seemed to imply the pportunity to *actualise* – in much the same way (I believe) as Ibn Arabi's Creative 'rayer between *'Abd* and *Rabb* – a divine marriage, one fundamentally based on ne dialectic of love.

To trek its path in material time and space, sing up country each step of its lorious way, would complete a circle of knowing, even if I had no idea what aid 'knowing' would reveal. It would be a voyage of discovery in the spirit of all explorers past present and future sailing *waters* unknown – courage, trust, and love their (and my) only requisite foundation (*stones*).

'The secret of divinity is yourself,' wrote the 9th century Sufi master Sahl Tostar whom Henri Corbin exuberantly quotes (b, p.225); a fact to which I append Thich Nhat Hanh's perennial wisdom: 'Drinking a cup of tea, the seeming distinction between the one who drinks and the tea being drunk evaporates. Drinking a cup of tea becomes a direct and wondrous experience in which the distinction between subject and object no longer exists' (p.42). Shakespeare could quite happily tag along on this mystic meander – a rose by any other name would smell as sweet.

Just as drinking a cup of tea or sharing breath with a smelly rose cannot be discounted as anything less than sacred ritual, sensately engaged, the psychoid unity inherent in replicating a *Malakut* journey in the material should not be underestimated for its own sake. The very *living* of life is *satori* after all. Time and again I have found that inner landscapes have their counterpart in the outer world of the senses, and that it is only when I make a commitment to manifesting some subtle learning in physical space that the final cathartic 'a-ha' resounds in the chamber of my heart.

Readying me for this 'event', perhaps, had been the long (physical) hours spent in reflection of our local creek before (figuratively) engaging its white-knuckled plunge hundreds of metres to gorge below, there to join the *Isorno's* frothing foaming, bruising bouncing, passage onward, out to engage the (wider) world. Equally I had been overjoyed to learn the specific geography of this *genius loci,* how our valley *chose* to make pilgrimage to the Venetian Lagoon before spilling into the basin of Adriatic, there to merge and flow with all (Seven Seas), before (re-) entering a cycle on endless repeat. So too did I marvel at the synchronicity of saint honoured by our village church one-and-the-same with *La Serenissima's* holy patron.

Purely (literally) and simply (substantively), water *defines* this precipitously contoured shed as compellingly and dramatically as the majestic mountain scape overlighting her whole of the whole. There was a reason I *desired*, beyond measure, to write an epic love song to this Beatrice of true-natured high wild; desire that could be summed up in two extraordinarily breathtaking and ordinary elemental phenomena – mountain and river, otherwise known as stone and water – combining in a singular *satori'd* event:

'In Song China there was a man who called himself Layman Dongpo ... A literary genius, he studied the way of dragons and elephants in the ocean of awakening. He descended deep chasms and soared freely through clouds. One night when Dongpo visited Mount Lu he was enlightened upon hearing the sound of the valley stream. He composed the following verse for his master:

Valley sounds are the long broad tongue.
Mountain colours are no other than the unconditioned body.
Eighty-four thousand verses are heard throughout the night.
What can I say about this at a future time?'

In giving this dharma talk – appropriately titled *Valley Sounds, Mountain lours* and delivered the same year as his Mountains and Rivers Sutra – Dogen ys: 'You may regret that mountains and waters *conceal* sounds and colours, t you may rejoice as well that the moment of enlightenment emerges *through* ountains and waters.'

In asking his students to open their minds to the possibility of 'hidden asure', he asks: 'Who can fathom this water? Is it a bucketful or does it fill ole oceans? In the end was it Dongpo who was awakened or the mountains and ters that were awakened? ... Once a monk asked: How do you turn mountains, ers, and the great earth into the self? The master said: How do you turn the f into mountains, rivers, and the great earth?'

Indeed.

Here I sit on a lowly novice cushion set before the great master's knee, his be cascading to the floor like a russet waterfall caught in the misted light of ate autumn's day, bounded by shadowed mountain ridges fore and aft, and gn to hear myself murmur in reply: 'Tis one and the same in the end for the e life we all share, is it not?'

Dogen's lesson and line of rhetorical questioning had reminded me of an counter, in the full material light of day, that I had had with a roe deer buck the forest years before. Reciprocal recognition pure, the Sacred had spoken rough this gentle sinewed creature. As we stared into each other's souls long, aring space, sharing breath, words formed:

Through your eyes I see myself.

Each of us, in seeing the other, had *become* the other, become the *true* self. One. moment for which a well-annotated hadith provides seamless translation, so o the immanent beauty of knowing that everywhere I turn is the face of God, ecited:

I was a hidden treasure and longed to be known, so created the world that I might known.

Its fundamental meaning is that only through *our* witness can the hidden od) be revealed; only through the loving 'eye' of *our* heart can witness (of and Him) be effected. The point being that the deer embraced such perception a natural matter-of-course, a perception which, in its innocence and purity of pression, it had gifted to me ...

Dogen's mountains, rivers, great earth, me. My light their light, their light

231

mine – all one and the same. *One Life,* I remembered, for which there is only *On* *Name* (yet giving rise to an infinity of same). My contemplations had returned m to the *Acqua Termale.* I devised a plan to gift my light to the waters of our river, a its source; I would physically add *my* light to *its* shed, and let our *shared* river c liquid light do what it will to effect blessings throughout the world, all the wa from source to sea, from source to sea to source. The moment when water *see* water, says Dogen, manifests complete understanding: 'You should go forwar and backward and leap *beyond* the vital path where other *fathoms* other.'

The bard yearned to get busy, the desire to create flooding mythopoies veins:

> *Dear Isorno flood, fedeli d'amore,*
> *entrusted grail. Through your eyes*
> *I see true Self: water (acqua), fire (termale) –*
> *my light your light, your light mine.*
> *Behold: Love's light, everlasting flame! – and*
> *our shared practice a molten stream of same ...*

Working the Sounds and Colours of Light

The reader may wonder about the expressions 'my light' and 'liquid light' to which I refer back to *The Wall* and *The Way of the Knight.* Concurrent with m musings about the *Isorno's* watershed, I had developed practices based on th opportunity to gift one's (excess, if that's the right word) self-light of love to th world. This centred on my observation of how the ball of light, emanating fron the spark of love at the core of each expression of sentience, *densifies* as a resul of its joyous desire to participate in the one-life-of-the-one-world.

We all do this unconsciously when we express our love for someone or thing so too in uplifting a memory of same. That 'warm glow' radiates out and touche all proximate beings. Proclus' heliotrope is an example, equally a child's wide eyed and open-mouthed wonder at discovering another facet of the beauty o the world for the first time. Yet to consciously harness this elemental fact of ou being works to *actualise* the flow of our light into the world in more concentrate and sweeping form.

Think of a lighthouse beacon emanating from our aptly-named solar plexu – a vertical (transcendent) structure spreading light out and across a horizonta (immanent) landscape effecting outreach to all others 'touched' by its ligh While standing in self-sovereignty as its own entity, at the same time it share the primal purpose of its existence with all sentience, as an act of solidarity, thu demonstrating the interconnectivity of *being* on a singular plane of consistenc with the *simultaneous* horizontal and vertical execution of its loving *flow* of ligh

232

As water sees water, as mountain realises mountain, so does light mirror light – through 'its' eyes we 'see' our self. My process of 'mirroring' joy is such a practice of light gifted to light, its intent to fill/infill/backfill the subtle reservoirs of Gaia's peace-sinks in the hope that bolstering these naturally-occurring *sequestrations* support her continued unfoldment and evolution of consciousness in resonant harmony with the cosmos.

Extending this line of thought, I had an inkling that the way elementals constellate and coalesce in the physical plane contributed to such process – implicated was a balance between geology and spirit, a necessity to ensure our physical engagement with the Earth reflected our spiritual aspirations and vice versa. A teaching by Mr1300BC (that: *Love in itself is Fire*) grafted onto Eastern philosophy (that: *All Matter arises from Aether*, i.e. the unmanifest becoming manifest), it traversed a path whereby 'I saw' Love in its molten form begin to circulate within my own being from the 'ball of light' at its core – its passage of 'becoming' and gradual densification thereafter actualised in the chakra-tunnels' of my *Volcano Mountain* before any (laval) flow into the world could be envisaged.

Working my *chi* was integral to the practice. *Central* to the equation, however, was the conscious 'holding' of divine Presence within. We each inherit the spark of love as a matter-of-course as incarnate beings, but unless we consciously honour and hold this divinity and acknowledge our incarnation as an expression of such divinity, we cannot release it back into the world with any *clarity*. The inner foundation must be sound before any outer practice engaged. Likewise are we challenged to honour and hold the divinity *inherent* in the elementals of our sacred sentient Earth for the practice of flow to 'flow'.

Our conscious sensing of Presence, of inner and outer divinity mirrored, begins the process; the ball of light 'grows' and densifies with our love. As a simple true-natured act, therefore, it cannot help but eventually expand *beyond* the boundaries of skin as joy shared with the world. Filling our self-reservoir seamlessly segues to gifting light to Gaia's reservoir when we mirror *simultaneously* our joy of the world and the world's joy of itself. *Through your eyes I see myself*: As simple as in-breath, out-breath, the practice ebbs and flows like waves on a sun-sparkled sea. No need of visualisation, or imagination, 'tis real, physical, embodied – embedded in the soil of the sanctity of our existence, flowing light is as sensate an experience as the circulation of oxygen through an (inner) blood stream or (outer) river system.

Follow the leylines, Mr1300BC had instructed long years past, an insight extended to mean the leylines of *self*, not simply the ones inscribed *within* landscape. Thus did I see these inner lines flowing, the *chi* of my own circuitry – liquid light I could now gift, as loving mergence, into the *Isorno*'s, its watershed an

233

(existent material) channel, a leyline in its own right, for flowing subtle energies out into the world.

Replicating the *Malakut* journey I had made to *Mandalay* in material space and time was integral to task. In Aboriginal-speak, for whatever reason yet to unfold, it constituted my personal 'stretch' of Ancestral song, a stewardship of territory gifted into my care in, for, by and to Love (a prepositional party if ever there was one!). The connection between myself and land, between spirit and geology, needed to be (re-) sung into physical existence for the *living* lines of energy and consciousness within the planet to be (re-) woken at this place, to flow on and out to the All:

'In Aboriginal belief, an unsung land is a dead land … if the songs are forgotten, the land itself will die,' writes Bruce Chatwin (p.52). I meditated on this wisdom in company of an aethereal prophecy I had once 'heard'. Uplifted from the very heart of Gaia's soul-self, 'I saw' her torn, wrenched from her planetary home by humanity's continued desecration of her mantle, by our unabated disrespect for elemental cohesion and energetic balance in our approach, as we (in Bateson's rhetoric) 'arrogate all mind' to ourselves … seeing 'the world around as mindless and therefore not entitled to moral or ethical consideration' (2000, p.468).

At this the voice spoke its wisdom: *When the Spirit is once again at One with the Third* … Gaian holism would be ripe for manifestation. My work – here, now – in support of actualising this profundity I understood to involve *re-singing* the connection into being between her bruised and battered spirit and her (equally) exploited Earth. To heal, the World Soul desired nothing more than to re-unite in divine marriage with the sanctity of her 'third rock from the sun', the material fact of our beautiful world.

By 'singing up country' (as Aboriginal dreaming describes the process), I saw my task as weaving 'light' threads between spirit and geology (verticality) and between material sentience and itself (horizontality) – yet my *depth* of engagement would only truly support Gaian holism if my 'spiritual' practice was enacted physically and my 'physical' practice likewise spiritually; I needed to walk in the footsteps of the Ancestors across the land, and leave my trail of 'song' as a gift permanently imprinted in Gaia's skin …

All of the above, of course, is simply a very longwinded explanation for why I felt called to replicate what I had learnt in the *Malakut* in the material world, to effect psychoid unity equally within myself and planet, microcosm macrocosm and all in between. Nevertheless, I worked to further my understanding, to harness the energy within the seclusion of retreat, over years of evolving practice before considering any outreach to the specificities of *valley sounds* and *mountain colours* in our high wild watershed. Yet once prepping complete, I felt confident to outreach my (liquid) gift to the source, that it would be accepted in the spirit of its offering – and decided to vest a blessing stone with the task to be the *container* for my light in physical space and time.

My reasoning? It has long been known that objects infused, suffused with sanctity, provide energetic transport for same – icons provide a classic example in the Western lexicon. Their tangibility works to *densify* the immaterial, to bring it into our sense-making orbit. An act of 'creation', any 'thing' has the ability to function similarly, to externalise sacred purpose; Mr1300BC described it to me in very simple language once, long ago: *We all breathe life into what we love*. And so it is. Just as we consciously 'hold' divine Presence within the very fact of our inner being, we may vest the same 'holding' function in an outer physical symbol.

Purpose therefore twinned between self and symbol, the object (in Italo Calvino's words) becomes the 'real protagonist of the story … charged with a special force … like the pole of a magnetic field, a knot in the network of invisible relationships' (p.32-33). And, when said protagonist is tossed into a small alpine lake which is the spring of the *Isorno*'s entry to outer world? 'Tis a network of 'invisible' relationships which exponentially grows; liberally diffused into the shed, liquid light is free to flow through a world without end – methinks message in a bottle by any other name would function just the same …

I may have worked through the proposition intellectually, and embedded a spiritual practice in my life involving the flow of liquid light experientially, but we still had to find the literal source of our river. Enter a (physical) map courtesy of one dear friend, a geographically-minded reading of same by another, and a joyous troupe of Gaian worldworkers known as *Amici della Montagna* (a sum history of whom, describing our entry into their subtle (and not-so-subtle) orbit recounted in the previous essay).

Following these treasured *Amici*'d encounters, we were keen to continue trekking the high wild headwatered country within their stewardship across the border where the (Swiss) valley road ends; however without a decent map, we had never ventured much farther than *Bagni di Craveggia*, the ruin of a thermal baths in use since the medieval until a pair of avalanches thundered down the slopes in the mid-20th century to halt the flow of its healing waters (in the minds of potential patrons, at least).

Now, the gift of a detailed *Club Alpino Italiano* map would ensure we knew where we were going throughout the watershed upstream of this locale; meanwhile, tracing an intelligent finger along all lines of contoured flight from the main river valley eventually located the small alpine lake into which pooled the water from our sacred mountains' heart before its (epic) journey made, out to join seven (and more) salty seas.

These events set in train a desire to begin walking the paths consciously, to sing up country and *Hello the House* to all sentience as a way to make myself (and future intent) known in 'new' territory, a becoming landscape with which I was clearly already acquainted in the *Malakut* but had to learn to read in the material. Here an example of one such outing:

> Easter Sunday; *Amici* hike day and the whole way up and back my mantra was: *Amici, Amici, Amici della Montagna – thank you for your work and your blessing of the paths!* Such was my outreach to both partners in this Alliance between Humanity and Faerie we are blessed to call friends on either side of the veil. I left a small white stone that has been by my bed-head these past years, fresh (still, I hope) with the energy of the mountains coupled with *Marianna*'s (and my) peaceful presence as well as D's energy of 'gifting' in the first instance. I left it on a 'standing stone' near a small grove of *Rottanne* growing in the soft river sand of the valley. I spoke with them, asked for their intercession on my behalf. Then later at the *Amici* hut, I 'realised' my spontaneous suggestion of leaving some Easter Eggs above the lintel for the next time they're there with their brushcutters likewise represented an 'offering' of food to subtle companions of the way. It made sense, 'twas a special human occasion we delighted in sharing ...

Malakut wanders also kept apace with these outer hikes during following months. In one, our family trekked up a narrow path, as if a side-valley, in single file – a place I didn't 'know'. Yet it seems we were heading to our new home (region) for along the way we were overtaken three times by different 'Amici' who were also home-owners from this upper end of the valley. Each time they stopped to introduce themselves and welcome us to the area. As a valley narrows, it leads toward the source; this much I know. But that it also represents home, that by undertaking this venture we would be symbolically walking home? Read on:

> Extraordinarily exhilarating lucid *Malakut* encounter ... with a wolf. We were hiking the back of the valley (*Amici* territory) in single file – me, D, then F with dog – when a wolf suddenly appeared on the path directly in front of me. Intriguingly we communicated completely in thought *after* I had completed a ritual toward which I was surface-resistant but deep-knew to be 'natural' – I had to kneel before her, bow down to her as 'keeper' or spirit-guardian of this wild place. Hence my hesitancy; I thought this could go horribly wrong if I ended up getting mauled!
>
> Nevertheless I knelt down, we literally saw 'eye-to-eye' as the ritual was conducted using the third eye (forehead-to-forehead) to enable our twinned communication thereafter. I called to D to come and greet her likewise but he (understandably) thought this was too 'way out' and weird to engage. So I said:

It's OK, she's a 'mother' (i.e. kind and gentle with children). He said: How do you know? But I couldn't explain it – it was the same sort of knowing as knowing her as a female presence, which, after effecting our 'link', I knew to include motherhood, like me. The interesting thing is that even though I bowed before her in this, her territory, once the ritual complete, I understood us to be 'equals'. We were both mothers, both keepers – guardians of our respective spaces. A very natural knowing but also exhilarating after I'd 'left' the space. I had 'met' a true sister in spirit. Thanks be!

Now, because D wouldn't come forward, she moved past me on the path to greet him. No need for ritual (I had completed that for our whole 'group', it seems) so he patted her normally. As preface to this meeting, I had 'mentally' introduced D as my child and I felt her treat him as lovingly as she did her own children. Then she looked past D to where F was reining in Pabey who was carrying on with his usual madcap barking routine (intriguingly he did not growl at any perceived 'menace'). She asked me who they were. I mentally introduced F, and with P said: 'It's OK, he's harmless.' In thought-image, 'I saw' her sigh of resignation, that he was like the aberrant child you ignore until he gives up through self-boredom. We shared a smile of parental knowing before she leapt away, off the path and back into the undergrowth, with a last message: *You are welcome here.*

Valley sounds, mountain colours: One day we sat by the river, near where WolfMother had welcomed us to her domain, to picnic, and I laughed to watch three boys attempt to dam an unstoppable flow. Her liquid light in the noonday sun was literal – each photo I took painted a still life far from still. Her frothing torrent held pearls of sunlight in each droplet, a prism of rainbow colours therein. All the way there (and back again) I held *conscious* Presence for the water's being, or the liquid light it flowed out into the world, and a mantra of blessing began to spontaneously script itself in my mind – to accompany me that day as well as all thereafter to sing up her beautiful country.

In specifically remarking the cyclical nature of water's 'quest' – all the way from source to sea, from source to sea to source, I was reminded of the migratory patterns of birds, or my own – crisscrossing the world between homes, each one both 'source' and 'sea' in terms of *my* own self's homecoming ritual. Was this the reason why in *Malakut* wanders we had been welcomed home by the *Amici* themselves as well as their overlighting *genius loci*?

In this context I had wondered when an appropriate container for my 'light' would cross the (material) path, for at some level I knew it would reference the practice by which I share blessings between home territories. The same year as the trek to source planned I carried a stone from the glacier-smoothed Cold

Mountain framed by *Marianna's* window down under with me, to be carried aloft a home-peak there, and deposited on its summit cairn. A greeting from one *genius loci* to another, 'twas a leyline of connectivity I intuited from Aboriginal ancestral dreaming, the songlines they had sung into spiritual and geological being over aeons. But I didn't know where, when or how the right stone of blessing for my *Isorno* task would intersect this particular trajectory. But, of course, it did …

In far western Queensland, our fifteen hundred kilometre road trip back in time nearing its end in this baking red and dusty scape, this inland sea of drought-ravaged plains, no hill within coo-ee, I feel the primal *tug* of land and sky, and know we will soon be gone from this place, on a plane back to coastal lushness, back to 'home-turf', gone.

It fulfills itself, this tug, in finding a place of pilgrimage to visit in the dry-cracked earth – to a 19th century cattle-duffing lookout. It takes us along a heavily corrugated track, past roos and emus and the occasional steer, all curious, we the only humanity it seems this day. I had felt the tug, the pull, to reach beyond the 'known' outback to its hidden repositories and wisdom scripts. I heeded, and this is where I find the stones.

Out here, the silence deep, heavy. We climb the lookout, rock outcrop fifty or so metres max above the surrounding plain, sit, *absorbed* by the landscape. It *slows* time for us all. On the return, therefore, I drive slowly, F hops out each now and then to check for new species of birds. At one almost-sucked-dry waterhole, the billabong of a creek long since driven underground by causes and conditions (unripened), he heads over for a look-see. A big coolibah on the banks and I look down, just there between car and waterhole …. The whole place littered with red pebbles, the whole inland of Australia it seems represented in this solitary catchment, a watershed no longer manifest, a potentiality in time and space. All these red rocks, holding the red of the red centre intact, and I think to take one as a keepsake of this part of the world, return to the north with a 'single simple stone of blessing', just like the one that waits in my bag to be carried atop *Wollumbin* next week.

But then I notice something. These stones are smooth, water-smoothed and -sanded by millennia spent being washed by the vast seas that *flooded* this landscape, over, over, over – how long since these rocks last *tasted* water? Yet here they all are, smoothed by the past, banished from the present. In the end I choose two, two at random amongst the millions lying here like acorns or beech nuts fallen from *The Tree of Infinite Knowing*, waiting for those never-arising causes and conditions, waiting in perpetual pause to sprout a vast russet forest … I choose two, swirled with the reds of now-landscape, threaded with the pale waters-of-memory, and return home with them to the north, to the ice and the snow and the perennial flow.

Now here, returned, to the ten-foot-square hut. And I know your shared fate, red river rocks (R3s). One shall remain in the wicker sacred pool, keepsake of promise, the other returned to bless the waters of life, chalice of liquid light since the molten birth of our Gaian home – you, R3, you with the face of an innocent child, sweet-expressioned, a-wonder, you it shall be to carry the light of my love into the *Acqua Termale* ...

Intent confirmed in a small ritual, purpose clear – my love, my deep, deep love for our beautiful, beautiful world, for dear Gaia and all her inhabitants, human and non- (animal, vegetable, mineral – physical and non-) – all building, building, building toward the performance of pilgrimage, my own *Way of the Knight* to fulfill. *WolfMother*, the *Amici*, my own family (and madcap dog) – everything would need to be in alignment, all causes and conditions fused in solidarity for this undertaking: Weather, terrain, fitness, motivation, path ... the all of it.

Final prepping complete, a brief ten-day (autumn school vacation) window loomed. I hoped and prayed the quest could proceed as planned; in the end though it would be in the lap of the (mountain and river) gods, and for nine solid days the rain pelted down. Had the river decided to come directly to us from out of the sky, no mediation required? The creek roared, the waterfalls howled, villagers feared the mountain itself would come down. What message should I derive from this *convergence* of spiritual intent and material watershed? All the way from source to sea, from source to sea to source?

I sat with R3 in meditation, felt his weight in my hand, communed with his spirit until we had fused to one being, one life, one simplicity of Bateson's ecology of mind. I communed until I felt his weight no more, till our body temps had met and melded. Till he was flooded with liquid light, my light his light, his light re-woken, and, holding this light as preciously as if it had always been part of his own, reclaimed a birthright immemorial ...

Emerson's Event

Weds. Late afternoon. A break in the clouds. A sniff to the west. The last possible day for the trek before called back to the north would be Friday, a slim 36 hours hence. That night, a *Malakut* scape. A small supermarket in the outback town whence R3 hailed. We are stocking up on provisions for a journey. Out in the car park, I meet the *Amici*. I hear a brushcutter loud in my ear and turn to find them busy at work. What on earth are they doing here? I recognise the energy signature of the fellow who spoke a little English but the rest are younger. He is leading them on a work detail – 'guerrilla-gardening', he grins.

It is today (Thursday) in the *Malakut* as well and I tell them joyously of our plan (if the weather holds) to try to make the trek up to the source. We're going tomorrow, I say. Oh, he replies, we've already come in today but we'll still be in the neighbourhood then. Maybe we'll see each other?

Friday dawns … A bank of low cloud still settled in the east, but Sun doing his buggy-best to peek through for the first time in a fortnight. We drive the valley road west, to where it ends, and begin to walk. If the path is still OK after all this rain, and the river crossings intact, it will take circa four hours even to reach a disused alpine hut marked on the map before the serious climb to lake. If not? We agree this to be simply a reconnaissance trip to the hut; for making the trek to the source this our initial scouting excursion given the prevailing conditions. Nevertheless I carry R3 in my pocket. It's a good opportunity for him to get to know future home territory …

We make it to the hut, we rest, picnic. We discover the hut is not disused, part of an abandoned summer farm after all (as the map indicated), but had been refurbished as a simple bivouac by – guess who – the *Amici* several months earlier. We wander inside (such *rifugios* are never locked) and find a diary on the dresser documenting the renovation and when the merry troupe had last been in residence to prepare things ahead of the winter – yesterday, Thursday. Today they had moved on to the next hut within their stewardship …

I shake my head at the beauty of synchronicity, *Malakut* and material twinned, laugh and dip my lid to their knowing presence, subtle and equally not-so. In such joyous spirit, I look to the map, to the day which has unfolded in our sight, and cannot contain my desire to press on to the AT. Now. Right now. It would take another solid hour or so of climb up to where the lake lay in the lee of the ridge but I was more than game …

Imagine. It *did* happen, it did *all* happen, everything that my loving intent had proscribed on my heart came to pass; energy completely sapped but oh! In the face of weather and other commitments, to think this day would even dawn as it did, and that it would all work out OK?

Oh!

Thank you to the *Amici*, thank you to the *House*, thank you to *WolfMother* and my blessed *Family*! *All* companions of the way, on this our homecome way. And imagine: At each step, a new revelation, all mirroring that which had been presented to psyche in the *Malakut* over *three* years since I had first been tasked this work to perform. Climbing the final slope to the lake and here revealed – the landscape of *The Tree of Infinite Knowing* intact. Right here, as I had seen it, as I *knew* it, here the spongey mossy ground, where rock and stone glistened with wetness, where small openings in the earth revealed the sacred waters within. And I looked out, round and about, to *all* chains of mountains in witness of this moment.

Oh! Joy!

Ah, but I worked hard to *still* the joy, to keep mountain *calm* over lake, to onserve energy for the final push up the slope (challenging, no path) to reach the rst and then the second (upper) lake. Here the *Acqua Termale* rose, entered the ,orld from its hidden source shafted deep in the mountain, here it pooled and here sent itself off, rushing over a lip of land down, down, down from an unpeopled nto a peopled watershed. I kissed R3, ancient repository of light-blessing, tossed im into the pool – red against all the green-grey-blues, he settled comfortably nto the silt basin of Being, sat there to wink his diversity in glee at this crystal-,ater'd heritage revisited, Nietzsche's *eterno ritorno* in miniature ...

Postscript

I often look back and marvel that this act completed my seven years in the ,ilderness, that following its completion I gained in confidence and spirit that I m not alone on the path, this Way of Love, and that my companions – a diverse :oupe of beings in various dimensions – manifest such joy to support my practice f living a one-life-in-the-one-world reality.

One day, as winter's dark approached, after this extraordinarily cathartic utumn trek 'home', I sat in meditation to again work at *The Wall*. Only to find gone – each time I had been in, till this specific moment, I had found my skills nproved, becoming more fluid and effective at each turn of the 'planing' tool, ut still I worked diligently in the spirit of the *I Ching* wisdom of *Gradual Progress*, elightfully expressed with such gems as:

Geese gradually proceed on boulders; they eat and drink happily. Good fortune ...
Geese gradually proceed in the trees, and may reach a level roost. No fault ... Geese
gradually proceed onto a mountaintop. The wife does not conceive for three years,
but in the end nothing defeats her. Good fortune.

This day, however, I looked about. No 'wall' anywhere on the horizon could spy (with this little eye). Three years – the counsel of geese a-waddle up a nountain – and yes, it had been exactly three years since the *Acqua Termale* had ntered this (wife's) imaginal world. *The Wall* had vanished, the landscape broad, lear, glacier-smoothed – calm, peaceful, Hemingway's 'clean well-lighted place'. he only thing I could 'see' was my *memory* of *The Wall*, and my work thereat, ow past ...

Earlier in this story I recounted my *Malakut* meeting at the hut four hours from he trailhead, the cave set behind the lake high above the hut, the place *Mandalay*, n which the monks lived and worked, the postcard I received while there with he pilgrimage route we had made inscribed thereon.

241

The summer following R3's submersion in the pool, our family, *in toto*, all three children and dog *unterwegs* in the high wild, engaged the selfsame trek as a multi-day wilderness adventure – sleeping on the floor of dusty attic in the *Amici* bivouac, making our own 'risotto' for tea. Its purpose? To fully bind the postcard's message to our shared familial soul-knowing, for me to introduce them in the material to the lake they all had visited (even if unconsciously, cosseted in my care like a mother roo's brood in her pouch) in the *Malakut*. For my part I was free to simply listen – to the long broad tongue of *valley sounds*, to the unconditioned body of *mountain colours*, to the roar of resonant hum within and beyond each pore of my skin, to the sublime fact of mergent life ever-lived afresh.

At the entry to *WolfMother*'s domain, at the stone 'gate' on the path just past the place where she had originally leapt out of the underbrush to greet us, I spontaneously lifted a stone and placed it atop, as a holder of blessing and presence, as a prayer for our safe return. And three days hence, found it there waiting – for my lift, and kiss, and thanks. Brought home to *Marianna*'s fireside it has been, another tale added to the *Book of Voyage*, the shy motif embossed on its skin for all the world like a marmot in profile or some other *Amici* spirit, cleaved to, embedded within.

The night of return to my bed (and pillow – godsend!), a lucid *Malakut* scape – somehow I had received a 'naming' of 'Sir', and I couldn't figure out why. Was this common in the *Amici*'s neck of the woods for women to be so-named? No, it seems not, but I was shown an official document and told this is what I would now be called: *Sir Anne*. It sounds ridiculous! I said. A word-image presented: *The Way of the Knight*. Alright, I shrugged.

But before the reader thinks this anything grand (indeed, I was beginning to feel uncomfortable in the space), it transpired to only define forthcoming task, my *next* assignment as 'assistant' to a group leader at a roundtable with others all focused on a specific undertaking. At the time I had no idea what this would involve; our discussions were project management-oriented.

But if the reader is interested in the extraordinary partnership to follow, it is the subject of its own text – a much longer one which goes by the name of *Awakening to Home*. Meanwhile, in honour of Gaia's blessed high wild, the first Canticle (Song of the Seasons) of the epic *Onsernone Long Poem*, has this bardic pen gambolling through meadows *Malakut* and material alike, on the way to the source, the sacred *Acqua Termale* – its *One Life* for which there is only ever *One Name*.

On that note, I bid all readers a fond adieu and *bonne nuit* from our merry band of *Amici della Luce*, singing up country with a perennial song of sanctity – of peace love and the light of grace, being and flowing the world with blessing …

Glossary

The following glossary entries relate to specific instances in the text where I feel it may be useful for the reader to have background definition or further information to assist with understanding of my approach. Clearly, there may be other cases of (self-) jargon for which the reader would care to have additional notes. In such an eventuality, a full glossary documenting how I apply a broader range of terms and expressions can be found at nestedfishes.org. Further, any essay or textual work of mine referenced in an entry below can also be found in one of the (several) nestedfishes.org libraries – all of course available for free download, as a contribution to the conversation on peace consciousness.

Alone with the Alone: A reference to Henri Corbin's seminal text on the 13th century Sufi mystic Ibn Arabi and his direct apprehension of the Unity of Being. According to Bloom's preface to this volume, such Gnostic revelation is 'to be acquainted with what is best and oldest in yourself, is to know yourself as you were, before the world was made, before you emerged into time' (Bloom, p.x).

Becoming landscape: As I navigate inner territories of the *Malakut*, I find that landscapes 'become' or constellate depending on the insights and stories being shared by subtle guides. Using the metaphor of the rhizome, I wander like a nomad into 'mobile arrangements of space where thought can settle for a time' (St Pierre, p.410), the 'spiritual topography' (Corbin a, p.33) thus emerging as it is explored.

Being-with: An expression coined by Irigaray in respect of reciprocal recognition which speaks to my task to unveil and cultivate a space of co-belonging, of 'being-with' (p.48), in order to create a 'context in which love can begin to flourish' (hooks, p.13). Equally, it references a comment of Mr1300BC's – long years past at a time when I was so eager to learn more, discover more, ask questions et al, I would self-sabotage my meditations. At which point he would sigh and say: *Just be with me. That is all.* Brilliant (of course); a technique to settle the grains of sand in the pool, to awaken self to the clarity of Suzuki's 'beginner's mind'. My work with the Stone Circle is just such a 'being-with' collective where, these days, I'm more than happy just to sit. And be ...

Bergkristall: Literally 'mountain-crystal'; in English: rock quartz – transparent, translucent, stunning in its purity. *"Look at them!" he says excitedly. "The scientist al-Biruni was enthralled by this material – crystal fast-frozen within its clay bed. Imagine – water frozen, never to unfreeze!"* And indeed, the perfection lies within this unity – the fineness of air fused with the clarity of water. Words I put into the mouth of Ibn Khaldun in *The Taste of Translation* (p.61).

Chi: The invisible force within all of life and nature, cosmic in origin sustaining everything in our known world. As essential to us as the air we breathe, the ancients called it by the same name – air or *chi*. There are many layers to *chi*, one of which is the unique signal of our own life energy: 'Each one of us is endowed with a piece of the one original energy, the Tao. This energy, through a series of transformations, becomes our *Chi*. Our body is made of dust (material) ... it is our *Chi* that holds us together, animates us, and makes us who we really are. ... Without it, nothing lives' (Lia 2009, p.3-4).

Cold Mountain: With each in-breath, each out-breath, Han-shan conceived of inner and outer spaces as one. Translated as Cold Mountain, the (perhaps 6th, 8th or 9th century Chinese poet-hermit took the name of his ten-foot square hut as his own. In each of his poems we find an osmotic existence described in full expressive flow, and wonder: Is it himself or his dwelling, which is the subject here (from Gary Snyder's translation, p.44)?

> *Men ask the way to Cold Mountain*
> *Cold Mountain: there's no through trail.*
> *In summer, ice doesn't melt*
> *The rising sun blurs in swirling fog.*
> *How did I make it?*
> *My heart's not the same as yours.*
> *If your heart was like mine*
> *You'd get it and be right here.*

All one-and-the-same, in the end, living the one-life-of-the-one-world...

Conversation partners: An expression to describe the interdisciplinary interlocutors – across fields as disparate as continental philosophy, eastern philosophy, psychology, translation theory, action research, interpretative ethnography, performance studies and other aesthetic paradigms, theology as well as the mystical traditions – whose thinking has contributed to my understanding of and approach to the *Malakut*. As unlikely as a particular reference may appear at first glance, a wide spectrum of research has helped make sense of my experiences as well as assisted descriptions of such phenomena – with the specific aim for my incoherent ramblings to be rendered more understandable to a third party. Whether still a part of this material world or already on their next (subtle or not-so) journey, our connection – across time and space via the wonderful resource of the written word – has given me a bibliophile's community of practice I am honoured to share further in the bibliography herein as well as via the nestedfishes org library.

(Meanwhile, as demonstration of a rhizomatic synapse: Writing 'bibliophile' into existence on the line above led to my recall this quote from the 19th century Scot Andrew Lang's The Library: 'The bibliophile asks about his books the question which the metaphysician asks about his soul.' This in turn led to the Andrew Lang Lecture Series and its most famous lecturer (JRR Tolkien, 1939) in which he waxes lyrically on mythopoiesis. Which returns me to the legends recounted by Sidhe companions, with a request to collaborate on transcribing these stories here in the material in the hope that mythopoiesis begets holopoiesis in the spirit of Tolkien's work. Thus is energetic interconnectivity ever-'live', as well as reminding me of incomplete tasks to boot!)

Demian: (From *The Taste of Translation* , p.398): 'I'll re-read the books though, she offers. Nothing bad ever comes from reading Hesse, and she reaches for the brandy bottle, lights a cigarette, and begins with *Demian* … Sinclair sits, sketches, sits, sketches, communes with the face he has sketched – a god-image arisen from half-serious scrawls: "This face had some message for me … it was making some demand … appeared to know me as a mother, as if its eyes had been fixed on me my whole life …" The candle on her cardboard altar sputters, wavers, suddenly flares. She looks up into the eyes of the Lady. No longer a sketch but the icon itself floods her memory. Baba's hand made those eyes. Baba's hand knew the light which cuts through winter-dark …'

Desire: I define desire as a productive and enabling energy, a creative force to bring potentialities into being. With its rhizomatic roots in 'energetic, constructivist, productive … desire' (Deleuze & Boundas, p.12), a central plane of Deleuzian philosophy is 'the articulation of a theory of transformation and change, … a theory of pure becoming' (ibid., p.4): 'Every assemblage expresses and creates a desire by constructing the plane which makes it possible and, by making it possible, brings it about (ibid., p.137). What Deleuze calls desire, therefore, expresses the same intent behind the creative force I experience to transform not-knowing into knowing, or to manifest *any* latency in time and space.

Ecology of mind: In his book *Steps to an Ecology of Mind*, Bateson defines 'mind' as 'the mental world … the world of information processing' (p.460). An individual unit of 'mind' is therefore a system, 'the relevant total information-processing, trial-and-error completing unit … be it DNA-in-the-cell, or cell-in-the-body, or body-in-the-environment' (p.466). Logically this extends to 'Mind in the widest sense (as) … a hierarchy of subsystems, any one of which we can call an individual mind' (ibid.). 'This larger Mind is comparable to God … but it is still immanent in the total interconnected social system and planetary ecology' (p.467).

Event: In my lexicon, this word holds a special (epiphanous) place: 'To the extent that events are actualized in us, they wait for us and invite us in' (Deleuze & Boundas, p.78). The French poet Bousquet understood his First World War experience thus: 'My wound existed before me, I was born to embody it' (ibid.). Equally, Emerson's insight about the soul containing in itself the event that shall befall it.

Feeling-tree: Gary Snyder's *feeling-wren* story (where I have taken the liberty to transpose 'tree' for 'wren') refers: 'To see a tree, call it "tree", and go on walking is to have (self-importantly) seen nothing. To see a tree and stop, watch, feel, forget yourself for a moment, be in the bushy shadows, maybe then feel "tree" – that is to have joined in a larger moment with the world (adapted from *A Place in Space*, p.179).

Firefly sparks: A reference to Laleima's speech in *The Taste of Translation*, imploring 'The Angel of History' to face the stream of time as she did, in full faith of Love's truth, her tiny firefly spark still one more than none – an inspiration that any one of us can make a difference. Her insight, and courage, ever reminds me that the one-life-of-the-one-world is a single rhizomatic plane of interdimensional consistency across which synapses of 'enlightenment' can occur (i.e. 'firefly sparks of meaning') when we are alive to the fact of synchronicity, the psychoid unity of two-as-one-become.

Ganz andere: A German expression (which I have appropriated from Mircea Eliade's seminal text *The Sacred and the Profane*) to mean 'the wholly other'.

George: We have met before in other *Malakut* encounters, so-named because his energy signature is like that of a responsible older brother.

Ground of Being: Essentially one of many names for that which is beyond names, beyond our limited human consciousness. Others, depending on the spiritual tradition, include: God-without-form, the modeless Godhead, the Void, the Sacred or Ultimate Reality, the Great Mystery, Big Mind: 'The divine Ground of all existence is a spiritual Absolute, ineffable in terms of discursive thought, but (in certain circumstances) susceptible of being directly experienced and realised by the human being' (Huxley, p.21). My profound introduction to same is documented in the essay, *One Life – a contemplation*.

Heliotrope: The 5th century Neoplatonist Proclus contemplated how a heliotrope's flowers exhibit diurnal motion by following the sun's passage across the sky – a natural process he likened to prayer. In so doing, he postulated that the consciousness with which each being approaches the ritual of thanksgiving may vary, but that does not lessen the *intent* underlying its act of love: 'Each thing prays according to the rank it occupies in nature, and sings the praise of the leader of the divine series to which it belongs, a spiritual or rational or physical or sensuous praise; for the heliotrope moves to the extent that it is free to move, and in its rotation, if we could hear the sound of the air buffeted by its movement, we should be aware that it is a hymn to its king, such as it is within the power of a plant to sing' (Corbin a, p.105-6). Thus is true nature followed.

Hello the House: The reader should not take 'House' too literally. For indigenous and nomadic traditions, the land itself is home – something Western thought must rediscover if we are to make any significant inroads into transcending the destructive relationship our culture has with dear Mother Earth. Indeed, *Hello the House* takes on a fuller, more powerful meaning if one calls it aloud from a mountaintop to all other mountaintops around; it becomes a greeting infused with the spirit of 'I see you' in all its myriad forms. The essay, *Homegoing*, shares more.

Im Einklang mit dem Universum: The literal translation of this expression – 'in harmony with the universe' – does not seem to go far or deep enough to describe a felt-sense of seamless harmonic resonance with the All, but then again neither does the expression 'Oneness' (for which the German is: *Einsein*). As ever, language has difficulty conveying the sense of something *outwith* language.

Interbirth: Gary Snyder writes: 'We are actually mutually creating each other and all things while living ... it may well be that (this) is the objective fact of existence which we (i.e. a western mindset) have not yet brought into conscious knowledge and practice' (from *Look Out: A Selection of Writings*, p.124).

I see you: The notion of reciprocal recognition, founding a relationship on truly 'seeing the other in oneself' is something I explore in depth in an essay of the same name. An embodied knowing rooted in the understanding that we are all sprung from the primal Ground, in popular culture the James Cameron film Avatar takes this literally with the Na'vi greeting: 'I see you'. In such form, cognition can be spoken all the way along the spectrum from 'I see you', through 'I see into you', to 'I understand you', and finally 'I love you'. The fact that the film demonstrates how we ignorant Earthlings need to be taught the importance of reciprocal recognition, and that it can be expressed by simply saying these three words with real feeling, seems aptly ironic.

I saw: 'I saw' is a signature phrase in the writings of religious mystics attempting to describe their lived experiences (Watson & Jenkins, p.7). This in no way suggests that I place myself in such auspicious company, only that it is the most accurate way to express the uprising of images in language.

Nachwuchs-Kookaburra: The largest in the kingfisher family worldwide, 'merry merry king of the bush is he,' this *nachwuchs* (junior/offspring) kookaburra was ever-perched (together with grandpa clan elder) on the telegraph wires out front of the rented flat around the corner from our future Little Cove 'home' each day following my meeting with *AncestorCouple*. As I pondered the signs, whilst staring into their inscrutable witness, a brief bardic offering was penned 29 April 2015, pre-7:00am ...

Old young, new-hatched, well-aged –
two kookaburras tripping their highwire
(grandfather ancestor divine child nachwuchs) –
silent your witness, your guardianship of
place. Through your eyes I see: Self.
This I know and cherish and want to share,
So repeat my prayer: Help me ...

Kisha: The chief protagonist in Panel Three of my major fiction, *The Taste of Translation,* she is a secular exile from the Bosnian War who learns to open to her past in order to embrace the future. Her role as facilitator to my own growing self-knowledge is documented in the essay, *Treasures Revealed 3.*

Laleima: The girl covered in blood in the halls of the Alhambra, the one whose words: *There is not enough love in the world,* propelled me to my first 'contract' with souls of the dead, to return their 'treasure' to the world of time. Our relationship is described in the essay, *Treasures Revealed 2,* and the contents of her beautiful inspiring life shared in *The Taste of Translation.*

Making: 'Making has seldom been considered as a work carried out *inside* subjectivity itself, starting from and upon what the subject already is and with a *becoming* in mind ... Such a work of *interiority* remains almost unknown to us. Perhaps because the relation with the other has not been sufficiently *recognised* as a decisive part of subjectivity' (Irigaray, p.115). This describes my practice of 'becoming product', whereby the act of writing bridges inner and outer spaces to realise an aesthetic product (physical artefact) linking and honouring the needs of both dimensions (i.e. *Malakut* source and material reader). It means welcoming the speech of the *ganz andere* (as a *decisive* part of subjectivity) and accepting their questioning of my translation. A process model of multi-step feedback loops is the result, amply demonstrated in the writing of *The Taste of Translation* (amongst others), and constantly reminding me of Beckett's lament in *Worstward Ho:* "Ever Tried. Ever Failed. No matter. Try Again. Fail again. Fail better" (p.101).

Malakut: The intermediate world of the soul in Islamic mysticism, the place 'where the body is spiritualised and the spiritual is embodied' (Corbin b, p.125). It is 'a dimension where meanings are embodied as images' (Helminski, p.26) and accessed 'through an awakened and purified heart' (ibid., p.29).

Maleny: The 24-acre parcel of forest, a deep nature peace-sink and refuge in perpetuity, I am blessed to steward in a quiet corner of the world. To describe something as a 'new Maleny' implies an equally profound connection to spirit-of-place as I engage in her domain. All I need say is *Hello – I'm home* to literally feel the swirling spirals of energy up through the earth, up through and into me as she returns the greeting. A soul hug from the purity of Gaia's font and one which sets all cells singing with the chi of shared circuitry every time.

Mantra: This refers to a shared mantra I invoke while (dog-) walking (amongst other pursuits); calling on *all* Gaia's children to join me in praising our beautiful home: *We are peace, love and the light of Your grace, being and flowing the world with blessing* ... I have several self-tunes I sing this to, but the one which arose in company of Sidhe was new, and *ganz andere* to my style of musical composition. The text of the mantra was set in train by 'writing-into-existence' (on a plane of intimate exteriority) my peace-sink insights years past, thus: 'I can imagine a time when peace and love is consciously directed out into the Gaiasphere to be circulated by the subtle energies of the world and sent where it is most needed. Maybe my prayer – *for peace, love and the light of Your grace to infuse every heart in this world* – could be sent up into the aetheric to rain down elsewhere?'

Mirroring joy: A reference to the following 'words formed': God is smiling on you today; *God is wanting you to enjoy the beauty of this world, not drown such joy in sadness at others' plight – here, now, mirror His joy!* which alerted me to our ability to sequester love, peace and joy in the subtle bones of the land by consciously *mirroring* divine grace, a teaching placed in context by the essay, *Peace Sinks*.

Mode-of-being: The expression coined by Aldous Huxley in his tome *The Perennial Philosophy* to convey the notion that *all* knowledge is a function of being where 'the thing known is in the knower according to the mode of the knower' (p.146). What we 'know' is a distinctly personal phenomenon according to our unique mode, thus determining the way in which universal consciousness interacts with our own. 'Tis essentially a Gnostic proposition for which Huxley's summary makes a useful one-liner. Christopher Bamford expands: 'It is the soul's *modus essendi* (mode of being) that determines its *modus cognoscendi* (mode of knowing) ... the great search is to meet, to

249

uncover, the true person that we are ... knowledge is not an abstraction derived in some way from sense-given percepts, but is an ontological "illumination" or assimilation of such percepts from "within"' (pp.xviii-ix). All of which basically means that even though the great Carl Jung expressed his frustration with the way in which his 'fantasies' presented, they could not have been presented in any other way for his mode-of-being. The following quote from his memoirs gives me the giggles every time I feel likewise: 'I wrote down the fantasies as well as I could ... But I was able to do this only in clumsy language ... "high-flown language" ... Archetypes speak the language of high rhetoric, even of bombast ... I had no choice but to write everything down in the style selected by the unconscious itself (p.202). Yep. Ditto ...

Mother'sHead: This I understood to be the Ancestral naming of the National Park headland, albeit presided over by a 'couple' as the resident genius loci. The whole stretch of coastline bears witness to a particular clan's Dreaming with this place – in my *Malakut* understanding – its northern-most reach i.e. the 'head'.

Nothing special: 'When you no longer want something, or when you do not try to do anything special, then you do something ... it is the expression of your true nature ... it is just you yourself, nothing special ... It is a kind of mystery that for people who have no experience of enlightenment, enlightenment is something wonderful. But if they attain it, it is nothing. But yet it is not nothing. Do you understand? For a mother with children, having children is nothing special. That is zazen. ... You may call it by many names, but for the person who has it, it is nothing, and it is something (Suzuki, p.32-3).

November fog: A compound noun that has entered my (antipodean) lexicon to describe a particular (Swiss) climatic phenomenon no matter what time of the year it descends to drench the landscape in grey; a thick pea soup it consistency, a bone-chilling damp its welcome. A mist that clings and in so-doing, invites one in – to seek what lies on the other side, to make the crossing to the *Malakut*. I describe Kisha's experience thus (p.327): *In the early days of this place, she had walked ... by the lake, the sky a heavy sheet of grey mirrored in its gunship metal surface. ... (She) stretched out her fingers into the fog that day, sent them as her scouts to the other side. The other world was always there, close enough to touch, beyond the blurred non-edge of lake ...* November fog is a perpetual reminder of how close the worlds are, that it is indeed one world whose visible and invisible elements fade in and out of focus depending on our acceptance of, attunement to, and appreciation for the existence of what cannot be perceived with the naked eye. November-fog encourages us to look harder, sharper, to squint into the mists and reflect on what we imagine to see. Things may not be as they seem on first reckoning. Slow passage is needed to remark the path taken – it is easy to get lost in the mists. Penetrating the unknown is best approached cautiously, with discernment.

Mr1300BC: For long years my principal *Malakut* guide, but why do I call him thus? Simply because the first time we officially 'met', I commented on his arduous journey through the 20th century. To which he responded: *Oh, that wasn't so difficult. I've been wandering since 1300BC!* The essay, Words Formed, drills deeper into our relationship.

One-life-of-the-one-world: Material and *Malakut*, life and death, self and other, on and on, married in a seamless whole as nestedfishes within the Ground of Being, Love – a vision of cosmic holism, all family, all One. 'Tis my expression to connote the felt-sense of the Unity of Being. The essays, *One Life – a contemplation* and *Amici della Luce*, relate further direct experiences and expressions of oneness.

Onsernone Long Poem: A very personal form of the epic, OLP is a verse narrative, woven around the seasons, directions and elements, documenting my enduring love affair with our planetary home. Specifically, it celebrates my experience of divinity in the Swiss-Italian border country an alpine stone's throw from the land of Dante Alighieri's birth, and death. Hence, in homage to this 14th century master of form, the work is composed in *terza rima*, his 'invented' three-line style which, according to some commentators, evokes the Holy Trinity. A constant work-in-progress, the first Canticle (*Song of the Seasons*) is complete (yay!), and can be found in the Poetry Corner.

Peregian: A tract of eastern sea wild shoreline ten kilometres south of National Park headland, itself part of the wider regional national park as well as home to ancestral 'old man emu' dreaming. 'Tis the place where my seven years in the wilderness began, a process of fully integrating soul-knowing into the *practice* of daily life, to *become* the one-life-of-the-one-world, as described (lovingly, blessedly!) in the essay, *self-naughting*.

Personal myth: Following Huxley, that all knowledge is a function of being where 'the thing known is in the knower according to the mode of the knower' (Huxley, p.146), what we 'know' is a distinctly personal phenomenon. Couple this observation with Jung's reflection on his own work – 'Whether or not the stories are 'true' is not the problem. The only question is whether what I tell is *my* fable, *my* truth' (Jung, p.17) – as well as the contention that to make sense of our lives, 'we are myth-making creatures' (Armstrong, p.142), and you may understand how I perceive my work as a personal myth being returned to collective consciousness via the nestedfishes web presence, and beyond.

Plane of consistency: An expression coined by the French philosophers Deleuze and Guattari to describe how a rhizome extends in any/all directions without negating its primal, *non-hierarchical* nature: 'All multiplicities are flat, in the sense that they fill or occupy all of their dimensions: we will therefore speak of a "plane of consistency" of multiplicities, even though the dimensions of this "plane" increase with the number of connections that are made on it' (p.9). Such a single never-ending plane assumes a cartography of 'becoming', of a landscape which *becomes* as it is *explored* much as the universe 'becomes' as our telescopes improve to detect further back and further out into space-time. Interestingly, the vernacular Deleuze and Guattari use for their rhizomatic model of becoming is analogous to how physicists talk about their discoveries – as 'waves (or) vibrations' (p.275).

Plane of intimate exteriority: The expression I use for my practice of journaling drawn from the work of French philosopher, Francois Zourabichvili. To document and reflect on *Malakut* encounters, a detailed journal is a worthy companion. Its function is to house data-gathering to the nth degree as well as provide a reflective and contemplative space, a plane of 'intimate exteriority', for my continued engagement with this raw material: 'The (inner) landscape does not return me to myself: it involves me in a becoming where the subject is no longer coextensive with itself, where the subjective form is inadequate when faced with the unformedness of becoming' (p.196) The plane is intimate, because its contents are too raw and unformed to be understood by any other than myself, implying further work beyond this plane to shape the inchoate into a form able to be publicly shared.

Psychoid unity: In describing the concept of synchronicity – 'the meaningful coincidence or equivalence of a psychic and a physical state or event which have no causal relationship to one another' (p.419) – Jung goes on to describe such occurrences as examples of 'psychic parallelisms, acausally related and connected via the contingency of events' (ibid.) Their purpose, he holds is to offer a glimpse of a pre-existent and unknowable psychoid unity, split between an outer physical phenomenon and inner psychic image – 'opposites that can now be recognised (… in) parallel events' (Jaffé, p.152).

Quickening: I use this expression to connote any practice which enlivens our connection to divinity, something I perceive with felt-sense. By way of background, Jean Shinoda Bolen provides a useful analogy: 'When new life stirs within the womb, and a mother has the sensation of her baby moving within her for the first time, it's called "quickening". The same word is associated with pilgrims, who go to sacred places to "quicken" the divinity within themselves, to experience spiritual awakening or receiving a blessing or become healed ... Pilgrimage to a sacred place is an in-the-body spiritual experience – as were my pregnancies ... the divine spirit is incarnate at sacred places ... places where the divinity penetrates matter, impregnating or quickening the divine in the pilgrim' (p.28-9).

Reciprocal recognition: 'The relation with the other cannot exist without (a) prior gesture of reciprocal recognition. A gesture that cannot be simply formal but will relate to a real content corresponding to the being of the other, and moreover of oneself' (Irigaray, p.88). Like nestedfishes each hosting a spot of the other's colour to enable their communion, it is this recognition that underpins and facilitates my *Malakut* encounters with non-physical presences, based on a way-of-love. Of course, such heart-centred approach is not only engaged in the subtle realms but for any and all interrelations in the one-life-of-the-one-world of Gaian consciousness.

Resonant hum: My expression for the deep and generative hum *beyond*, yet *within*; the 'foundation-breath' *beneath* all sound, *shared* by all universal sentience, and onto which their own extant 'self-note' is grafted; thus do I feel the permeability or porosity of *my* self with all *other* selves living the one-life-of-the-one-world. The essay, *Universal Resonance*, contemplates this blessed connection I have to the fundamental *sruti* note of creation, as described by Sri Ramana Maharshi, among others.

SacredKingfisher: Maleny's *genius loci*, and a wonderful companion of the way since beginningless time, his lesson in selfless gifting and the thanksgiving at the *heart* of Grace (its constancy of *praise* an act of true-natured being moment-by-unfolding-moment) is told in the essay, *Lessons in Gifting*.

Singing up country: An Aboriginal expression for the walking of ancestral dreaming 'songlines' across the land. See Bruce Chatwin's seminal text.

Ten-foot-square hut: See essay of the same name for a rhizomatic universal journey conducted in a very small physical space.

Thematic plateaus: A reference to those doyens of French philosophical thought of the 1970s, Gilles Deleuze and Felix Guattari, whose rambunctious non-adherence to anything remotely mainstream at the time was a godsend to this lass composing an academic dissertation about forging relations with *Malakut* presences (not an easy task, I assure you!). Even though they would probably be gobsmacked to learn their theory of knowledge production based on rhizomatic interdimensionality was appropriated in this way, it proved eminently fit to purpose: '... unlike trees or their roots, the rhizome connects any point to any other point, and its traits are not necessarily linked to traits of the same nature ... It is composed not of units but of dimensions, or rather directions in motion. It has neither beginning nor end, but always a middle (*milieu*) from which it grows and which it overspills. ... the rhizome pertains to a map that must be produced, constructed, a map that is always detachable, connectable, reversible, modifiable, and has multiple entry ways and exits and its own lines of flight' (D&G, p.24). Roll on ant armies, I say!

The Taste of Translation: A major work of prose fiction through whose conception and execution I began my journey toward understanding the Unity of Being. 'Tis no more or less than a personal Axial myth of compassion, of unconditional care for the suffering other. From the dust jacket: "A Muslim princess learns to die to self, a Christian translator learns there are other ways to write, and a secular exile from the Bosnian War learns to open to her past in order to embrace the future. Across a shifting landscape spanning Europe and North Africa, and bridging more than six centuries, their pilgrimages to the centre of being are told in this triptych. A three-panel work of art, *The Taste of Translation* tells a single story – of what it means to love." Like all other resources in the nestedfishes.org library, the e-book is available for free download as a contribution to the conversation on peace consciousness.

True nature: 'Something which comes out of nothingness is naturalness, like a seed or plant coming out of the ground. The seed has no idea of being some particular plant, but it has its own form and is in perfect harmony with the ground, with its surroundings. As it grows, in the course of time it expresses its nature. ... For a plant or stone to be natural is no problem. But for us there is some problem. ... To be natural is something which we must work on' (Suzuki, p.97). An essay of the same name contemplates this principle in detail.

Unity of Being: Although he never used the specific expression himself, the medieval Sufi philosopher Ibn Arabi is noted as the prime exponent in his faith tradition of the doctrine of *wahdat al-wujud* ('unity of being'), which argues that we are all unique expressions of a single divine life, each an infinite display of the absolute and unitive truth – oneness by another name.

Unseen hand: An expression I use to connote the felt-sense to act in some way when mind and rational decision-making have exerted no influence. Rather, action is informed by heart-knowing pure and literally felt as a tug on the 'heartstrings'. It is a phenomenon I explore in Panel Two of *The Taste of Translation* – here, in the voice of the Brother's witness (p.189):

> *I knew not what pulled him onward, forced his passage from the known to unknown. Our path held no meaning or logic and I wondered if he were guided,*

drawn, to this place or another by a voice, perhaps, a soft buzz in the ear. As dust rose in our wake over all the long years, I pondered the strange journey his inner guide led. And yes, at times thought to see the tug of an unseen hand at his breast, at times thought to witness with my waking eye the line it held, and his wince each time the hand tugged, pulled taut on a string hooked into his heart, which ripped and tore at his flesh. It was his fate – to hear the unheard voice, to heed the unseen hand, to follow the line uncoiling before his dirty-heavy boots. His fate, and mine. I had said I would stand by him and so it would be. Till the line self-cut, till his place of rest found, till his bloody wound licked clean and healed.

Way-of-love: An expression coined by French philosopher Luce Irigaray to describe the intent one must bring to an encounter with the 'other' to be ever-respectful of inherent difference, 'welcoming the speech of the other in oneself and … accepting that this speech questions us' (p.115). In the French original, Irigaray's way of love encompasses both *la voie de l'amour* and *la voix de l'amour*. The essays, *Making the Crossing* and *Reciprocal Recognition*, contemplate in more depth the spirit of engagement I bring to my encounters with subtle beings.

Wei wu wei: *Wu wei* literally means non-ado. *Wei wu wei* is thus doing through non-doing, action through no action, a basic principle of Taoist philosophy. Anything we *do* (or strive for) is against the natural harmony of the universe. The metaphor of water and its yielding nature is often cited – water is without *will*, yet creates great landscapes. 'Tao never makes any ado, and yet it does everything … All things will grow of themselves … When the desires of men are curbed, there will be peace, and the world will settle down of its own accord' (Lao Tzu, p.83).

Welcome to country: The expression used for the ritual Aboriginal greeting whereby one clanship group welcomes another to its stretch of country; 'reciprocal recognition' by another name.

Words formed: 'Words formed in my understanding' – the expression used by the 14th century mystic, Julian of Norwich, for a mode of revelation which her editors consider to be 'evidently not heard physically but in some sense' (Watson & Jenkins, p.78). In this context, they cite St Gregory's 6th century assertion that 'the heart (is) informed … the speech … rather made or performed than heard' (ibid.). My 'words formed', as well as offerings by inner voices not my own, always appear in italics in my writing in acknowledgement of the completely contrary nature of such arisings from normal thought processes. The essay, *Words Formed*, contemplates in more depth the way in which such mystical experience constellates for my Huxleyian mode.

Writing-into-existence: An expression to describe the process by which I shape the 'inchoate' into a form communicable to a third party. I find the physicality of pen to paper is the only thing slow enough to bring the depths of my inner experience out, on a plane of intimate exteriority, as it own manifest 'existence'. I draw inspiration from ethnographic researcher who suggest that 'writing is not only inscription but discovery. It is a kind of nomadic inquiry in which I am able to deterritorialise spaces in which to travel in the thinking that writing produces' (St Pierre, p.407). Such an approach confirms the writer's place as 'neither historian nor prophet: (s he is an explorer of existence' (Kundera, p.44). And, like TS Eliot, I hol that: 'We shall not cease from exploration, And the end of all our exploring Will be to arrive where we started, And know the place for the first time (Eliot, p.43).

YMM: A specific self-practice developed to facilitate the streaming of light involving yoga, tai chi, meditation and more.

Bibliography

Without question, the two most fundamental volumes which assisted my preparation of this text are the *Card Deck* of the Sidhe and *Conversations with the Sidhe*, both published by Lorian Press and brought into being by David Spangler, Jeremy Berg, and Mariel of the Sidhe. I have quoted liberally from their pages, with good reason, and immense gratitude!

Beyond these foundational works, however, I drew inspiration from the range of scholarly texts listed below. As well as comprising a wash-list of references quoted throughout the book, they are offered as original pearl wisdoms or thought fragments in their own right. In this way the reader has the opportunity to return to each source document for further elaboration of relevant concepts without the mediating influence of my own writing.

Indeed does each work represent a conversation partner whose thinking has contributed to my understanding. As unlikely as some of these bedfellows may appear, such a wide research spectrum has been integral to my approach – to make sense of direct experience as well as attempt the translation of same. It is a community of practice I am honoured to share further, with the hope that it may bring complementary insights to others' own practice. It goes without saying (but I shall say it anyway) that a more extensive bibliography is ever-available for perusal in the nestedfishes.org library.

Ag Assarid, M 2006, *Y a pas d'embouteillage dans le desert: Chroniques d'un Touareg en France*, Presses Renaiss, Paris.

Armstrong, K 2005, *A Short History of Myth*, Canongate, Edinburgh.

Atwood, M 2002, *Negotiating with the Dead*, Cambridge University Press, Cambridge.

Bamford, C 'Introduction: Esotericism Today: The Example of Henri Corbin' in Corbin, H 1998b, *The Voyage and the Messenger: Iran and Philosophy*, North Atlantic Books, Berkeley, CA, pp.xiv-ix.

Bateson, G & Bateson MC 1987, *Angels Fear: Toward an Epistemology of the Sacred*, Macmillan, New York.

Bateson, G 2000, *Steps to an Ecology of Mind*, University of Chicago Press, Chicago.

Beckett, S 1989, 'Worstward Ho', in *Nohow On*, John Calder, London, pp.99-128.

Berry, T 2006, *Evening Thoughts: Reflecting on Earth as Sacred Community*, Sierra Club Books, San Francisco.

Blake, W 1790, *The Marriage of Heaven and Hell*, http://www.blakearchive.org/

Bloom, H 1998, 'Preface' in H Corbin 1998a, *Alone with the Alone*, Princeton University Press, Princeton, NJ, pp.ix-xx.

Bolen, JS 2004, *Crossing to Avalon*, HarperOne, New York.

Calvino, I 2009, *Six Memos for the Next Millennium*, Penguin Classics, London.

Chatwin, B 1988, *The Songlines*, Penguin, London.

Cleary, T (trans.) 2005, *The Taoist I Ching*, Shambhala, Boston.

Corbin, H 1998a, *Alone with the Alone*, Princeton University Press, Princeton, NJ.

Corbin, H 1998b, *The Voyage and the Messenger: Iran and Philosophy*, North Atlantic Books, Berkeley, CA.

Daido Loori, J 2008, *Becoming the Mountains and Rivers*, http://archive. thebuddhadharma.com/issues/2008/fall/becoming.php

Dante Alighieri, 2014, *The Divine Comedy* (trans. C James), Liveright, London.

de Certeau, M 1988, *The Practice of Everyday Life*, University of California Press, Berkeley, CA.

Deleuze, G & Boundas, CV 1993, *The Deleuze Reader*, Columbia University Press, New York.

Deleuze, G & Guattari, F 2004, *A Thousand Plateaus*, Continuum, New York.

Dogen, 1240, *Mountains and Waters Discourse*, accessed from: www.abuddhist. library.org.

Dogen 1240 *Valley Sounds Mountain Colours*, in Tanahashi, K (ed.) 1999, *Enlightenment Unfolds: The Essential Teachings of Zen Master Dogen*, Shambhala, Boston.

Eliade, M 1987, *The Sacred and the Profane: The Nature of Religion*, Harcourt Brace Jovanovich, New York.

Eliot, TS 1944, *Four Quartets*, Faber&Faber, London.

Emerson, RW 2003, 'Fate', in RW Emerson, *The Collected Works of Ralph Waldo Emerson, vol.vi*, Belknap Press of Harvard University Press, Cambridge, MA, pp.1-27.

Forster, EM 1910 *Howards End*, Project Gutenberg e-text.

Forster, EM 2005, *Aspects of the Novel*, Penguin Classics, London.

Gambling, A 2011, *The Taste of Translation: A Triptych*, nestedfishes.org e-book.

Helminski, K 2000, *The Knowing Heart: A Sufi Path of Transformation*, Shambhala, Boston.

Hesse, H 1969, *Demian*, Grafton Books, London.

hooks, b 2000, *All About Love: New Visions*, The Women's Press, London.

Huxley, A 2009, *The Perennial Philosophy*, HarperCollins, New York.

Irigaray, L 2002, *The Way of Love*, Continuum, London.

Irwin, L 1996, *Visionary Worlds: The Making and Unmaking of Reality*, State University of New York Press, Albany.

Jaffé, A 1983, *The Myth of Meaning in the Works of CG Jung*, Daimon Verlag, Einsiedeln, CH.

Jung, CG 1995, *Memories, Dreams, Reflections*, Fontana Press, London.

Kundera, M 1988, *The Art of the Novel*, Faber&Faber, London.

Lang, A 1881, *The Library*, Project Gutenberg e-text.

Lao Tzu 2006, *Tao Teh Ching* (transl. JCH Wu), Shambhala, Boston.

Liao, W 2009, *Chi: Discovering Your Life Energy*, Shambhala, Boston.

Matthiessen, P 1998, *Nine-Headed Dragon River*, Shambhala, Boston.

Muir, J 1938, *John of the Mountains: the Unpublished Journals of John Muir*, http://www.sierraclub.org/

Nhat Hanh, T 2008, *The Miracle of Mindfulness*, Rider, London.

Selimovic, M 1996, *Death and the Dervish*, Northwestern University Press, Evanston, IL.

Smith, D 1970, *The Starlight Barking*, Puffin, London.

Snyder, G 1995, *A Place in Space*, Counterpoint, Washington DC.

Snyder, G 2002, *Look Out: A Selection of Writings*, New Directions, New York.

Snyder, G 2009, *Riprap and Cold Mountain Poems, Counterpoint*, Berkeley, CA.

Spearing, AC (ed.) 2001, *The Cloud of Unknowing and Other Works*, Penguin, London.

Steinegger, H 2013, *Innerschweizer WildmannliSagen*, Riedter Verlag, Schwyz.

St Pierre, EA 1997, 'Circling the text: nomadic writing practices', *Qualitative Inquiry*, vol.3, no.4, pp.403-418.

Suzuki, S 2011, *Zen Mind, Beginner's Mind: Informal Talks on Zen meditation and practice*, Shambhala, Boston.

Tanahashi, K (ed.) 1999, *Enlightenment Unfolds: The Essential Teachings of Zen Master Dogen*, Shambhala, Boston.

Virgil 1986, *The Aeneid* (trans. C Day Lewis), Oxford University Press, Oxford.

Watson, B (ed.) 1994, *Four Huts: Asian Writings on the Simple Life*, Shambhala, Boston.

Watson, N & Jenkins, J (eds) 2006, *The Writings of Julian of Norwich: A Vision Showed to a Devout Woman and A Revelation of Love*, Pennsylvania State University Press, University Park, PA.

Zourabichvili, F 1996, 'Six notes on the percept,' in P Patton (ed.), *Deleuze: A Critical Reader*, Blackwell, Oxford, pp.188-216.

CPSIA information can be obtained
at www.ICGtesting.com
Printed in the USA
FSOW04n2028121017
39855FS

9 780936 8788